ERNIE
O'MALLEY

To my eternally helpful, loving wife Susan, and to
Cormac O'Malley, guardian of his father's flame.

From an emigrant Irish family, **Harry F. Martin**
graduated from Harvard University and Law School.
His career included time as a Wall St lawyer, and an
officer in the US International AID programme. He
was CEO of Merrill Lynch Bank, London, an Arab
consortium bank in NYC, and the shareholder entity
that owns Cargill, America's largest family company.
He lectures on literary and historical subjects.

Cormac K.H. O'Malley was born in Ireland but
went to the USA to live with his American artist
mother, Helen Hooker, when his father died in 1957.
Apart from his career in international corporate law,
he has focused on the literary and artistic heritage of
both his parents, including the publication of books
not published during their lifetimes.

ERNIE O'MALLEY

A Life

HARRY F. MARTIN
with
CORMAC K.H. O'MALLEY

MERRION
PRESS

First published in 2021 by
Merrion Press
10 George's Street
Newbridge
Co. Kildare
Ireland
www.merrionpress.ie

978-1-78537-390-9 (Paper)
978-1-78537-392-3 (Ebook)

A CIP catalogue record for this book is
available from the British Library.

Typeset in Sabon LT Std 11.5/16

Unless otherwise stated, all images are taken
from the Cormac O'Malley Papers and are
used courtesy of Cormac K.H. O'Malley.

Merrion Press is a member of Publishing Ireland.

TABLE OF CONTENTS

ABBREVIATIONS

Blake Papers	Collection of Frances-Mary Blake Papers, UCDA
Cathal	C. Hooker O'Malley
CBS	Christian Brothers School
COMPP	Cormac O'Malley Private Papers
EOMP-AIA060	Collection of Ernie O'Malley Papers at NYUL
EOMP-UCDA	Collection of Ernie O'Malley Papers
IPP	Irish Parliamentary Party
IRA	Irish Republican Army
NYUL	New York University Library
RIC	Royal Irish Constabulary
UCD	University College Dublin
UCDA	University College Dublin Archives

FOREWORD

I first encountered Ernie O'Malley's writings in the 1980s. Research into Irish republicanism meant reading many activist memoirs, but none of the others possessed the compelling power of O'Malley's 1936 book *On Another Man's Wound*. I read and re-read it zealously as a PhD student, and indeed for years afterwards. And when I had the privilege of meeting O'Malley's son Cormac, I began to explore the incredibly rich legacy of materials that had been left to the scholarly and wider world by this early-twentieth-century Irish republican figure. Much of that legacy has been preserved because of Cormac's impressively committed work over the years; in this new book with Harry F. Martin, he again makes a valuable contribution to the O'Malley story.

It's a very different book from my own *Ernie O'Malley: IRA Intellectual* and – as usual – it's good to have diverse voices of interpretation and understanding on the bookshelf. As Harry Martin's authorial Preface makes clear, Ireland has a precious place in his own family too. And O'Malley's significance here in Ireland remains clear. This is the case both because of his role in the 1916–23 Irish Revolution, and also because of his important and revealing writings and papers, which remain of enduring relevance to the understanding of those fractious years. Martin's book, however, also rightly attends to Ernie O'Malley's non-Irish years and connections, to his cultural, intellectual and personal interactions in the USA and beyond. The story is one that features Edward Weston, Paul Strand and Hart Crane, as well as Michael Collins, Liam Lynch and Dan Breen.

It was often enough a turbulent life, even after O'Malley's Irish Republican Army years. To the injury, bloodshed, imprisonment and hunger strike of the Irish Revolution were added post-Revolutionary libel, ill health and painful marital collapse. But Harry Martin deals fondly with his subject, and the lightly written narrative tells its story with obvious affection for the man at its centre. The account in this book draws on fascinating published and unpublished sources. It will be enjoyed by sympathetic admirers of O'Malley, and also by those who are keen to hear a gently told story of someone who lived at the centre of one of Irish history's most significant periods.

Richard English
Queen's University Belfast
April 2021

ACKNOWLEDGEMENTS

My special thanks to our publisher, Conor Graham, whose continued support and belief in our book made it possible. Patrick O'Donoghue's useful edits and constructive additions made this a better book. Richard English, for his continued support and fine 1998 biography of Ernie; our invaluable editorial advisors, Stuart Vyse, Patrick J. Mahoney, David Leeming and Jason Knirck; Cathal O'Malley, for frank family recollections; Mary Feehan, for her valuable, early tough love and guidance; Mary-Francis Blake, RIP, for her devotion to Ernie; Cormac O'Malley, for everything.

In recognition of the following consummate commentators, among others, on Ernie's warring period and later life in Ireland: Nicholas Allen, John Crowley and fellow editors of *The Atlas of the Irish Revolution*; Gavin Foster; R.F. Foster; Glucksman Ireland House, New York University; Peter Hart, RIP; Michael Hopkinson; J.J. Lee; Des MacHale; Fearghal McGarry; Jerry O'Callaghan; John O'Callaghan; Meda Ryan; and Charles Townshend.

Harry F. Martin

Thanks to Harry Martin for his deep dedication and insights in presenting my father's story. My gratitude to those Harry has not already recognised who helped us with this book: Síobhra Aiken, Anthony P. Behan, Mary Burke, Marion R. Casey, CBS O'Connell Schools and its Allen Archives, James S. Donnelly,

Conor Graham, Tim Horgan, Timothy V. Johnson, Peter Katz, Roísín Kennedy, Tanya Kiang, Lynn Kidney, Kilmainham Jail Museum staff, Trish Lambe, Margaret Leeming, Ivan Lennon, Pascal Letellier, Críostóir MacCárthaigh, Patrick J. Mahoney, Kate Manning, Eve Morrison, Miriam Nyhan, Ruan O'Donnell, Colette O'Flaherty, Eunan O'Halpin, Shannon O'Neill, Denis Tinsley and R. Bryan Zehngut-Willits. A special thanks to my family: my beloved late wife Moira, and my children Bergin and Conor, who were so supportive from the start.

Cormac K.H. O'Malley

MY IRISH GRANDFATHER

My grandfather, Dominick Martin, left his home in Galway and shipped out of Queenstown, Cork to Boston on the Cunard liner *Samaria* on 29 April 1890. Thirty years old, he was listed on the ship's manifest as 'labourer – reads and writes'. Six years later, in Lynn, Massachusetts, he married Nellie Callahan, 21 years old, listed on their marriage certificate as a 'domestic from Ireland'.

He built a small construction firm and bought two acres of land with an old wooden house in Lynn. Beside the house, in a field surrounded by a stone wall, he planted potatoes. We grandchildren loved digging up the potatoes. Dominick and Nellie had seven children, and there are now close to one hundred of their Irish American descendants here in the United States.

We were brought to grandfather's house to see him on holidays. He would sit in his wooden chair set in the kitchen corner with his black, twisted shillelagh cane balanced against it. He would beckon us over, and we were sometimes frightened when he asked us questions about what we were doing.

When I was 16 years old, my father somehow arranged for me to go to a boarding school in Massachusetts. This horrified grandfather, who thought I was going to be corrupted by the 'English on the hill' who sent their children to such schools. Irish immigrant families like ours certainly did not. I stood in front of his chair while he gripped my knees with his strong hands. He was then 89 years old.

'I have two things to tell ye, Mickey,' he said, 'and I want you to never forget them.' He called all his grandsons Mickey. 'First, nothing is good enough for your friends, but nothing, nothing, is bad enough for your enemies. Did you hear me?' 'Yes, grandfather,' I answered. 'The second goes along with the first. Never let any man ride over ye.' I have tried to follow his advice throughout my life.

CHAPTER 1

BOYHOOD TO EASTER RISING, 1897–1916

When he joined the Irish Volunteers in 1916 at 19 years of age, it's likely he was known as Earnan Ó Máille. When travelling around Ireland as an organiser in 1918–20, local men called him the staff captain from Dublin. To the British who captured and tortured him in late 1920, he remained Bernard Stewart, the alias he used. The Free State soldier who saved a severely wounded Ernie from being summarily executed by another soldier in November 1922 called him O'Malley. 'That's O'Malley,' he said, 'and you'd better leave him alone while I'm here.' Travelling in Europe in 1925–6 with a false British passport after being released from an Irish Free State prison, he called himself Cecil Edward Smyth-Howard. Afterwards, in America, when newspapers and prospective publishers of his first book addressed him as 'General', he replied, 'I'm not a general now.' To his friends, the poet Hart Crane, the movie director John Ford and the painter Jack Yeats, or his American heiress wife Helen, he was simply Ernie. At his 1957 state funeral with military honours in Dublin, he was described as 'Our Irish hero'.

Ernie was born on 26 May 1897. He was the second child of Luke and Marion Malley, a conservative Victorian-era couple from Castlebar, County Mayo in the west of Ireland. He had ten brothers and sisters. Ernie and two of his brothers, Charlie and Dessie, called themselves O'Malley, whereas the rest of the family went by the last name Malley. Their mother and father were serious parents who gave them the best educations they could and brought them up to be responsible people. However, they were not particularly warm, emotionally supportive or outgoing. They expressed little interest in Irish nationalism, although they may have favoured Home Rule for Ireland. Ernie believed, for all he heard from them on these issues, that his family might as well have been living in Wales. They were not literary people, nor did they express much interest in Irish history.

Luke Malley had been a legal assistant and then an administrative officer to the Crown Solicitor for County Mayo. This was a respectable position in the British system, which ruled Ireland through a series of official posts primarily manned by Irishmen loyal to them. Three years before Ernie was born, the Malleys moved into a fine three-storey house on the main street of Castlebar, just across from the Royal Irish Constabulary (RIC) police station. The RIC officers and men, most of whom were Irishmen like Ernie's father, provided a key element of local support for British rule in Ireland. They often tipped their hats to Luke when they passed him on the street.

The Malleys home in Castlebar had a back garden area for flowers and vegetables, with a pony and trap to take them on local excursions. They also rented a house for the family in the summer that looked out over Clew Bay on the Mayo coast near Westport. It was there, as a boy, that Ernie grew to love the ocean, to feel comfortable sailing small boats on the bay and fishing, and to visit the people who lived on Achill Island just off the coast. He enjoyed these activities throughout the rest of his life.

During this period, Ernie and his older brother Frank played pirates using a rowboat. They captured prisoners, including their sister and other local children, followed maps to dig up treasure, did what they thought real pirates would do, and acted out sea stories they had heard. It was a delightful childhood by the sea.

The Malleys were part of the respectable Castlebar community and raised their children as Roman Catholics. Ernie remained committed to his religion all of his life. At one point his mother had hoped he would go into the priesthood, a normal route for a bright Irish boy in a large family. His father and mother both had siblings in various religious orders, but Ernie successfully resisted their efforts. The Malley family attended Mass on Sundays in the new Castlebar church erected in 1901 where his mother's parents, the Kearneys, had dedicated a stained-glass window in memory of her grandparents, Patrick and Mary Kilgir of Castlebar. Ernie's mother Marion came from a family with one hundred acres of land, which gave her meaningful status.

According to Ernie, Castlebar was a 'shoneen town'. A shoneen was a little John Bull – that is, anyone who imitated the manners and ways of the English as represented by the anglicised Irish. In his estimation, this community had turned away from the culture of the original Irish people. Luke and Marion did not create a family environment conducive to producing sons who might later fight to drive the British from Ireland. They would never have expected that one of their boys would become a famous leader of the Irish Republican Army (IRA) in his early twenties.

Ernie later regretted that his family did not speak Irish at home, even though it was taught at school. When he became dedicated to understanding the significance of Irish culture and history, he realised this lack of fluency presented limitations in his quest. When young men like Ernie became convinced of the Irish nationalist cause, they sought out their own culture, its language, literature, dances and folklore. They complained that the Irish people had not been able to fully develop the uniqueness of their culture because Ireland had been dominated by a foreign power, the British, for centuries. These occupiers stifled the appreciation of ancient Irish heroic tales. This made it more challenging for Ernie and other leaders of the Irish independence movement to convince their countrymen that they had a heritage worth preserving and fighting for.

Ernie was brought up as a Roman Catholic and continued in his faith, although he was not always a consistent, faithful practitioner. He wrote, 'My recollections of home life are not always pleasant, all due to lack of religion, for growing boys are not naturally religious, and if mother and fathers do not show the good example it is hard for the young people to learn to love their God.'[1]

Later, as an active IRA soldier captured by the Free State, Catholic priests often refused to give him communion. In spite of this, he remained a Roman Catholic for the rest of his life. In jail he read religious materials and attended Mass when he could. Ernie was married in the Roman Catholic Church and sent his children to Roman Catholic schools. He was also willing to criticise the Church when he thought it necessary.

One compelling person in Ernie's early life who brought him back to his Gaelic roots from the pressures of shoneenism was Mary Anne Jordan, known as Nannie, the Malleys' Irish-speaking family nurse. She took care of Ernie, Frank and the other children when they were young. Nannie had a special status in the Malley family. She regaled the children with ghost stories that kept their heads under the blankets. She encouraged them to explore nearby land owned by peculiar, old Lord Lucan, who benignly patrolled it on his tricycle. The brothers looked for green-coated leprechauns under the trees, hoping to hear the sound of their silver hammers, while they also hoped to see fairies dancing their rings in the glades. Nannie defended the children when challenged by their parents. She made a lasting impression on Ernie.

Nannie's most important contribution to Ernie's development of nationalistic feeling for Ireland as a boy were the stories she told his older brother and himself about ancient Irish heroes. He remembered one in particular. It was their favourite. This was the epic of the fabled cattle raid, the *Táin Bó Cúailnge*. It not only inspired him but also mirrored Ernie's own later experiences fighting against the British. He remembered this tale:

> Maeve, soldier queen of Connaught, arrogant and womanly and strong, had a long pillow talk with her husband, Ailell. Disputing their belongings, jewel by jewel, shield by shield, Maeve was a bull short. In the hostile North was a great brown bull she must have. She gathered her troops and off with her for the country of the Ultonians, Ulster. Then began the famous cattle raid, the *Táin*. Nannie described the fight at the ford between Cuchulain, defender of the Ultonians, and Maeve's champion, Ferdia of the Firbolgs. The two had been trained in arms together [and] had taken vows of friendship and brotherhood. Day after day they fought … When evening came they kissed each other, exchanged wound herbs and salves, and sent presents of food and drink. At last Ferdia fell in death and we cried. Was he not from Erris in our own county of Mayo, and was it not sad to see two brave friends fight to the death of one?[2]

His mother wished to maintain the family's social status by ensuring that Ernie did not associate with the wrong kind of local children. Ernie and his siblings were directed to keep to themselves after school. This isolation may have contributed to the social awkwardness that limited Ernie later in life. He and

Frank were even told not to play football with the local boys, although they did whenever they could get away with it. Ernie later wrote, 'Few [children] were "good enough" for us ... Many with whom we were not supposed to mix passed our tests ... Our chief admiration was for a boy who could use stilts and a tomboy who could walk on her hands. The most interesting of all our illicit acquaintances was a beggar woman, who was double-jointed.'[3]

Ernie's descriptions of his boyhood in Mayo demonstrate the keen observational abilities he developed as a boy. He appreciated colourful scenes present in rural villages: 'On market days we could sense the roughness of country people. Awkward men drinking pints of frothy porter ... Shawled, barefooted women selling eggs and yellow, strong, salty butter in plaited osier baskets ... Old women with pleated frills to their white caps ... rosy girls in tight-laced boots, which some had put on at the entrance to the town.'[4]

The Irish mourning ritual observed in rural Ireland, known as keening, fascinated Ernie. Women wailed and beat their long wild hair as they walked after the casket procession. Townspeople lifted their hats, shopkeepers respectfully closed the shutters of their stores, and no one walked closer than three steps behind the corpse. A box of clay pipes with tobacco or snuff was left outside the church door when the body was lying inside. He absorbed the dramatic scene of death in the countryside with a sense of awe and wonderment.[5]

The Malleys belonged to the stratified social life of smaller towns in the provinces. Its distinctions made an impression on Ernie – they seemed silly to him, and he subjected them to his critical view. Some of his observations might have come from one of Dickens's novels: 'Gentility flourished easily in Ireland; very little wealth nourished it. In the towns tuppence-ha'penny looked down on tuppence, and throughout the country the grades in social difference were as numerous as the layers of an onion.'[6]

His curiosity led Ernie to insights about the relationship between men and women, including the notion of who really directed the family. He observed how his mother could turn his father around by pillow talk, so by morning he had changed to adopt her point of view, forgetting the firm position he had taken only the night before. The boy noticed the effective, quiet matriarchal domination exercised by mothers and grandmothers in Irish households.

Although his family moved him away from country life in the west of Ireland early in life, Ernie had been brought up in rural County Mayo and retained a respect for country people for all of his life. He recognised their inherent kindness to children, supporting and watching over them in the villages. It was impressed upon him at this early age that one had to respect and understand the differences of the local people in the various Irish counties, something he never forgot. Initially, as a child, he had been awed when Nannie described the fierce mountainy men who lived in certain areas of Ireland. This was soon reinforced when he first encountered mountainy men who came down to villages for the weekend market days.

In 1906, when Ernie was 9 years old, his father moved the family to Dublin, where Luke expected to have a more important civil service position. This job didn't materialise immediately, but he was eventually appointed as a senior clerk in the Congested Districts Board. The family moved into a comfortable house large enough for their growing family at 7 Iona Drive. This was in Glasnevin, a new development designed to accommodate Dublin's growing middle class. His mother, Marion, nevertheless became concerned that her family in Dublin did not enjoy the same social position they had enjoyed in smaller Castlebar.

The Malley parents had always focused on their children's education and continued to do so to the best of their ability. They committed their children to private secondary education in Dublin, and five of the boys, including Ernie, went on to university. The boys first went to the O'Connell Christian Brothers School (CBS) on North Circular Road. This school was founded in 1820 for Catholic boys in Dublin who might otherwise not have received an education.

Funds were sometimes short for the Malley family, considering the number of children to be educated. There were times when Ernie went without books he needed. Although he knew his father would say yes if he was asked for them, he also knew his father really couldn't afford the additional expense. Ernie sometimes couldn't see the blackboard on the school wall and needed glasses, but he realised they were expensive and was afraid to mention his problem. Instead he learned to memorise the assignment when the teacher first announced it verbally, or to do the math problems from the teacher's initial oral description. He was beginning to demonstrate what a resourceful young man he could be, even when deprived of needed resources.

The choice of the Christian Brothers School was important for Ernie, guiding him in his early teens towards the republican principle that Ireland deserved to be free from British rule. CBS and its teachers had developed an independent nationalist spirit. The school did not depend on government funding, so its teachers could select and write their own books. They had freedom of expression, and Irish history and culture was an important part of the curriculum. This included a strong interest in Irish nationalism, which Ernie began to embrace.

It was during this period at CBS that Ernie learned about Irish history. In the narrative he was taught, Ireland had been invaded and suppressed by a series of invaders, Vikings, Welsh, Flemings,

English and lowland Scots. From Tudor times, continued attempts were made by the British invaders to subdue the country. Native Irish control of their own land and law was broken down by the English system. They suffered from severe subjugation of their Catholic religion, their language and their education.

Oliver Cromwell's Parliamentarian force reconquered Ireland in 1649–52 after a decade-long war. Many Irish men, women and children were slaughtered and viciously oppressed by Cromwell's army. Land was confiscated from Catholic landowners and granted to Protestant Adventurers and members of Cromwell's New Model Army. However, after the land acts of the late nineteenth century, even though some large Protestant landholdings remained, Irish Catholic farmers owned 60 to 70 per cent of the land in Ireland.

This long history of Ireland's political and cultural domination made a deep impression on Ernie as a young man. It sowed the seeds for a life-changing decision that he would make after the Easter Rising of 1916.

Ernie was only 14 years old when his parents asked him, in 1911, to take a younger sister and brother to see King Edward's procession during his visit to Dublin. This was the first time he would openly demonstrate his disdain for the British, illustrating not only how his political feelings had developed at this young age, but also his confidence in carrying out a public act of defiance. 'We stood in the front rank of the waiting people. I said we would keep our hats on. Scarlet-coated Life Guards with shining helmets cantered past; but we alone of the crowd looked at the carriage with hats on. To show my intense conviction I spelt King with a small letter. I did not like the English.'[7]

Although he had failed the exam to enter his senior year at CBS, Ernie was allowed to finish, graduating in June 1915. It's not clear why such a talented young man went through such academic difficulties. Two years earlier he had received honours in English, French, history and geography, but he only received passes in Latin, Irish, arithmetic, geometry and science.

Ernie was a lean young man with dark red hair. He had distinct chiselled features with a prominent nose and jaw. He was an intense lad, always focused on the job at hand. There was little boyishness about him. His serious demeanour was impressive to his elders.

His father asked him what he wanted to do with his life, suggesting he might wish to go into the law. Ernie was uncertain but said he would prefer to become a doctor. He remembered his father had previously said that in Ireland the system believed one was guilty until proved innocent. He decided to study medicine, but he still may not have had a clear view of what he should do with his future. Fortunately for Ernie, in June 1915 he was permitted to sit for a Dublin Corporation University Scholarship examination. He won one of twenty-four scholarships, thus allowing him to enter University College Dublin to study medicine in October 1915.

Ernie was only 18 years old and a first-year student in Dublin when the Rising began on Easter Monday, 24 April 1916. The rebels seized various points around the city to create a defensible perimeter. They attacked Dublin Castle but failed to take it. However, they were able to capture the General Post Office and used it as their central base of operations. The Rising ended six days later when the rebels surrendered to overwhelming British forces.

The Rising had the advantage of occurring when the British were fighting a major war in Europe. It had the disadvantage of being regarded by the British as a treasonous act, deliberately initiated with German assistance when Britain was fighting Germany. It was led by brave men and women totally devoted to procuring freedom for their country, but it was also doomed from the start by poor planning and execution. Its leaders failed to fully anticipate how Britain's vastly superior naval and army forces, armed with artillery, heavy machine guns, and armoured cars not available to the insurgents, would immediately amass to quell it. Dublin city centre was seriously damaged by the bombardment that followed.

The historic background to the Easter Rising goes back to the British general election of 1885, in which a majority was won on the premise of giving Home Rule to Ireland. This Home Rule bill proposed a limited amount of self-government for Ireland in the form of a devolved assembly, but it was enough to secure the support of the Irish Parliamentary Party (IPP). The first two bills for Home Rule failed, but in 1912 the IPP managed to influence the introduction of a third Home Rule bill that was expected to pass into law. The second Home Rule bill (1893) was passed by the House of Commons but defeated in the House of Lords; the Parliament Act, introduced in 1911, limited the powers of the House of Lords so that they could only veto this latest bill for up to two years. Finally, Home Rule seemed an imminent reality.

This shift sent shock waves through Ireland's Unionist community, which was predominately Protestant and had strong links to Britain. It was particularly feared by the concentration of Unionists in Ulster. They feared they would become subject to rule by the Roman Catholic majority in a new Irish parliament located in Dublin, losing the protection they now received from Parliament in London.

The Ulster Volunteers were formed in 1912 in the northern counties to protect their rights if Home Rule was enacted. In 1913 the Irish Volunteers were formed in Dublin as a counter force to the Ulster Volunteers.

In 1914 the Home Rule bill was passed into law. However, the introduction of the Suspensory Act, passed simultaneously, postponed its enactment until the end of the First World War. At this time, many thought the war would be of a short duration – they didn't expect it to go on for four long years.

Given the assurance that Ireland would soon have its own parliament, John Redmond, the IPP leader, proposed that the Irish Volunteers, who had spread throughout the country, should volunteer in the British army to help fight Germany. This caused a split in the movement. The vast majority – an estimated 188,000 or 93 per cent – followed Redmond. The balance – an estimated 13,500 – refused to join and continued under the Irish Volunteers flag.

When the Easter Rising occurred in April 1916, in the middle of the First World War, everything changed. Those who had been waiting for years to obtain Ireland's freedom from Britain used the Rising to galvanise open opposition to British rule.

The Rising resulted from decades of activity by Irish men and women from various groups who believed it was time for Ireland to declare its independence and become a free republic. From this emanated the popular term 'republican', designating anyone willing to use violence to gain Ireland's freedom. The term originated with the United Irishmen of 1798 through their association with the new French Republic, and it was reinforced by the formation of the Irish Republican Brotherhood, a secret society created in 1858.

The Irish Republican Brotherhood's aim was to free Ireland from British rule by physical force, not through gradual constitutional change. They promoted republicanism while waiting for an opportunity to use force to obtain Ireland's freedom. They provided the key political leadership behind the Rising.

The Irish Volunteers, diminished in number since the split, made up most of those who participated in the Rising. They were partly armed by a shipment of German Mauser rifles smuggled in to Howth, a Dublin suburb, two years earlier in July 1914. This occurred when Erskine Childers and his American wife Molly brought the rifles in on their large sailing yacht, the *Asgard*, which had picked up its cargo from a German vessel in the North Sea.

The Childers, early supporters of the republican cause, were from unlikely backgrounds for revolutionaries. Erskine, a former British naval officer, was from the Anglo-Irish Protestant Ascendancy; Molly was from a wealthy American family in Boston. The Irish Volunteers were waiting at Howth harbour to receive the arms. By this time the Irish Republican Brotherhood had infiltrated the Irish Volunteers, enabling them to plan for a rebellion.

Not all of the Volunteer leadership had been committed to the idea of staging a rebellion. Several had argued in the days preceding that it was an ill-considered expedition that should not happen. These men had to be prevented from disclosing the proposed rebellion to the British authorities. Eoin MacNeill, Chief of Staff of the Irish Volunteers, had been left in the dark on plans for insurrection until the last minute.

The Irish Citizen Army, another key force in the Rising, was formed by James Connolly in 1913 to defend Dublin's striking workers from the police when they were locked out of their places of employment. It was a more militant republican force than the Volunteers. Connolly became an important member of the military committee established to manage the Rising. From the beginning he was an advocate for using force; he had military experience, and as secretary general of the largest trade union, the Irish Transport and General Workers' Union, he controlled a large segment of Dublin's workers, who would be key during the Rising.

Roger Casement, another key figure, continued right up to the Rising to contact German officials in efforts to receive additional military support for their eventual rebellion. He managed to secure guns and ammunition from Germany, but much less of it than he had hoped – and the shipment was eventually intercepted by the Royal Navy. Casement travelled back to Ireland at around the same time as this shipment. It is believed that Casement did so in an attempt to prevent the insurrection, perceiving that the support was inadequate. He was soon captured in Kerry; he was later charged with high treason and hanged in London.

As Fearghal McGarry effectively demonstrates, the leaders of the Easter Rising did not take strategic locations in Dublin, such as Dublin Castle or Trinity College, which they could later defend, or minimise destructive consequences to the civilian population.[8]

For example, the Volunteers placed one of their garrisons in the South Dublin Union, the largest poorhouse in Dublin; it contained more than 3,000 sick and infirm inmates, and some of them became casualties. About 450 people died in the insurrection. Approximately 50 per cent of these casualties were civilians, including many women and children. Another 2,600 people were wounded, many seriously. The Irish rebels counted for less than 20 per cent of the dead, whereas British army fatal casualties comprised another 30 per cent. Assignment of responsibility for the civilian casualties should include the British forces, who bombarded densely populated urban areas with gun boats and heavy artillery.[9]

The Rising did not result from a democratic process voted on by a majority of the different groups involved. Instead, it resulted from a secret decision by the military committee. The committee also had to deal with the challenge that the Rising became known to the British authorities just before it was about to occur.

Some of its key leaders, including Tom Clarke and Seán MacDiarmada, had been planning an insurrection for some time. Clarke was a committed republican who had lived in the United States for years, returning to Ireland in 1907 to rejuvenate the Irish Republican Brotherhood. He and MacDiarmada believed if they did not strike now in 1916 – when Britain was diverted by the war in Europe, and they might also get help from Germany – their cause for freedom would wither away. The desire of certain Irish men and women to seize this opportunity drove the Rising – not a set of well-planned actions that could fight the British to a standstill. Many of its leaders actually predicted they would die in the Rising or soon afterward.[10] They also held out hope that the rebellion would radicalise the Irish public, the majority of whom supported the constitutional methods of the IPP.

After the Rising was crushed, the British made the mistake of interning the resulting prisoners for a period in a camp in Wales called Frongoch. This effectively brought republicans from all over Ireland together in the same location, allowing them the chance to plan for future resistance against Britain. Michael Collins, a lower-level player in the Rising, began to demonstrate leadership abilities in his interactions with comrades imprisoned at Frongoch. After the Rising, during Ernie's role as an 'organiser' and then as a commandant-general in the War of Independence, Collins became Ernie's key commander and mentor.

The Rising galvanised the Irish revolutionary spirit that led to the War of Independence (January 1919–July 1921). This did not happen, as some argue, because of the bloodbath in Dublin. Instead, the public reaction that motivated Irish men and women to continue the fight against Britain primarily emanated from the immediate execution of fifteen of its leaders by summary British army courts-martial. The executions were carried out by firing squads in the prisons. This signalled a shift in Irish society

– a shift that became more distinct as the European war went on, Home Rule was further postponed, and the British government eventually attempted to impose conscription in Ireland.

Another factor explains why Ernie and many others were motivated by the fifteen men initially executed by the British. Ireland was a small country. One hundred years ago, within certain circles there, almost everyone knew each other. In this way, paths sometimes crossed – a personal connection that lent greater significance to these events. For example, one of the fifteen men executed by the British was Major John MacBride, who had been drawn into the Rising almost accidentally while visiting Dublin. MacBride, even though he had republican sympathies, was a good friend of Ernie's parents from years before in Mayo. Ernie later recalled that he had been there when MacBride visited the Malleys in their Dublin house just weeks before the Rising.

John MacBride was also the husband of Maud Gonne, a leading feminist. The poet W.B. Yeats, future Nobel laureate, had tried to marry Gonne before MacBride did. Ten years later, when working with the Basque separatists in Paris, Ernie would frequently visit Seán MacBride, who was John and Maud's son. A decade after that, Ernie would become a close friend, supporter and collector of the painter Jack Yeats, the younger brother of W.B. Yeats.

The expression of the revolutionary spirit built up over the years in Ireland is exemplified by the two poems Yeats wrote about the events, both of which are still often quoted today. 'Sixteen Dead Men' begins with the lines:

O but we talked at large before
The sixteen men were shot,
But who can talk of give or take,
What should be and what not

While those dead men are loitering there
To stir the boiling pot?

And 'Easter 1916' ends with the following:

Now and in time to be,
Wherever green is worn,
Are changed, changed utterly:
A terrible beauty is born.[11]

For Yeats, green became the symbolic colour of the Irish revolution against Britain. The 'terrible beauty is born' was the dream that Ireland could be a free republic. This dream persuaded Ernie, and many other Irish men and women, that they should risk their lives to make Ireland free. Ernie's life thereafter was 'changed, changed utterly' by the Rising.

R.F. Foster, a noted historian, outlines three characteristics shared by many of the young men from ordinary middle-class backgrounds who became IRA wartime leaders: 1) they were educated by institutions like the Christian Brothers, whose school teachers were proponents of Irish nationalism that continually told their boys how Britain had suppressed Irish culture; 2) they were rebelling against their conservative parents who supported the British establishment ruling Ireland; and 3) they were relatively inexperienced men in their twenties, who, with a few exceptions, did not possess university degrees. Ernie O'Malley fits perfectly into each of these categories.[12]

Ernie's older brother Frank had joined the Dublin Fusiliers, a British army unit, as an officer in 1914. In contrast, Ernie had been moving towards supporting Ireland's demand for freedom during his school days. After the Rising occurred, he turned completely against British rule, becoming a soldier in the Irish

Volunteers. He was infuriated by the executions, bringing his nascent nationalism to a fever pitch. Britain had become his enemy. Had Ernie been a few years older, he too might have become an officer in his brother's British unit.

When the Rising began, he was a student at University College Dublin. Another medical student at the more upper-class Trinity College had asked him on Easter Monday to join a group of Trinity student cadets who were arming themselves to protect the campus from expected attacks from the Irish insurgents. Instead, that evening Ernie crawled out of the window of his parents' home to join a friend who had a rifle. Together, without any military guidance, they began firing on British troops near the River Liffey on the north side of Dublin.

After the Rising, while he was still living at home, Ernie joined F Company, 1st Battalion, in the North Dublin Brigade of the Irish Volunteers, which had begun training secretly. His F Company sergeant in 1917, Liam Ó Briain, remembered that Ernie was demanding and appeared to be more of a Trinity College student than one from the more middle-class University College. Ó Briain, who went on to become a professor, also recalled that Ernie was critical of the training process, appeared to view him as a relatively ineffective military superior, and therefore paid little attention to him.[13]

It soon became difficult for Ernie to focus on his medical studies. His medical school had become, in a few weeks, not only a place of training to become a doctor but also a seat of resistance involving his fellow students. He and many of his contemporaries went on exercises in the nearby Dublin mountains, pledged their allegiance to freeing Ireland and promised to fight and die for the cause. Ernie had begun a journey that would lead him in his early twenties to become a fighter rather than a medical man.

CHAPTER 2

IRELAND PREPARES FOR WAR,
1916–1918

After the Rising, Ernie joined the Irish Volunteers. He followed this by serving in a new challenging role as organiser, travelling all over Ireland at Michael Collins's direction to train men for future possible operations against the British.

After its leaders were executed by the British in 1916, Irish opposition grew against supporting the British cause in the First World War. The nationalistic spirit to abstain from the war was supported by Sinn Féin, the political counterpart to the Irish Volunteers that developed vital momentum after the Rising. Sinn Féin candidates were elected in four by-elections, including Count Plunkett, for North Roscommon; Joseph McGuinness, for South Longford; Éamon de Valera, for East Clare; and William Cosgrave, for Kilkenny.

As the popularity of Sinn Féin was growing, the British created a conscription crisis. Conscription had already been established in England, Scotland and Wales, but in the spring of 1918, the British government attempted to extend it to Ireland, requiring Irishmen to serve in the War effort in Europe. This met with significant opposition in Ireland – an opposition that received the backing of religious leaders. The British retaliated by arresting Sinn Féin leaders while also claiming there was a pro-German plot hatching in Ireland. They eventually dropped their effort for conscription in Ireland when it was clear the United States was entering the War in force. But what had transpired served to intensify nationalist feeling and boost Sinn Féin's popularity.

Sinn Féin soundly defeated the IPP in the December 1918 elections, gaining 73 of the 105 Irish seats. Nevertheless, they refused to take their places in the House of Commons. They formed their own parliament, or Dáil, in Dublin. It first gathered in the Mansion House on 21 January 1919 and Cathal Brugha was appointed as its president on a temporary basis; Éamon de Valera was to take over from Brugha in April.

An early example of Ernie's audacity while still living at home after the Rising was demonstrated when he obtained his first revolver. He describes how he was able to accomplish this:

> One day I decided to get some arms so I borrowed Frank's uniform whilst he was out, changed into it in a house [in] town, and after considerable trouble in which I had to visit the Police Dept., and finally the office of the Provost Marshall, where I had to interview him and another Command Officer, I obtained a permit in the name of an officer I knew and purchased a .38 Smith and Wesson and 100 of ammo. I felt very proud ... My brother never discovered I had used his uniform ... [Michael] Collins RIP was highly amused when, by some means, he heard of the incident a year or so later.[1]

After joining the Irish Volunteers late in 1916, Ernie continued to live with his parents. Living at home and climbing out of the window at night to participate in training with the Irish Volunteers must have been extremely trying. Somehow he managed to keep this activity from his parents. His younger brothers knew what he was doing and supported him. The Dublin house where the

Malley family lived still has a slanted low roof, just below an upstairs bedroom window, coming down close to the ground. Ernie probably used this route when leaving and returning to his parents' house. Continuing to participate in his medical studies in a non-committed fashion couldn't have been easy.

He was frustrated; his older brother, Frank, had become an officer, and his next younger brother, Albert, had also enlisted in the British army. Both were respected by his parents. Ernie felt he would be looked down upon as a son if he were known to support the rebels. To his parents he would become 'a mere Irish black sheep'. In March of 1918 he finally decided to leave home permanently. He entrusted his rifle there to be kept by his younger brothers. It was later discovered by his father and turned over to the British.

Ernie would not see his family again for over three years. This included his four younger brothers, who followed him by subsequently joining the revolutionary cause. He completely broke ties with his father and mother, which indicates how politically estranged he had become from them. Ernie had already been living a separate life for several years as a young man. In many ways, he had already become a loner, able to live his life without any discernible support. This was the psychological profile of someone who could later be sent out alone on difficult military missions because he had already learned to survive by his own wits.

He had become a young man moving alone through the countryside and training men to oppose a superior power supported by his parents. Years later he described why he believed Ireland finally deserved to rule itself:

> Ours was the country of broken tradition, a story of economic, social and mental oppression, propped up by a

mythological introduction ... We were a nation of saints and scholars, we had often been told, but our experience had disproved this cliché. If sainthood was intolerance, we had our share of it. If scholarship was living on the unearned appreciation of people who wrote or taught eleven hundred years ago ... then we were scholars ... The laws of aristocratic tradition were in our teeth. We favoured the royalists in the English Civil War, the beaten South in America, and the Irish battalion that had fought against Italian freedom ... Cut off from scientific and intellectual eddies, we had built a world of our own, an emotional life but no philosophy or economic framework. Physically we had never had control of the land in peace.[2]

In March 1918, Ernie was first appointed as a second lieutenant and sent to help organise Volunteers in the Coalisland district of County Tyrone in the north of Ireland. On returning to Dublin from this first assignment, Ernie began his new life by living in secret safe houses set up by the Volunteers. Later, he was promoted to captain as his role as an organiser increased in importance.

Back in Dublin his activities were directed by the two senior leaders of the Irish Volunteers, Richard Mulcahy, chief of staff, and Michael Collins, director of intelligence. Both men had been involved in the 1916 Easter Rising, but because they had not been amongst its leaders, they escaped execution. Ernie reported directly to Collins, who next sent him to organise a brigade in Offaly, where he knew no one. Collins only gave him the names of a few good men in its primary town, Tullamore.

Ernie was then 20 years old with less than two years of informal training with the Irish Volunteers. Most of this training had taken place at night, and few of the officers or non-commissioned officers had significant military experience. He was now being sent to hold brigade officer elections and develop a fighting unit in an area seventy-five miles south-west of Dublin. Offaly was part of the prosperous midland counties, which were generally not militant in 1919–21. This made it inherently more difficult to build the support from the local people required to develop an effective fighting unit there. At that time a brigade could muster between 800 and 900 fighting men, depending on terrain and local support.

Mulcahy and Collins did not necessarily determine that Ernie had extraordinary abilities transcending his limited experience, giving him the capability to achieve results in the daunting circumstances he would face. There were simply not many officers available to the Volunteers. Ernie himself observed that there were not many men in Dublin who had any military background and could commit themselves to the cause full-time. Ernie and a few others, whatever their limited experience, were the only resources available in early 1918 to be sent out into rural Ireland as organisers.

Ernie also had a number of other limitations, considering the challenges of what he was asked to accomplish. He lacked the natural social affability and relaxed humour that would make it easy to communicate with men in counties with different accents and local loyalties. He was bookish and had recently been a university boy in Dublin, which did not go down well in the countryside. Ernie himself admitted he was a perfectionist who was impatient with anyone who didn't give military training their complete focus, follow specific instructions, or complete assigned functions on time. These were not qualities natural to rural men with little formal education – who may have spent many hours that day working at their small businesses, farms or in the local creameries. Military training usually took place only late at night.

As his role as an organiser developed, Ernie began to be described by officers in the field as the 'staff captain from Dublin', a term not used favourably by fighting men in the country with their own ideas about how to undertake military engagements. He was trying to create effective military units out of untrained men in areas dominated by the British army and the RIC, the highly developed armed force of Irish constables who supported British rule in Ireland. However, he was often challenged by the local Irishmen, who resented taking orders from a Dublin university boy.

Soon after his service in Offaly, he was assigned to organise more distant Irish counties, beginning with Donegal in the far north-west. He sent reports to Dublin on the military capacity and limitations of the brigades he visited. He received no guidance or instructions when sent out to organise a brigade, later recalling, 'Collins would hand me a pile of copies of the organisation scheme and add some typewritten notes reminding officers that their reports were long overdue; then I was left to myself.'[3]

Each county and its brigade could be vastly different in its reception to Ernie. Each also differed in its ability to raise and train a meaningful fighting unit. Some counties in the south, like Cork, Kerry, Limerick and Tipperary, had a long history of Fenian opposition to British rule. They were often able to create effective brigades whose officers and men were spoiling for a fight. Other counties in the north or west might be less receptive to taking on a stronger British or RIC unit, or even accepting Ernie's input. In each area, the men governed themselves and elected their own military leaders. Ernie observed later that he was training the officers and men in the countryside for another uprising, like 1916, that could be even more meaningful in achieving freedom for his country. His training helped form effective guerrilla units to attack British and RIC barracks, and otherwise effectively harass British forces – even though an uprising like that of Easter 1916 never occurred. Another uprising would probably have failed, whereas the IRA activities were effective.

When he was sent as an organiser to north Donegal, his initial encounters there were not welcoming. The elders regarded him as a spy who was recruiting their sons for dangerous activities of which they did not approve. He was made to feel unwanted, with the local men indicating that they would be happy if he moved on to another place. His assignments to an area often did not last more than two months. Even at best, it was difficult to achieve much in so short a time. Ernie described his enormous challenges as an organiser:

Gradually I got accustomed to the discomfort ... to lack of companionship as I was always alone. There was no one to talk to ... Few had their heart in the Movement, and responsible officers were satisfied with devoting two hours' work a week to the Movement. I was very sensitive and shy. The people knew I was not of their own particular class and were diffident. The elder people thought I was mad, as they had little sympathy with us. The men were raw and did not know anything about military work ... I generally managed to do several hours study each day at military work ... but, by constant reading and thinking and by working my knowledge on the men in lectures and field work, by the end of 1919 I had a pretty all round knowledge [of military tactics and training] ... Progress was slow and heartbreaking. Men simply would not carry out the simplest instructions. I had issued ... the duty of each officer, had helped to ... supply them (when I had money) with books and maps, but it was not until 1920, when the fighting really started that men ... began to become more confident and independent.[4]

In understanding how Ernie could have become a senior IRA leader at such a young age without formal military training, his contemporaries' observations of how he operated in the field are helpful. One of his early comrades, Tomás Malone (alias Seán Forde), reported on Ernie's visit to Tipperary in 1918:

> The fact that he was young made no difference to us because we were all young … but he was a strict disciplinarian … He wanted to get down to business straight away … He was a wonderful organiser but still a real soldier … People wouldn't take offense at him – not while he was there any way! They were a bit in awe of him … The reaction of the women towards IRA men at the time was that they adored them! Ernie was not a city man. He was a real country man. His sense of leadership was to lead by example. He'd be the first in a fight every time![5]

Risk was present from natural as well as enemy sources, as Ernie often travelled by night across the countryside. One night in Donegal, while riding his decrepit bicycle, he took a wrong turn. When he reached the top of a hill, his bike began running wildly down the steep incline on other side. The brakes failed, and he jumped off. He heard a crash far below. The next day locals found the remains of his old bike smashed on the rocks under a high cliff. Ernie had narrowly escaped death.

Ernie had to endure these challenges without much guidance or support from senior officers. Mulcahy and Collins didn't risk travelling to the field, preferring to remain in Dublin, and there were no secure telecommunications available. There were few senior officers in the counties he could trust for support; Ernie was supposed to be the staff captain instructing them, but they had their own clannish loyalties. Written communications took time to arrive and could be captured by the enemy – a disaster that occurred from time to time. Ernie had also cut himself off completely from his own family.

Often he felt quite alone when visiting brigades in less receptive counties. The people could show their reserve in many subtle ways: by their silence, by looks between them, or by their indifference to following his instructions. Some demonstrated their resistance by the expression on their faces, or more directly in their speech. Ernie had the determination to carry on with his duties as an organiser in spite of these challenges. It became clear that one of his most valuable qualities was simply persistence, the ability to continue where others would have given up. He followed his orders to organise each new area, to raise companies and build them into battalions, and to elect officers who would carry out the training exercises he had worked to instil in them.

Many practical limitations affected Ernie's living conditions as he travelled to different counties. His hours were extremely irregular. It was almost impossible to keep clean. Often he slept on the floor of the kitchen of a farm cottage, where he was given a basin with only a few inches of water to wash in; his clothes became ragged and verminous. There was no local transport readily available. He had to carry all his gear on his back, travelling by bicycle from one assignment to the next. He wore a heavy trench coat in the winter and could be wet with sweat and rain, bicycling in the dark with local maps and mending his tyre punctures by candlelight.

By degrees I lost all my clothes and had to depend for a change of shirt (I had to dispense with underclothes) on the generosity ... of the males in the house ... Gradually the men in the country began to think for themselves ... At the beginning great courage was needed to enable a man to leave home for some hours in the busy season. To leave it for a day was wonderful and, at any time one chose, nothing short of marvellous.[6]

The psychological strain of training often-reluctant Volunteers without local senior support also took a toll on Ernie. He observed that while in normal armies a bonding occurred that gave the men a sense of belonging and security, this was not available to him when working with the local Irish Volunteers. There was no base he could return to where he felt he was in a safe haven.

Some of these feelings may have been inherent to Ernie himself. At first, he wasn't able to create close relationships with the men he was training; he held back from intimacy. Perhaps this inhibition came from the early formal upbringing by his parents in Castlebar and Dublin. He had not grown up with the country men; he now came from Dublin, which was almost an alien world to them. Ernie was a loner who found it difficult to relate easily to others, even when working with them for a common cause.

Young organisers in the field, like Ernie, operated under other limiting conditions. Little money was provided for their needs, and they had almost no funds of their own. They had to depend on local people they had never met before to give them food and shelter. Ernie noted, 'I have always, and have still, a terrible antipathy to the IRA taking money and though Mick, now and again, offered I only took it when I was destitute or needed it for railway fares.' The organisers were also not necessarily provided with weapons by Dublin headquarters, 'It was not till January 1920 that I got a .45 Smith and Wesson.'[7] Before, Ernie had to depend on his .38 revolver, which had a faulty spring. By this time Collins had begun to realise that Ernie had good judgement and often asked his opinion of officers he had worked with in the field.

The men in the countryside had formed their own brigades well before Ernie arrived, but their leaders were unfamiliar with standard military tactics. Ernie had learned these rules – marching order, musketry, proper movement in battle over different terrain, expertise in using explosives, and other necessary knowledge – from reading and rereading British military manuals on his own. Little formal military training had been available to him from the Irish Volunteers.

He was a persistent teacher and worked hard to help the men master these military principles, even if his manner was off-putting for men in the country. His challenge was to instil in the company and brigade commanders the discipline and tactics they had to pass on in turn to their men. Otherwise their men would never be able to attack effectively the British forces and the RIC supporting them.

Instead of training officers and men who woke up every morning to the highly disciplined life of an established army barracks, Ernie had to train local tradesmen, farmers and workers at night in the countryside, where they could not be observed by the RIC. It was slow going, but in time Ernie could begin to point to some counties where his training was beginning to bear results. When he revisited these areas, he could see that the officers were in place and that the military training was beginning to create meaningful companies and brigades.

During his service as an organiser from 1918 through 1919, another limitation surfaced that Ernie, in his role as a combat leader, would have to overcome. This was his natural reluctance to resort to violence except under conditions where each party had an equal chance. This fair approach to using deadly violence could make it difficult for Ernie to survive, as there is nothing fair about war.

One example of this occurred in Ballymoe on the Galway–Roscommon border in June 1918. At this time, Ernie had only been working as an organiser in County Roscommon for a few months, and open hostilities had not yet broken out between the Volunteers and the RIC and British forces. Ernie had been sent to organise and train the Roscommon brigade. The RIC had identified him as a troublesome character stirring up opposition locally and had just issued a warrant for his arrest.

Travelling alone one night in Galway with his ineffective .38 pistol, Ernie's bicycle chain broke. He was walking his bike along a muddy road when an RIC sergeant and constable stepped into the footpath to confront him. They told Ernie to halt and read out a warrant for his arrest that claimed he was an instigator of trouble in the area. Ernie and the constable drew their revolvers, and the sergeant shouted, 'Fire'. Ernie's instinctive sense of chivalry made him believe he should wait until the other man fired. He held his fire, and the constable shot and wounded him twice. Ernie bled profusely but escaped through a thick bramble hedge – he got away without being captured.

A few months later, in Killygordon, east Donegal, Ernie was again confronted with a difficult decision. He had yet to experience combat. He and his small local team were about to attack an RIC barracks, force their way in and seize rifles and arms. Just before the raid, however, Ernie heard that the wife of the RIC sergeant in charge had spent the night in the barracks. He reluctantly postponed the attack, noting that she might have been injured or killed if shooting had occurred.

The most egregious example of Ernie's early reluctance to shoot to kill without worrying about outdated chivalry occurred in Ennis, County Clare in late spring 1919. His men, armed with shotguns, waited at night at the road's edge for an RIC patrol to pass. At Ernie's command they planned to shoot the police patrol. But he could not give the command: 'I knew my men would shoot to kill ... I could not give the order; shooting like that did not seem fair ... We waited until the patrol repassed, and again I let them go, cursing myself for the second irresolution ... I did not explain to them, but I knew they were disgusted.'[8]

The Irish Volunteers had been preparing themselves, with assistance from organisers like Ernie, to make effective assaults on the British and RIC whose barracks held the armaments they so desperately needed. In 1919, the Volunteers became the Irish Republican Army. In supporting the first Dáil, they had taken an oath to uphold the Irish Republic. Within a period of two and a half years, they would find out if their scattered groups of Volunteers could drive the British out of Ireland or get them to bargain for peace.

CHAPTER 3

WAR OF INDEPENDENCE, 1919–1921

The first notable act of violence in the War of Independence against the British took place in Tipperary in January 1919. After that, IRA actions against the RIC and British army developed gradually. At this point, there was a vast difference in military capacity between these opposing forces. The IRA could field thousands of men, but they were volunteer officers and soldiers, most of whom had regular day jobs. They assembled for particular actions only when called. Even by 1921 only a few of their senior officers were paid, none of the men were. They did not operate from established barracks and travel in organised columns of military vehicles; instead, most of them arrived for attacks by foot, travelling from their homes in villages or farms, and then melted back into the countryside after the engagements. Sometimes they had to cover many miles at night over rough countryside. They were not always adequately armed with modern rifles, carbines, revolvers and grenades.

When open hostilities broke out against the British, the IRA forces may not have had more than 3,000–4,000 rifles and handguns between them throughout the country. Arms were so limited early on that their rifles sometimes had to be passed from brigade to brigade in different counties for a particular action.

Ammunition was scarce. For many their military training had just begun.[1]

The British had at least 37,000 troops in Ireland by the end of 1919. They were housed in their own protected garrisons and had a wide range of armaments, including modern rifles and carbines, machine guns and grenades, and even a few armoured cars. The British were also supported by up to ten thousand RIC strategically positioned in 1,300 protected barracks across the country. These veteran Irish police officers provided British units with information on local IRA movements.[2]

Due to the number of resignations from the RIC – owing to armed attacks and social boycott – early in 1920 the British began enlisting demobilised British officers and men from the First World War to be sent to Ireland to strengthen the RIC. Some of these ex-soldiers were effective counter-insurgents, others could be less effective when they were not well led. They began to make brutal attacks on members of the Irish populace suspected of harbouring IRA forces, especially in response to the growing number of IRA ambushes on RIC forces in 1920. These IRA attacks began a year earlier, in January 1919.

These new British recruits became known as the Black and Tans because of their motley uniform – a hybrid of military and police attire. Indeed, the War of Independence against Britain became better known to many Irishmen as the Tan War. In 1920, as the violence increased, the British augmented the Black and Tans with a supposedly more elite, higher-paid force of volunteers from Britain, composed of ex-officers, known as the Auxiliaries.

The first notorious open attack on the British establishment by the IRA occurred in Soloheadbeg, County Tipperary on 21 January 1919. Dan Breen, a local fighter, led a group of nine men who attacked and deliberately killed two RIC constables guarding the transport of explosives to a quarry. It was ironic that the first victims of the War of Independence killed by the IRA were not British soldiers but Dan's fellow Irishmen.

Ernie and Dan later fought together in several attacks. The two young men were quite different. Ernie was a university student who was initially reluctant to kill the enemy. Dan Breen was a natural, impulsive lad from the countryside who had no such inhibitions. He wrote, describing his attack on the explosives convoy, 'Our only regret was that the escort had consisted of only two Peelers [RIC] instead of six. If there had to be dead Peelers, six would have created a better impression than a mere two.' Breen left the two dead RIC men on the road, seizing their weapons and the cart of explosives and making off with the lot. He left Patrick Flynn, a county employee accompanying the 'Peelers' and the driver, unharmed. Unfortunately, Breen had neglected to take the electric detonators to the explosives that Flynn had hidden in his pockets.[3] Breen's account is disputed by Séumas Robinson – the local brigade commander – who was with him that day.

Breen had initiated this first attack without approval from IRA headquarters. He took this bold step to show the British and his fellow Irishmen that the IRA was a real army, not just 'toy soldiers'. Afterwards he and his group travelled for weeks in the countryside to escape large groups of British and RIC forces sent to find them. A reward of £1,000 was put on his head by the RIC, a large amount for that time. The reward poster described him as follows: '[Breen has a] sulky bulldog appearance ... like a blacksmith coming from work.'[4]

Early in 1920, the senior IRA leaders in Dublin, Mulcahy and Collins, determined it was time to organise systematic attacks on RIC barracks all over Ireland, many of which were vulnerable. This formed the context of the attacks Ernie began organising, and then leading, beginning with Ballytrain in the north, then proceeding to the west and down to the south, where many of the barrack operations were carried out during that year.

Ernie was organising IRA forces in County Monaghan when he participated in the attack on Ballytrain barracks on 14 February 1920. On his way there, two armed RIC men tried to halt him in Clones. In response, he flattened one to the road by kicking him, then knocked the other out with a punch. Ernie and his men then moved on to blow a hole in the Ballytrain barracks wall. They made off with nine new carbines, and bayonets, revolvers and ammunition.[5]

Peadar O'Donnell, one of Ernie's early IRA comrades, described an experience he had witnessed with Ernie prior to the raid on the Ballytrain barracks:

> Ernie insisted on marching up the town wearing two guns quite openly. The IRA battalion commandant felt he had to walk with him. The RIC were on duty on the streets at the time, trying to keep out of the way. Somebody said to Ernie that was a strange thing to do, and he said, 'Well, it's good for the morale of the people that they should see an IRA man walk around openly armed.' The battalion commander added, 'It may have been very good for the morale of the people, but it was damn bad for my morale, I can tell you.'[6]

Throughout 1919, and well into 1920, Ernie began performing a dual role in counties in the north, eventually making his way down to Munster in the south. He continued his duties as an organiser, the role he had begun in 1918. Officially he was still the staff captain from Dublin, but as the attacks on barracks took on increased momentum in 1919 through 1920, Ernie began participating in them, first as an advisor, then as a participant, then as a combat commander. He previously had difficulty bonding with the men he was training. Now, in his new prospective role as a combat commander, he needed to demonstrate he could become their effective leader.

One Tipperary battalion badly needed to arm themselves with weapons. The battalion had only ten rifles and thirty shotguns compared to the 1,150 rifles and other weapons available to the local police and military. Another battalion had only three rifles and fifteen shotguns as opposed to eighty police carbines.[7]

The local commander of the IRA's Tipperary No. 3 Brigade in May 1920 was Séumas Robinson, a key man in Dan Breen's earlier Soloheadbeg attack. Ernie was visiting the Tipperary area in his staff organiser role. The brigade officers there were not sure at first whether they should even inform Ernie of their plan to attack the Hollyford RIC barracks. Ernie had not been directed by Dublin to participate in the Hollyford operation, but the local men realised he had had useful experience in participating in barrack attacks in other counties. They brought him in to help plan this operation.[8]

Séumas Robinson began consulting with Ernie about how to make the Hollyford attack work. Ernie helped Séumas plan it and then led it together with him. This would test whether Ernie could perform as a combat commander as effectively as he had been able to perform as an organiser.

The Hollyford attack took place on the night of 11 May 1920. The RIC barracks was a well-fortified, two-storey building with steel shutters protecting its windows and loopholes cut for defenders to fire out at attackers. It was a difficult objective. Ernie and Séumas put up the double ladders Ernie had designed and climbed to the roof, burdened down with heavy hammers, revolvers, grenades, inflammable paraffin and petrol. Their men assembled below to cover them with rifles. Ernie and Séumas broke holes in the roof, poured down their paraffin and burning petrol, threw in grenades and fired their revolvers.

Flames surrounded the two men. Ernie remembered, 'My hands and face were burning hot, my hair caught fire ... My coat was alight.' Ernie looked at Séumas thinking, 'This looks like the end,' and shouted, '"Good-bye, Séumas."'[9] Somehow they survived, climbed down from the roof at dawn, and led their men to safety in the countryside before RIC reinforcements could arrive. On the ground, Ernie stopped to criticise one of the men for having excessively fired his rifle, wasting precious ammunition that would be needed later.

Séumas and Ernie, now comrades, were badly burned, their clothes scorched, but they were pleased with what they had done together. Ernie later reported, 'We laughed at each other whilst we wrung our hands in pain. We had failed to capture any rifles, but we had driven in that post.'

They made a good team and built up their momentum attacking other RIC barracks. Their next objective, a month later in June 1920, was the Drangan barracks close to the Kilkenny border. When some of the local IRA brigade officers were overcome by fumes from the nitro-glycerine they were making into bombs, Ernie was asked to manage the attack. His leadership ability had been accepted by the local men. Ernie, Séumas and their men attacked the barracks with mud bombs and burning oil siphoned up to the roof and down into the building. Ernie told his men not to threaten the RIC men inside with death because he wanted them to surrender.

A white flag came out, and the RIC inside signalled they would consider surrender if they were allowed to live. Ernie assured them safe passage but insisted they throw out all their arms first. He persuaded them to do so, and they walked out with their hands up. Their names were taken, and they were told they would not be given a chance like this again if they went back to other barracks. Ernie ordered them to walk single file out of the village and not to look back. Ernie's team had captured all of their shining carbines, new Enfield rifles and ammunition without loss of life.[10]

Tomás Malone gave an account about Ernie's qualities as a combat commander: '[Ernie] had a superiority complex with regard to the enemy. He considered … that they had more reason to be afraid of us than we had reason to be afraid of them. He was very conscious of his own ability to deal with any situation … He wouldn't consider that he was outnumbered unless it was ten to one or more than that. He was absolutely fearless … Physically … he was like an athlete. It was amazing how he was able to keep going. He could also walk miles and miles over any terrain.'[11]

The takeover of the Mallow barracks in north Cork in September 1920 was one of the IRA's most successful operations in the War of Independence. Mallow housed the famous 'Death or Glories' British Lancers Regiment. One way the British army brought their troops to Ireland was to dispatch an entire regiment, consisting of up to 800 men, to a particularly sensitive area where they wanted to maintain security while also creating a symbolic presence. The regiment would be housed together in a significant military establishment rather than in one of the smaller buildings housing modest groups of RIC. These smaller buildings had constituted the RIC barracks previously attacked at Ballytrain, Hollyford and Drangan.

The British regiments had often fought together as a unit; they had their own permanent officer cadre and displayed good morale. This was true of regiments that had retained their cadre of officers and non-commissioned officers. Now, after the First World War, many of the ordinary soldiers in these units were new recruits. Their barracks could not be attacked nearly as easily as the more vulnerable RIC barracks, not only because of their physical defences but also because they held a larger group of well-armed British troops than the IRA could muster against them. However, a successful operation might yield considerably more armaments for the IRA than an attack on RIC barracks, and if successful would also be a big morale boost for the IRA.

The Mallow operation was carried out by the Cork No. 2 Brigade led by Liam Lynch.[12] The barracks was too large and well-fortified for the usual IRA frontal or roof attack. Liam and Ernie planned the action together, using a column of twenty-four men from Lynch's brigade – this was an example of the IRA 'flying column', a small group of well-led men able to take initiative when the opportunity arose. They found that most of the British Lancers went out for cavalry training at a certain time each morning.

Just after the cavalry group left, Ernie approached the barrack's gate alone, telling the guard he had an important letter for the commanding officer. The armed guard let him in and stood facing Ernie with the bayonet of his rifle pointing at him. In the background, Ernie could see groups of Lancers standing around. It looked like they had stacked their arms on entering the building. By putting the letter for the commanding officer in his left hand, Ernie made the guard stretch for it. He then deftly put the man's rifle's catch on safety and simultaneously snatched it from him. Slipping off the safety catch, Ernie pointed the rifle at the guard and shouted, 'Put up your hands!' When he did, Ernie quickly opened the gate and his armed men rushed in. Some held the unarmed Lancers at bay, while their colleagues ransacked the guard room for weapons. The column from Lynch's brigade made off with over thirty rifles, several machine guns, many revolvers, bayonets and over 4,000 rounds of ammunition.

The Mallow raid was a successful, symbolic IRA measure against the British army, demonstrating how a much smaller IRA unit could capture meaningful arms and ammunition from a larger, better armed British force. However, like many such actions against the British and RIC during 1920 and early 1921, it resulted in sustained military reprisals against the Irish population in the area. Liam Lynch and Ernie were concerned about whether they could depend on the promise of the British colonel that there would not be reprisals against local civilians because of the Mallow attack.

Their fears were realised when they looked back at Mallow from a hilltop during their retreat and saw the town hall and what may have been the creamery burning. The creamery provided three hundred jobs for the community. They realised that local families with their women and children were probably being driven from their homes. Liam and Ernie felt terrible: 'Our elation at success ebbed away; we felt cowardly and miserable; in silence we journeyed on amongst the hills.'[13]

Seán Lemass, another of Ernie's IRA comrades, who later became taoiseach (prime minister) of Ireland, expressed in 1970 what he believed had made Ernie an exceptional military leader: '[Ernie] had these [daring] characteristics. I suppose they were born in him ... The gap between decision and action in his case was always very small ... Leading men in actual action, in combat, he'd be excellent. He'd have the capacity to inspire them to do things that they [would] otherwise not attempt. He'd have the initiative to seize opportunities ... One of the other things ... was his fantastic organisational ability to write commands in minute detail to each and every person ... He would be writing ten to twenty maybe thirty each day.'[14]

Ernie described how he operated in mid-1920, moving from brigade to brigade in different counties:

I had overhauled my kit and books. I carried two guns; one was a Mauser automatic. Steel waistcoats often worn by police and officers could turn most bullets, but the Peter the Painter bullet, with its high initial velocity, would go through. I had a prismatic compass, prismatic binoculars around my neck, a map case, ammunition pouches and haversacks, a series of wrist straps for a fill of cartridges, a whistle and a luminous watch. I had a book, sewn together and bound in soft leather, of selections from English military training manuals with my written notes and sketches; I carried it in a waterproof case. My coat was burnt, torn and scratched ... patched with odd cloth, and the pockets, its most important part, were lined with moleskin. They could support the weight of notebooks, books, maps, pencils and medical supplies. I was my own base, and I looked it ... Jerry Kieley ... came with me. He carried my Winchester rifle ... We walked through east Limerick, from the wooded glens beyond Doon.[15]

As his experience developed as a military commander who could bring off successful raids, Ernie became more realistic about when he had to shoot to kill in order to protect his men and himself. But, as the attacks on Ballytrain (February 1920), Hollyford (May 1920), Drangan (June 1920) and Mallow (September 1920) demonstrated, he often managed operations where significant armaments were captured without any loss of life on either side. As Ernie mentioned later, he harboured no hatred of the British people; he merely believed they should not be ruling his people in Ireland.

In late July 1920, before Mallow, Ernie had been involved in a one-on-one episode illustrating his continuing aversion to killing the enemy. When walking by himself across Limerick, he came across a British captain moving through the field with his pistol strapped in its holster. He hadn't seen Ernie, who got up to ten yards away from the captain before drawing his pistol, pointing it at the ribbons on the British officer's chest. The captain must have thought his life was over. Instead, Ernie waved him safely away, pointing his pistol at the ground.

Shortly thereafter, in August 1920, during the continuing interim before Mallow, Ernie had a different experience with the British in north Cork, which ended the idea he could defeat them without personally killing them. This was an open field firefight rather than an attack on RIC or British barracks, or the individual encounters characterising so many IRA operations that year.

As they travelled over the countryside towards a council meeting of the North Cork Brigade, Ernie and his orderly, Jerry Kieley, encountered a unit of British troops moving above them. The British sighted them lying in the field below them. Ernie and Jerry were armed with an automatic Winchester rifle and a German Parabellum automatic pistol with a stock transforming it into a light rifle.

Ernie and Jerry began firing at the khaki soldiers rushing towards them with fixed bayonets. They brought at least five of their attackers down, and then another. They came across one soldier lying dead in the grass. As he fought alongside Jerry, reloading their weapons, Ernie reported, 'I felt a great warmth in my body and a rich joy as I filled my magazines ... The Winchester made the hell of a noise and the Parabellum sounded like a baby machinegun.'[16]

After repelling the British attack effectively, instead of immediately escaping across the countryside as most men would have done, Ernie told Jerry they still had ammunition and should charge the remaining British troops above them. The two men did so, shouting as they climbed the hill. Ernie had been nicked under the eye by a bullet and was bleeding, but he and Jerry were then able to escape the British force, which apparently had not expected their attack and was in disarray. Ernie was beginning to live up to his belief that he and his men could not be defeated unless the enemy had a huge advantage against them. In the terms of war, Ernie had finally been 'bloodied' in combat.

During the War of Independence, from 1919 to mid-1921, Ernie was constantly in grave danger, even though he participated in many barracks attacks without being seriously wounded, killed or captured. Often travelling at night, he might turn back to find a safe house rather than going further, only to find that an ambush had been laid at the next crossroads. Or he would avoid a house where he was supposed to sleep to find later it had been raided that night. Once in mid-1920 a young girl from Cumann na mBan, the Irish women's auxiliary supporting the IRA, had stopped him on the Ballyporeen Road to warn him the police were lying in wait for him on the road ahead.

Ernie described how Cumann na mBan supported the IRA men: 'The girls came on foot, on bicycles, in ponies and traps, some of them in uniform. Always they brought presents: honey, homemade jam, freshly churned butter, griddle or large white oven cakes, a flitch of bacon, packages of cigarettes.'[17]

The brave women of Cumann na mBan did more for the IRA than merely bring them food. They were active couriers of secret messages between IRA units during both the War of Independence and the later Civil War. They used every available source of transportation to deliver their information, often outwitting the British and the RIC who questioned or searched them. Women and girls also took great risks hiding IRA men from either British and RIC forces or, later, pro-Treaty forces. During the War of Independence only seventeen Irish women were imprisoned for supporting the IRA. This number increased during the Civil War that followed.

British and RIC forces became frustrated by the mounting incidents of IRA violence against them in late 1920. The IRA had developed an effective programme of identifying and executing British intelligence officers. On Sunday, 20 November 1920 an IRA squad directed by Michael Collins assassinated thirteen British intelligence officers in Dublin. Several were shot in bed beside their wives, who had just woken up beside them. Ernie was in Dublin that evening and had holed up in a safe house after being advised by Collins the day before to lay low. Increased allocations of troops being sent to Ireland, including the Black and Tans and Auxiliaries, were not able to prevent the onslaught of IRA hit-and-run guerrilla tactics. British soldiers assigned to Ireland increased to 40,000 in March 1921, peaking at 60,000 by that summer.[18]

Another violent IRA attack occurred shortly thereafter. On 28 November 1920 at Kilmichael in West Cork, Tom Barry's flying column killed seventeen Auxiliaries out of a force of eighteen, leaving one survivor comatose; Barry only lost three of his men. Peter Hart, a historian and critic of the IRA, claimed the killings represented a slaughter of helpless British troops. Barry claimed that he ordered his men to finish off the Auxiliaries only after they had fired on his men after a false surrender offer, but Hart argues that this was false.[19]

In December 1920, Ernie had been summoned to Dublin for a briefing with Richard Mulcahy, the IRA's chief of staff, its most senior officer. Previously, before the Easter Rising, Mulcahy had been a medical student senior to Ernie. He was clearly aware of Ernie's ability to take the initiative in challenging situations.

Ernie was asked by Mulcahy to take the Inistioge barracks, the headquarters of the Auxiliaries in County Kilkenny. Mulcahy also wanted to insert meaningful IRA activity into Kilkenny, a 'slack' area in Leinster where aggressive action had been lacking. Based in Woodstock House above the village, the Inistioge barracks was a formidable target to overcome. Ernie was to draw his attacking force from the Kilkenny Brigade and the adjoining East Waterford Brigade. Neither brigade had done much fighting so far, and experience in combat was one of the factors that measured the effectiveness of any IRA group. Ernie was concerned with their level of unpreparedness, as they had no flying column action experience and he did not know any of the IRA officers in either brigade. He suspected this assignment may have already been turned down by local IRA commanders. He understood the challenges presented but immediately answered Mulcahy, saying, 'Yes, sir ... I'll take Inistioge.'[20]

Shortly thereafter, in December 1920, Ernie was captured by the Auxiliaries in a safe house near Inistioge, which he had been using as his local command post to plan the attack on Woodstock House. This capture appears to have partly resulted from Ernie's own negligence. Apparently he had been warned that this safe house was under scrutiny and might be raided. Ernie also had papers on his person when captured; they contained the names of IRA men and stores of their arms in Kilkenny. Local resentment continues to this day for the reprisals on men in Kilkenny that Ernie's capture occasioned.

Under severe questioning at Inistioge, Ernie refused to tell his tormentors anything other than that he was Bernard Stewart, an IRA Volunteer with no rank. The Auxiliaries continued to pressure Ernie to talk, but he refused. '"Who gave you [that pistol]?"' one asked him. '"If you don't answer by the time I count to three, we'll blow your God-damned brains out." He counted to three with the pistol at his head but did not fire. '"I'm ready to die,"' Ernie said. The sergeant said, '"Stewart, you will be shot at dawn tomorrow."' Then the British brought him to another room:

> A few [soldiers] walked in their heavy boots on my stockinged feet. My toes were crushed; some stamped hard with the full weight of their legs on instep and toes ... Two guards jabbed me a few times with their bayonets ... I could not walk ... The guard lifted me, carried me along and flung me into a room. My head struck the stone floor.

The injuries to his feet bothered Ernie for the rest of his life. He was later told that most of the garrison at Inistioge wanted to execute him but a General Wood had intervened to spare him.

The next day, Ernie was taken from Inistioge to Dublin Castle, the centre of the British administration in Ireland. Here he went through a round of even more serious torture by two experienced British intelligence officers, Major William King and Captain Jocelyn Hardy. Ernie may have been identified as a particularly recalcitrant prisoner, or one who had possibly been involved in the Sunday massacre in Dublin. The British officers were enraged at captured IRA prisoners like Ernie, not only because of Collins's gang's recent killing of British intelligence officers in Dublin but also because of Tom Barry's attack on the Auxiliaries at Kilmichael. Other IRA prisoners were beaten up, and three were summarily executed by the British in Dublin Castle during November–December 1920.

After further questioning, Captain Hardy started in, '"I have a little plan." ... He walked ... to a stove and picked up a poker ... He dug the poker between the bars [of the stove] ... The crimson glow ran up close to the handle. 'Now you'll talk.' ... [He] angled the point forward as if to dig it into my eyes ... My eyelashes curled up ... "Will you answer?" I shook my head.'

The ordeal went on. Major King shouted, '"Do you think you are going to beat us?" … He hit me hard in a passion, smash after smash … I swayed on my feet … The blood in my eyes made the room a distorted jumble of reds and blues … My tongue seemed to loosen my teeth … I snorted when I exhaled. I felt myself trying to sing.'

Captain Hardy then held a Webley .45 mm revolver to Ernie's head and threatened to fire if he didn't give information. When Ernie refused, Hardy pulled the trigger, but it was a blank cartridge. Ernie gave them nothing. To the lifelong injuries to his feet had been added long-term injuries to his eyes damaged by the heat from the red-hot poker.

By late December 1920 Ernie was removed from Dublin Castle to Kilmainham Jail, which already held many IRA prisoners. The British still had no idea who he was. However, British intelligence men had recently raided an IRA safe house in Dublin. A newspaper reported that important documents of Michael Collins and a new unknown IRA leader named E. Malley had been found in this house. This led to inquiries by the British as to where this new dangerous IRA leader could be found. They had no idea he was already their prisoner, Bernard Stewart.

Late in January, a British intelligence officer in Dublin Castle sent a request for information about Ernie to London:

To Lt Col Beatty, Colonial Office, Whitehall.

There is a notorious rebel and officer of the IRA who has been concerned in many attacks on barracks, named E. Malley. He has a brother, I believe, named Frank F. Malley, 1st King's African Rifles … Can you tell me anything about him? … E. Malley is on the run and I am anxious to locate him. [signed] Col. — Police Adviser.

Someone, possibly a guard, in Kilmainham Jail who must have known that Bernard Stewart was actually Ernie O'Malley secretly slipped the newspaper report under the door to Ernie's cell to alert him. This was the first of several cases where jailers from the opposing army went out of their way to help the imprisoned Ernie, often at great risk to themselves.

Most men in Ernie's severely damaged physical condition would have remained in jail without chancing escape, hoping they might be released at the end of hostilities. Ernie continually thought of escape. He began to understand the basis for the sympathy he engendered from some of the British enlisted men serving as his jail guards. He realised that these men's resentment towards the officer class who ruled them could be turned to his advantage. Some identified with his plight even though he was an enemy soldier.

Michael Collins and his men outside the jail had identified Ernie and a few other men as priority prisoners to be freed if possible. It's believed they bribed several of Ernie's guards, who were already friendly towards him when they were approached to assist in helping Ernie to escape. Time was short, as the imprisoned IRA leaders could be brought to the courtyard to be executed at any time.

Ernie described what it was like to be in the prison: 'The cell walls were crusty with age, dirt, and misery ... boots beat out a noise that hit back off the walls, cell doors opened and shut in iron strength ... [Jail] was at first a half-world of bone-cold, smells, muddy light and crushing walls. I would stand up to yell with a high sustained note or sing songs.' Nevertheless, he kept his spirits up by reading: 'I read *The Brothers Karamazov* ... I began *Crime and Punishment*. I was so excited that I could not sleep well. The mental excitement of Dostoyevsky came over to me, it put my mind in a whirl of delight and warmth and over-stimulation.'

In February 1921, Ernie and a fellow prisoner, Frank Teeling, who had been captured on Bloody Sunday and was sentenced to death, began to devise a plan of escape. If someone left their cell doors open, they could quietly walk at night down two flights to a distant yard in the jail. It had a gate that was only secured with a thick bolt which could be cut with heavy bolt cutters. They also needed a gun to overcome guards if necessary. They gave a note to one of their sympathetic British guards and asked him to deliver the message to the IRA leaders outside in Dublin. The guard was then supposed to smuggle in the bolt cutters and revolver.

Soon afterward the British guard walked into Ernie's cell and closed the door. 'He opened … his tunic and took out a long package … "And here's something you'll like," he said.' It was the bolt cutters. Then he drew a revolver from his pocket and gave it to Ernie. It was a fully loaded Smith and Wesson .38.

There was one more obstacle to overcome. Ernie needed three men in the escape group, plus another man to be the lookout-advance person looking for guards. The outside IRA command insisted that Frank Teeling, a young prisoner destined to be hanged, and Ernie be in the final escape group. Ernie didn't have his fourth man – the lookout. He told the British guard he needed four men but only had three. The soldier came back to his cell soon after. '"Four", said the soldier, "I'm your fourth, Ga blimey." … I felt a rich, happy glow … Our soldier would find out the strength of the guards, their hours of relief, and the best way to the main gate.' Ernie was determined, 'I had no intention of being hanged. I was going to escape, dead or alive.'

The British guard came to their cell doors, unlocked the padlocks, and then fixed the shackles so they appeared to be fastened. One evening Ernie, Teeling and Paddy Moran left their cells and took the long walk to the gate. However, they could not cut the outside bolt with their special tool or scale the wall, and so they returned to their cells.

Teeling came to Ernie's cell the following night. He excitedly reported that he and the British guard, working together, had just managed to cut the bolt on the outer gate. It was time to escape. Ernie and Teeling went to another comrade, Simon Donnelly, to pick him up. They walked to Paddy Moran's cell to take him along. Paddy had changed his mind and refused to leave, believing that the charges against him would be dropped. He was also not willing to let down the witnesses who had just testified for him. Ernie later felt terrible that his close friend had not been willing to escape with them, as Paddy was executed shortly thereafter.

The three men went down to the gate and walked free into the night on Valentine's Day. At first, they were worried they would have to fight their way through the British soldiers, who seemed to be posted along the outside walls, but it turned out those young men were only locked in embraces with their local girlfriends. They didn't even notice the IRA prisoners who had just come out through the gate.

Ernie and his comrades couldn't believe they were actually out. They got on a tram and paid with a sixpence Ernie had just borrowed from a fellow prisoner, Desmond Fitzgerald, who had been the IRA Director of Publicity. On the tram, they chatted.

> We felt inclined to sing and shout ... The wind was cold, it blew clean and sweet in our faces ... Simon got off the tram by himself. Ernie and Teeling went on to Malone's in Heytesbury Street. The Malones were a sympathetic Republican family who would shelter them in time of need.

The family's daughter, Aine, opened the door. They said: 'Hello, we're paying a call.' 'Oh, oh, oh,' she said, pulling us in by the hands ... Mrs. Malone wept and smiled by turns; she ran her hands over my face. 'They hurt you ... But it's all right now.'

Soon after Ernie escaped in February 1921, Michael Collins sought him out, and when they met, he shook Ernie's hands for a long time. He then said, referring to the practice at Kilmainham Jail of hanging IRA prisoners, 'Well Earnán, you're born to be shot, you can't be hanged.' The two enlisted men who helped him escape, Privates Ernest Roper and J. Holland of the Welsh Guards, were court-martialled and sentenced to eight years of penal servitude.

Ernie and his IRA comrades continued attacks on barracks and convoys all over Ireland during late 1920 through June of 1921. IRA losses increased proportionately. The conflict began to escalate sharply during early 1921. It was concentrated in Dublin and Munster, and in sections of the west- and north-midlands.

The IRA had become adept at making effective, demoralising assaults and then vanishing into the supportive countryside in spite of the overwhelming forces they faced. After these attacks and ambushes, the British and RIC forces would rally from the entire district to hunt the IRA down. They rarely succeeded, because local people, at risk to their own lives, helped the IRA. The women and girls were particularly effective in either assuring searchers that the fugitives were not hidden on their premises or warning their men to flee just before soldiers arrived.

An example of how the IRA was able to survive fighting against vastly superior British forces is provided by the engagements that began in March 1921 between the British Essex Regiment in Cork under the command of Major Percival, including Black and Tan forces, and Tom Barry's IRA West Cork flying column, which numbered only 104 men. Percival first sent a force of several hundred men with rifles and machine guns in lorries to Crossbarry, a town twelve miles from Cork City. They were to hunt out and attack Barry's force. Barry had carried out a highly effective ambush there, killing more than ten men belonging to a British unit and capturing much-needed weapons while losing only a few of his own men.

Percival ordered his remaining forces to continue to engage and ambush Barry. But then the larger British command in Cork saw an opportunity to surround and eliminate Barry's column. The British forces were ordered to abandon their encircling positions and road blocks for an all-out effort to surround Barry's force. Realising what was happening, Barry ordered his men to break into small groups or act as individuals, to stash their weapons where necessary and simply vanish into the countryside. Crossbarry was a relatively long, meaningful engagement. Many other IRA actions during this period were smaller attacks or individual assassinations.

Barry described his men: 'The greatness of those men of the Flying Column had a double-edged effect on me. One knew they could be relied on to the last, but on the other hand, I grew to have such an affectionate regard for them that I worried continually in case I failed them.'[21] Just two months later Percival would miss a prime opportunity to capture Barry when he released him from custody without knowing he had his arch-enemy safely in his hands.

Many IRA flying columns were not always as fortunate or successful in battle as Barry's unit at that time, as historian John Crowley notes: 'Spectacular IRA victories were rare in 1921, and there were some crushing defeats. Flying columns were far from an unqualified triumph ... There were a number of narrow escapes when whole units came close to being rounded up or wiped out in one fell swoop. Few escaped at Clonmult in east Cork on February 20, however when the location of a house full of Volunteers was betrayed: twelve were killed.'[22]

Cork and its adjoining counties had a long history of supporting the Fenian movement for independence. It was not surprising that this area in the south was also the centre of warfare and violence during the War of Independence. Much of Ernie's activity in 1920 occurred there, including several attacks on barracks in Tipperary and the takeover of the Mallow barracks in north Cork.

The Cork brigades and flying columns carried out the most striking attacks on British power, such as killing Brigadier General Cumming in a convoy ambush, kidnapping Brigadier General Lucas while fishing, and assassinating Gerald Smyth, the hated RIC divisional commander, while he was drinking brandy in the Cork County Club. These audacious IRA actions were among the reasons why Cork and its adjoining counties suffered more sanctions and attacks – on various civilian activities, businesses and homes – than any other area in the country. Ten of the twenty IRA Volunteers executed by the British came from Cork.[23]

Before the War of Independence was over in July 1921, the IRA had captured about thirty RIC barracks. The RIC and British forces eventually abandoned nearly four hundred of their barracks. Usually the IRA burned these buildings to ensure they could not be used again.

The savageness of the British responses deeply troubled Ernie. He cursed when he heard stories of what to him were examples of excessive torture or killing. One involved an IRA man who was dragged behind a lorry in east Limerick until he died. Other stories emerged of IRA men who were beaten or whipped until almost dead; mutilated, they were then buried in a field where their family might never find them. In anger and desperation, the RIC, Black and Tans, Auxiliaries and British forces began killing men suspected of being IRA members, even when there might be no evidence of their affiliation.

The British response was not limited to killing. At least forty-eight creameries, representing major markets that purchased local products and employed local Irish men and women, were attacked and some were burned to the ground. Most of the creameries producing butter and milk products were located in the southern counties. Of the forty-eight attacked or burned, Tipperary had sixteen; Limerick, thirteen; Kerry, seven; and Cork and Sligo, four each. The destruction of a creamery usually meant the destruction of the livelihood of many citizens living around it.[24]

In addition, homes that may have housed IRA forces, or were known as safe houses for them, were torched or blown up. This could occur in front of those still living there. Michael Collins's mother was forced to stand by as her home was burned down in Cork. Sections of country villages were destroyed if they were considered strongholds for IRA support. In retaliation, the IRA in Cork burned down the houses of some prominent supporters of the British, who were often wealthy pro-establishment Protestants.[25]

The cruel activity of the British should have come as no surprise to Ernie and his comrades. Violence begets violence, cruelty begets cruelty. The British and RIC may have been guilty of more atrocities, particularly against civilian communities, but the IRA had to continue to use the only weapon it had to drive the British out of Ireland: continued, unpredictable violence. The IRA in Cork were particularly brutal and were reported to have executed at least seventy-eight Irish civilians for allegedly aiding the British forces. They were called spies or informers. In addition to these executions, the IRA executed sixteen civilians in Tipperary, eight in Kerry, seven in Limerick, and one in Waterford. There were also fifteen civilian IRA informers killed in Dublin, though the execution of civilians was primarily limited to the southern counties.[26]

The situation got so bad that, on 10 December 1920, the British declared martial law in Cork, Tipperary, Limerick and Kerry. In many areas, the people were forbidden to leave their houses at night. A curfew was imposed in Dublin as well. Measures included carrying IRA men as hostages in military vehicles with British and RIC forces. English public opinion began to voice its concerns. The English Labour Party Commission issued a report on the escalating violence: 'The IRA is formidable because it is intangible … It is everywhere all the time and nowhere at any given moment. Without the support and sympathy of the vast majority of the population, it could not exist.'[27]

Before the new divisional structure had been created, the IRA units and command were scattered. Sixty-five brigades had been formed all over Ireland, with the highest concentration of combat-ready men located in the southern counties under martial law. Actions taken by brigades were often coordinated with units in nearby counties, but there was little if any coordination between the southern counties and their fellow units in the west, east and north of Ireland. When Ernie was concentrating on organising units in a particular county, he had limited knowledge of what was happening elsewhere. He operated on his own. There was no effective communications system, and leaders in the Dublin headquarters found it difficult to visit their forces in the counties. Nevertheless, early in 1921 the IRA was a decentralised but effective revolutionary force.

***

By late 1920, the IRA headquarters leadership had realised the need to create a more manageable command structure throughout Ireland. They came up with the concept of having sixteen IRA divisions. Each would have the brigades in its area reporting to it. It would take time to create and staff these divisions, but Mulcahy and Collins must have thought that they had time to do so. No one knew how long the war to drive the British out of Ireland would last. They decided to begin implementing their new command concept where the IRA had its strongest presence – the southern counties: Cork, Kerry, Limerick, Tipperary, Waterford and Kilkenny. Liam Lynch had been chosen to lead the 1st Southern Division, based in Cork and Kerry. This was to be the IRA's largest combat command.

One of the objectives in creating IRA divisional commands was to ensure that these regional units developed independent leadership, empowering them to operate without direct guidance from IRA headquarters. Each division could become an army in itself, capable of surviving if the IRA headquarters in Dublin were captured or destroyed. Mulcahy and Collins were aware of the vulnerability of its brigades all over Ireland – how they were without the benefit of direct communication by phone or wire from headquarters, and how they differed in fighting capacity, arms and leadership. They were trying to build a more modern army without the benefit of the infrastructure enjoyed by their opponent, who controlled transportation and communications all over Ireland. They believed the creation of divisions might also assist the IRA in developing more military proficiency.[28]

In March 1921, soon after he had escaped from Kilmainham Jail, Ernie was summoned by Michael Collins to a meeting. There Ernie found the senior leaders of the Irish republican cause: Éamon de Valera, President of the Republic, who had just returned from America; Richard Mulcahy, IRA chief of staff;

and Michael Collins, director of intelligence. De Valera would become the senior political leader of Ireland in 1932, a decade after the warring period ended. They talked with Ernie for more than three hours and then gave him his appointment – at age 23 – to command the 2nd Southern Division. His new command's brigades would be situated in the counties surrounding Cork and Kerry's 1st Southern, including Kilkenny, Limerick and Tipperary. It would have 7,000 men, the second largest IRA command after Liam Lynch's 1st Southern.

When de Valera left, Mulcahy and Collins talked with Ernie. Collins asked him what he thought of the interview. Ernie replied that the president did not know much about his army in the south. Mulcahy and Collins burst into laughter. Ernie was concerned he had been critical of de Valera; after all, he thought to himself, other senior offices at headquarters, like Mulcahy and Collins, also didn't know first-hand what was going on in the field. The IRA field commanders were aware of this.[29]

What factors led the IRA leadership in Dublin to choose Ernie to lead the 2nd Southern? There were many other effective IRA military officers in the south, including Tipperary No. 3 Brigade commander Séumas Robinson; Ernie's comrade from Hollyford and Drangan, Dan Breen of Soloheadbeg fame; Cork No. 1 Brigade commander Seán O'Hegarty; and West Cork flying column leader Tom Barry. These men were battle-tested. They were known and respected by the men in the south, who would readily accept their promotion to the new division title. By this time, Ernie had already participated in, and led, successful attacks on British and RIC barracks in Cork and Tipperary. He had also previously served as an organiser in many counties in the west, east, and north of Ireland.

Lynch and Robinson, military commanders from the south who had fought with him, respected Ernie as a combat commander, but apparently some key IRA military leaders in the southern counties did not. The ongoing rivalry between Cork and Dublin could also have affected the opinions of many IRA officers from Cork and adjoining southern counties.

Opinion leader Tom Barry indicated how Ernie was received at a meeting on 21 April 1921, when he came down from Dublin headquarters to report that Liam Lynch would lead the 1st Southern Division. Barry still referred to Ernie as a staff captain from headquarters, whereas he described Dan Breen, from adjoining Tipperary county, as 'that splendid fighting officer'. He noted that Ernie's presentation 'left no doubts in the minds of his listeners that he had read a military book of some sort'. As Ernie spoke, Cork brigade commander Seán O'Hegarty interrupted him and basically told Ernie to sit down and shut up. In contrast to his critical references to Ernie, Barry described O'Hegarty as 'an implacable enemy of the British and had faith only in armed action as the way to his country's freedom'.[30] Ernie may have been a born combat commander, but in a situation like this his lack of social and communicative skills showed that he had limitations as well as strengths.

Ernie's courage, his ability to lead men, and his audacity and cleverness in combat had all been demonstrated, but other IRA leaders in the south, like Robinson, O'Hegarty and Barry, had also shown they were fine combat leaders. He had become knowledgeable of the counties where the 2nd Southern was located, but there were other eligible IRA officers whose knowledge exceeded his on this point. Finally, Ernie had exemplified his tenacity by persevering through consistently tough challenges, but fighters like Dan Breen had also become known as unshakeable survivors.

There were two other valuable qualities that Ernie had which his competitors did not share. First, he had trained and developed men in many different Irish counties, giving him the opportunity to understand the capacities and limitations of the emerging IRA. He became so effective as a training officer that Ginger O'Connell had asked him, in late 1920, to take on the IRA headquarters position as director of training – Ernie had refused, since it was not a combat command. Second – and perhaps most telling to Mulcahy and Collins – he had, through intellectual ability, curiosity and discipline, developed an understanding of many aspects of military science. None of his colleagues in the field had achieved this, and none gave it much attention.

Ernie had already written a comprehensive description of what real 'soldiering' entails. He had provided a detailed outline of what goes into mounting a meaningful military effort. He had listed the various disciplines involved and how they worked together; to list a few, these included infantry training, engineering, intelligence, medical services, signalling, munitions, artillery, chemicals, organisation, training, transportation, logistical support and quartermaster support.[31]

Ernie's intellectual capacity made him a more effective leader. His grasp of both concept and detail, his ability to discuss various military functions coupled with his ability to issue many clear orders to his men, distinguished him. Ernie's understanding of military science had been gleaned only from studying British military manuals completely on his own.

There has been much speculation about why Ernie did what he did. What was his psychological makeup, why was he so willing to leave his family to become an organiser, why did he move from being an organiser to becoming a combat leader? Why was he always exhibiting such bravado, trying to prove he was a man, trying to become accepted by his IRA comrades, trying to outdo his older brother who joined the British army?

The answer is simple. Once he was totally devoted to a cause, Ernie gave everything in himself to it. He was driven and obsessed as a trainer of men, a soldier and a military leader. His early comrades Tomás Malone and Seán Lemass acknowledged this. He didn't have to prove he was a man; he didn't seek or need praise or acceptance. He did what he thought had to be done with almost no regard for his own comfort or safety. He said to Molly Childers, 'I ... taught that one should always be ready to give one's life for the big as well as the small issues ... I risked my life consciously and unconsciously at all times.'[32]

Ernie is so interesting because he was not an ordinary man driven by ordinary motivations or needs. The things that most men need and seek, he did not necessarily need or seek. He marched to his own drum. When he left his family, he became a loner, totally dependent on himself. This characteristic was helpful to him while working in hostile counties where many of the locals resented and disliked him, often refusing to follow his directions.

By noting what most disappointed him compared to what disappointed most of his colleagues, we can understand one key reason why he was chosen to command the 2nd Southern Division. He was not depressed or hurt by the lack of operational or moral support from above or below in his various roles, or by a lack of recognition or respect from seniors, colleagues or those he was trying to train in the countryside. He bore that easily. What hurt him was anything that hurt the cause he was serving.

Describing his frustrations as an IRA trainer and later as a commander, he notes, 'In general things began to improve, but I made few friends ... My heart was nearly broken daily by petty meanness, by lack of energy and by the lukewarmness of the officers and men. One could forgive and understand either extreme – a good worker or a thorough slaker – but a face saver is hard to deal with. I never spared any of them.'[33] For Ernie the cause was more important than anything, including himself. It appears Ernie may not have immediately announced his own new command on his trip to the south in April 1921, when he delivered notice of the new division structure created by Mulcahy and Collins. He had at first only conveyed Liam Lynch's appointment as commandant-general of the 1st Southern at the meeting described by Tom Barry.

Shortly thereafter, as a new commandant-general, Ernie travelled to his new command in Tipperary. But he did not make use of the special transport one might think would have been available to a general officer. Instead, he went incognito on an ordinary train. As a revolutionary leader operating in territory controlled by the enemy, he and all his fellow IRA senior officers travelled undercover. This subjected him to considerable risk. Police peered into the carriages of his train as it stopped at various stations along the way. Just the day before, two trains on this route had been stopped and held up while all the passengers and their belongings were thoroughly searched by British soldiers. Ernie carried a briefcase full of maps and other incriminating material about his new assignment. Although police got on the train at several points, they did not search passengers or their luggage. For him, this was just one more fortunate but narrow escape.[34]

This new responsibility motivated Ernie to do his best. He gradually overcame any local resistance to his appointment that may have existed. He had shown he could integrate himself into the southern IRA units for the past year as he participated and led many attacks and ambushes. It became apparent Mulcahy and Collins had made the right choice.

In May 1921, after a few months in command, Ernie's leadership ability was challenged in an unusual way. Near

Thurles, in Tipperary, he was approached by the local IRA company commander for help. The Volunteer responsible for sentry duty that night had simply refused to follow orders. A direct refusal to obey orders was a serious offence that should have been immediately dealt with, but when the man told the company commander to go to hell, the commander simply couldn't handle him.

Ernie went to the sentry, who said he was tired and wouldn't do his job. Ernie was tired too – tired of telling reluctant men to do their duty. He took off his Sam Browne belt, which held two revolvers slung in open holsters. Ernie told the man to take one of the guns; they would simply fight it out together beyond a nearby clump of trees. The man looked at the belt, the two revolvers, and at Ernie. He then told Ernie, 'I'll do my share of sentry work.' They shook hands and Ernie moved on.[35]

Another challenge presented itself in June 1921. Three armed British officers had been captured in his command area. Ernie decided they would be executed the next morning.[36] This decision went back to a meeting he had had with Liam Lynch shortly after Ernie had assumed command of the 2nd Southern. Lynch had asked for the meeting in order to discuss the increased uncivilised violence they were experiencing from British and RIC forces in their areas. Captured IRA men were being summarily executed and houses of suspected IRA sympathisers were being blown up; other atrocities against civilians had also increased. The two young generals decided to show the British and RIC they could not get away with this cruel behaviour. They agreed that any armed British officer captured by their forces would be executed until such time as the enemy ceased killing their captured IRA prisoners.

As he developed as a military leader, Ernie did not lose his aversion to killing, but he did not flinch in this sensitive situation.

He spoke directly to the British officers, explaining what he and Lynch had agreed. When Ernie learned that IRA prisoners had just been executed in Cork, he noted that it was his duty to execute these three British officers in reprisal. The officers argued that he did not have the authority to carry out the sentence. Ernie told them this was not a personal decision. He would follow the agreement he had made with his fellow general to protect their own men.

Ernie asked the British officers if they wanted to see a clergyman of their own religion. They did not. They were given writing paper and told they could write confidential letters to their loved ones. They could include their personal valuables and seal the package themselves if they promised not to disclose military secrets. The three British officers told Ernie he should send their letters and valuables to Major King, then in charge of a military unit in Fethard, Tipperary. This was the same British intelligence officer who tortured Ernie severely at Dublin Castle in December 1920 when he was posing as Bernard Stewart.

Early the next morning, on 20 June, Ernie and his armed men took the British officers to a field. He told them that none of his group wished to do this. He shook hands with them and stood back. The volley crashed sharply in the clear morning. The three fell to the ground.

Ernie was encouraged by the progress he was making with the 2nd Southern Division. Positive results were beginning to show: it was becoming easier to form flying columns that could take on the enemy; the increasing attacks on British and RIC barracks and increased movements of enemy troops in his area boosted his support from civilians; his Volunteers had created training areas in the countryside, with dugouts holding supplies; firing positions were secured in the high banks on many roads; brigade and company staff were more efficient; the morale of his troops was steadily improving. The Irish people could feel proud that a real army was being formed all over Ireland to beat the British out of Ireland.

The young commandant-general relished his assignment with the 2nd Southern. Later, in a 1923 letter to Molly Childers, he described his leadership duties there:

> The previous years [1919–1920] were for me one long Purgatory but last year [1921] was sheer joy ... My first duty was to get a Battalion Staff elected and [then] a Brigade Staff. I then inspected each Company on parade and after having held a Battalion Council, addressed the men and taught them something ... Here and there one met men eager to work ... A company consisted of as many men who could be raised locally generally – 20–35; 4 or more Companies, up to 7, comprised the Battalion, the [headquarters] of such being determined by the proximity of a town or railway station, or predetermined by the presence of an enemy force ... I generally endeavoured to pull a member of the Brigade and Battalion Staff round me to show them what the area was like and to make them get in touch with the men ... I ... put my soul into writing [military dispatches], endeavouring to build up esprit de corps, strengthen discipline, love of country, inculcate an offensive spirit, make them play the game by the country and their comrades.[37]

Describing what he knew was the other side of his demanding leadership, which often asked more of his men than they could give, Ernie went on to write:

> [Even though] I seemed to have a charmed life so far as immunity from raids and bullets, fatal ones, were concerned,

I was hated thoroughly ... I was feared in an area even more than the enemy ... Fighting was so easy compared with that awful, soul-numbing, uphill fight against one's people's ignorance and prejudice ... I was able to overcome my fear in action and the men who actually fought under me were always anxious to do so again, as I nearly always succeeded – due to method and superior tactical knowledge and nothing else.[38]

On 9 July 1921, Ernie received a messenger from Dublin headquarters who had been told not to give his important order to anyone other than the division commander himself. The typed order from Mulcahy read, 'In view of the conversations now being entered into by our Government with the Government of Great Britain ... active operations by our troops will be suspended as from noon, Monday, July 11.'[39]

Ernie was stunned at this news of a truce. No other explanation of this momentous decision had been shared with him. He wondered why this should have happened without consultation between Mulcahy, Collins and the division commanders like Liam Lynch and himself. Why should it have occurred just when he was making real progress in building his division's capacity to fight. He had no idea how long the truce would last, or why it was agreed to by IRA headquarters. Ernie wanted to keep up the pressure on the British that he and his men had worked so hard to develop. Soon he would have been able to use his flying columns to carry out more meaningful attacks in chosen areas. He had no choice now but to wait, wonder and worry.

CHAPTER 4

TRUCE TO CIVIL WAR,
1921–1922

Before Ernie received the formal truce notice on 9 July 1921, it seems clear that he had received no previous information from Dublin headquarters that, in May, June and early July, a truce with the British was being discussed among the Dáil Éireann (the revolutionary parliament of the Irish Republic), the senior officers of the IRA headquarters and the British authorities. If Lynch had been informed of the truce discussion, he would have shared this knowledge with Ernie. Much of the IRA headquarters' knowledge came from regular reports received from the quartermaster or supply officers of each division, making them aware of the generally low level of weapons, ammunition and supplies. However, headquarters had not asked either commandant-general, whose divisions included the majority of effective combat-ready troops, to come to Dublin to discuss a possible truce. How then did the IRA leaders in Dublin assess the IRA's military strength in the field to decide whether a truce made sense?

The answer is provided by Tom Barry, who reported to Lynch. Barry was summoned by President de Valera to appear at the IRA headquarters on 19 May 1921. Barry was amazed to discover that it was located in the centre of Dublin. The

IRA headquarters, where all of its key leaders met, passed as an ordinary business enterprise. These IRA senior staff officers came to work each day dressed as ordinary businessmen carrying false identities and papers in their attaché cases and pockets in case they were stopped. Barry was informed that he would be required to give a 'detailed, first-hand account of the military position in the South'.[1]

He was a wanted man who would have been executed if caught by British forces or the RIC. He travelled by foot and pony cart disguised as a second-year medical student, having prepared himself with all of the appropriate documentation.

Much of Barry's time at IRA headquarters was spent with Collins, whom he described as, 'without a shadow of a doubt, the effective driving force and backbone at GHQ of the armed action of the nation against the enemy'.[2] Barry noted that Collins was also meeting separately with men from five different IRA divisions throughout Ireland at that time. Presumably these officers, like Barry, who worked below the divisional commander rank, were summoned to give information on the military capacity of their units.

After being questioned for seven days by Collins and others, Barry was finally summoned to meet with President de Valera himself. Barry respected de Valera but reported, 'The unworthy suspicion, already planted in my mind, was that de Valera was about to end the struggle.'[3] It does not appear that Barry informed Lynch of his visit to Dublin. Both Lynch and Ernie were left out of the information cycle until they received formal notice of the truce on 9 July 1921.

Ernie looked at the truce from the standpoint of a newly appointed general who commanded IRA troops in a district with a historically Fenian background of opposition to British rule. Ernie's division was gradually developing its ability to engage the British successfully in larger engagements. They had strong support from the people living in their districts. Why sign a truce just now, he wondered. His comprehension of the overall strength of the IRA relative to the British–RIC presence was limited, and from his vantage point in the south, where the IRA was making progress, he believed it made no sense to be negotiating now.

Ernie had no previous experience working in business or government; he had limited exposure abroad, and no experience working with or observing the Irish and British political systems; he had incomplete knowledge of the relative military capacity of the IRA throughout Ireland compared to the British military's strength, or of the additions the British could make to their present forces. He knew the capability of his opponents only from his direct encounters with them in various counties, and from intelligence reports. Finally, he probably had no direct knowledge of how British political leaders in London regarded their position in Ireland relative to the other dominions they controlled, such as India. Ernie's experience profile reflected that of his colleagues running other IRA divisions throughout Ireland. All but one were under 30 years of age, and none were university graduates.

Michael Collins, on the other hand, had the broader knowledge required to understand that the truce with the British was necessary and appropriate in July 1921. Collins came from a strong republican community in Clonakilty, West Cork, and as a boy he had idolised the early republican leader Jeremiah O'Donovan Rossa. Collins went to London as a young man to work in the civil service system. He made friends with both Englishmen and his own people there. This is where he first became actively involved with the republican cause. He then returned to Dublin in anticipation of the Easter Rising. Collins joined the rebellion, was captured, and began his ascendency to IRA leadership at the Frongoch internment camp in Wales.

When he was released by the British, Collins returned to Dublin and later became the director of intelligence – first for the Irish Volunteers and then their successor, the IRA. His acumen in understanding the British intelligence system in Ireland and his increased leadership capabilities in recruiting and directing young Volunteers like Ernie became apparent. As the conflict with the British developed, Collins grew to understand not only the capacity of the British forces compared to the IRA but also what the British would likely do to maintain their position in Ireland. He enjoyed a well-earned reputation as a leader. Collins was also a tall handsome man blessed with charisma; he could be as convincing chatting with a small group as when addressing the large crowds who came to hear him speak.

As Collins understood, the struggle had become frustrating and challenging for the British, who therefore might be willing to make a truce in spite of their superiority in arms and men. He was aware, as Ernie may not have been, that the British army regarded the troubles in Ireland not as a war but as an insurrection that could be regarded as a nuisance assignment for the professional British army officers and men assigned to it.

With his intelligence background, Collins was also informed of the limitations of each of the four distinct military groups fighting the IRA. There were the British army regiments, who had less than their usual troop strength and sometimes suffered from low morale; the Irishmen in the Royal Irish Constabulary, who were continually resigning because of the difficulty in being forced to fight their fellow Irishmen; and the Black and Tans, who had mixed training and morale. The Auxiliaries operated as separate units and often supported the RIC; although paid double what the Black and Tans received, one of their limitations had already been demonstrated by their loss of seventeen out of a unit of eighteen men being transported in military vehicles at

Kilmichael in 1920.[4] However, they could be highly effective and were respected by Ernie as a formidable opponent.

These four British groups did not receive coordinated leadership or training, which reduced their effectiveness against the much smaller but highly motivated IRA forces fighting for their country with the active support of their own people. But Collins also knew, as Ernie might not have known, that in spite of these advantages, the IRA could not beat the British out of Ireland and should therefore seek a truce. Collins would also have been aware of the backchannel diplomatic communications that had been going on between Sinn Féin and London for some months, as well as of the international publicity created by the British reprisal policy in Ireland. All of these factors gave the Irish an advantage in seeking a truce at this time.

Collins made it clear why he supported the truce in early July 1921: 'We had prevented the enemy so far from defeating us. We had not, however, succeeded in getting the government entirely into our hands, and we had not succeeded in beating the British out of Ireland, militarily. We had unquestionably seriously interfered with their government, and we had prevented them from conquering us ... We had reached in July [1921] ... the high-water mark of what we could do in the way of economic and military resistance ... We had recognised our inability to beat the British out of Ireland, and we recognised what that inability meant.'[5]

He had made a convincing case for the truce, which he believed would be a stepping stone to the eventual freedom that could not be achieved for Ireland in December 1921. In his short book *The Path to Freedom*, written early in August 1922, Collins told the world why the Treaty with Britain, supported by the Irish people, made sense for his country, and why the anti-Treaty leaders like Ernie and Lynch should have supported it.

But his manifesto went beyond these political arguments, expected from a key negotiator of the Treaty. He made a compelling case to the nations of the world that after its inspiring struggle for freedom, Ireland had achieved the status of a nation deserving the respect of its fellow nations.

Mulcahy and Collins also had an important area of responsibility and understanding not shared by most of the commandant-generals who reported to them. They had both been elected to the Dáil and, unlike Ernie later, actually served there. This meant they were responsible to the people of Ireland who had elected them, giving them a better grasp of the people's wishes and beliefs as Ireland went through this difficult period. If they had been able to share this broader view with the field commanders reporting to them, it might have been an added persuasive element in helping these young men to understand why the truce was necessary and why a negotiated peace agreement made sense for Ireland. When the next, much bigger challenge of getting these IRA field commanders to accept the Treaty came up, an important precedent would have been set. Division commanders like Ernie and Lynch would have had more confidence in Mulcahy and Collins. They might have been more receptive to arguments urging them to accept the Treaty. Instead, they became accustomed to being completely ignored in important decisions seriously affecting their commands.

Treaty discussions with the British went on for almost five months after the July truce – first, in written communiqués between Dublin and London, and then in London after the Dáil sent its Treaty delegation there in October 1921. President de Valera deliberately stayed in Dublin, it is often said, to give himself future leverage to object if the final treaty displeased him, as he asked the plenipotentiaries to report back to him before signing. His demands for total independence for Ireland's thirty-two counties could never have been agreed to by the British, since the Government of Ireland Act of 1920 had already created a parliament in Northern Ireland to govern six of the nine counties in Ulster. The Irish representatives sent to London to negotiate the Treaty were led by Arthur Griffith, with Michael Collins as his deputy.

The Prime Minister of the United Kingdom, David Lloyd George, led the British treaty delegation, which included Winston Churchill, then secretary of state for the colonies. The British began by insisting that there could be no Irish republic, that the government of Northern Ireland must continue, that Irish parliamentarians must swear an oath of allegiance to the British sovereign, and that the British would occupy three strategic naval ports at Cobh, Berehaven and Lough Swilly – and that Ireland would have to provide all other ports to Britain 'in time of war'.

The Irish people were fed up with the violence that had been ravaging their country from 1919 until 1921, and the British were tired of sending more and more men to Ireland well after the First World War had ended. One would think that after the truce of July 1921, it would have been relatively easy for the two sides to arrive at a mutually acceptable treaty.

There were many reasons why this proved to be so difficult. Ireland was only one country in the large British colonial system – which included their largest colony, India. If Britain allowed Ireland to be a fully independent republic, as desired by Irish nationalists, this permissiveness would be a dangerous precedent for India, where an independence movement was already established. Any such action would also be a bad example for other British colonies now beginning to agitate for their independence.

Continued control of the Irish ports in the event of a war with European powers was also important to the future defence of Great Britain. The fully independent republic demanded by de Valera and young IRA commanders like Ernie would not be achieved for many years.

The six counties in the north could not be included in a future Irish republic. Their position had been sealed by the Government of Ireland Act of 1920. The Irish Unionists in the six counties had lobbied the British government to enact this into law so that they would retain their union with Britain. Ernie never conceded publicly that the partition of Ireland was legitimate. He continued in his belief that the Irish republic included the thirty-two counties.

In mid-November 1921, well after the July truce and almost at the end of the treaty negotiations carried out in London, Ernie – still commander of the 2nd Southern – travelled to London with Johnny Raleigh, one of his men from Limerick. They went to see if they could buy war materials from the British Disposal Board, which was selling excess war materials from the First World War no longer required by the British military. With a few £5 tips to the right people, Ernie and his companion managed to buy prismatic compasses, range finders, artillery knee boots, Sam Browne belts and other equipment. They were also able to order three tons of an explosive base with no questions asked. He was surprised that the higher-level English people in charge accepted bribes to look the other way.[6] Ernie was planning to use these military resources for his command when the truce was over.

When Ernie was invited to lunch in London by Desmond Fitzgerald, then the head of IRA publicity, he was surprised to run into Michael Collins at the premises occupied by the Irish Treaty delegation. Collins asked him, '"What the hell are you doing in London?"' Ernie replied that he was 'having a break', and Collins responded, '"That's the way with you bloody fellows … I suppose you think the truce is a holiday."'[7] Collins told him the negotiations would end shortly and gave him an important package concerning the Treaty to take back to de Valera. Ernie noted to himself that Collins appeared worried, looked unhealthy and had clearly been drinking. This was an ominous foreshadowing of the worsened relationship Collins and Ernie would begin to experience when Collins returned to Dublin with the results of the negotiations in early December.

However, Ernie wrote of Collins, 'He drank, but I never saw signs of drink on him, except in 1917. Now he neither smoked nor drank, but later he began to drink, especially when in 1921 he lived alone. He had difficult tasks to carry out. He led a harassing life, and we who had given up drink had always a soft spot for Michael's use of drink.'[8]

Near the end of the negotiations, Lloyd George challenged the Irish team by saying that if they did not accept his final proposal, he would initiate an 'immediate and terrible' war against Ireland. The Irish delegation debated through the evening of 5 December whether Lloyd George was bluffing or not.

Griffith and Collins knew that substantial benefits for Ireland had been achieved in the draft Treaty. This included recognition of a state – the Irish Free State – with dominion status, the prompt withdrawal of all British troops from the Free State, and a process they hoped would eventually lead to independence of the Irish Free State. They wished to avoid another bloody protracted war with Britain, and the consequences felt by the Irish people. Griffith signed initially; Collins, after some delay; the rest of the Irish delegation, after more deliberations early on 6 December 1921. The Treaty was returned to Dublin for approval by the cabinet, the Dáil and the electorate.

Opposition to the Treaty was led by republican politicians who had supported the Easter Rising, including a number of prominent nationalist families and the more militant IRA commanders, such as Ernie and Liam Lynch, who believed swearing allegiance to the British Crown was unacceptable. Any result less than the independent Irish republic they had been fighting for was unacceptable. Most of the senior IRA headquarters staff, like Collins and Mulcahy, supported the Treaty, as did six division commanders outside of Dublin. Eight division commanders in Munster, including Ernie and Lynch, and the two Dublin brigadiers went anti-Treaty. Frank Aiken eventually went anti-Treaty, and Wexford 3rd Eastern Division was split.

The cabinet approved the Treaty with a four to three vote. The Treaty was submitted to the Dáil on 14 December. Debates went on until 7 January. De Valera continued to oppose it, while Collins said it was the beginning of a gradual process that would eventually give Ireland its freedom. Every woman in the Dáil voted against it. The final vote was sixty-four in favour of the Treaty, fifty-seven against.

Two days later, on 9 January, a separate but closely related issue was debated, namely the election of a new president. De Valera had walked out of the Dáil to protest the vote supporting the Treaty. Re-electing him would have been a repudiation of the positive vote a few days earlier to support the Treaty. This time de Valera was defeated by only two votes: sixty against electing him, fifty-eight for. The margin for approval of the Treaty had shrunk, but it was approved.

National elections held in Ireland in June 1922 gave a plurality to those favouring the Treaty. Michael Hopkinson describes what happened:

> The Republican side received less than 22 percent of the first-preferences votes ... a high proportion of the vote represented a protest against Sinn Féin and their management of affairs both during and after the Treaty negotiations ... [The result]

... demonstrated a popular realisation of the need for stable government, and the acceptance of realistic compromise with regard to Anglo-Irish relations. The electorate had at last been able to show that social and economic issues ... were of greater import to them.[9]

The Irish war against Britain was over, but the war between Irishmen was lurking in the shadows. The forthcoming Civil War would eventually prove to be more shattering for Ireland than their war for independence.

The anti-Treaty republican group's basis for opposing the Treaty was rather one-dimensional, although based on deeply held patriotic beliefs. It was expressed by Ernie in simple terms: 'There were two parties now, Republican and Free State, those who believed in an absolutely independent Ireland and those who wished to become a dominion of the British Empire.'[10]

A helpful study of the differences between the two opposing groups just before the Civil War has been made by Gavin Foster.[11] He reports how the 'trucileer' element glorified the IRA resistance during the six inactive months. He also outlines the social, economic and political differences between the IRA and the Free State supporters. Many pro-Treaty supporters began referring to the republicans as a group of lower-class younger men without meaningful education, employment or family, creating a negative image for those opposing the Treaty. Republicans made much of the government jobs that pro-Treaty supporters would obtain from the new Free State government, inferring that the motivation of their leaders was heavily influenced by their economic and social gains. The Irish business and political establishment basically went pro-Treaty.

When a republican leader happened to be a well-educated, thoughtful man like Éamon de Valera, or a distinguished representative of the Ascendancy like Erskine Childers, thus negating the pro-Treaty image of republicans as an underclass mob, Free Staters marginalised these republican leaders by calling them 'extremists'. When formerly respected IRA leaders such as Michael Collins, Ernie's former mentor, or Collins's superior, Richard Mulcahy, urged their countrymen and women to support the Treaty, they were dismissed by anti-Treatyites and branded as 'turncoats' who had abandoned their former republican values.

These biased views of republicans and Free Staters in the months before the Civil War limited Ernie's ability to work together with Free State supporters towards a common cause for Ireland. Instead of recognising the validity of the other side's arguments for supporting or opposing the Treaty and reconciling them in an acceptable compromise, the two Irish groups accused each other of bad motives, failing to impartially evaluate the merits of their opponents' arguments. When the time came later for Ernie to consider whether a truce followed by peace with the Free State made sense, his biases made it difficult for him to observe the military situation with the required objectivity.

If, during the critical period between the signing of the Treaty on 6 December and its approval by the Dáil on 7 January, Mulcahy and Collins had been able to persuade Lynch and O'Malley, commanders of the two largest IRA divisions, that they should support the Treaty, the Civil War may not have occurred. There simply were not enough other anti-Treaty IRA units to carry out a meaningful conflict.

In fairness to Collins, late in December 1921 in Dublin he sent four messengers in one day asking Ernie to come to him for consultations. Ernie refused, and instead returned to his 2nd Southern base in Tipperary. The differences between the four senior commanders – Mulcahy and Collins, and Lynch and O'Malley – regarding whether the Treaty was good for Ireland was so entrenched that perhaps further negotiations would have been fruitless.

***

From 7 January 1922 until late June, an uneasy standoff existed between forces reporting to commandant-generals who opposed the Treaty, like Ernie, and the larger troop units now part of the Free State's newly created National Army. The provisional government of the Irish Free State and its army began to exercise control over the twenty-six southern counties. One of the most practical areas of difference, and potential conflict, was which military group would receive the significant handover of British barracks and arms provided for in the Treaty. It was agreed in principle that each division commander would take over the British and RIC barracks within the territory he commanded. Over the next few months, though there was an apparent initial solidarity within the IRA, in reaction to the developing split in the IRA headquarters, some local commanders at various levels were deciding to take their troops to either the pro- or anti-Treaty side.

Ernie understood the daunting challenges he would face in confronting the growing strength of the Free State army. He realised it would be difficult to keep men in barracks, to feed them, and to receive the required new sources of arms or ammunition. The men would have to return to their homes and support themselves.[12]

The new Free State army was now recruiting men with the promise of regular wages, which were not available before to IRA Volunteer forces. The Free State had received most of the arms and ammunition from the British government (though the British forces did not fully depart until December 1922); they controlled transportation and communications systems throughout Ireland; and they had the support of the majority of the Irish people, the business establishment, the powerful Catholic Church and the press.

One of the first open armed confrontations between pro- and anti-Treaty forces was carried out by Ernie. He had refused to play a role cooperating with the divided headquarters staff, returning to his command of the 2nd Southern. There, on 26 February 1922, he led a raid on the RIC barracks in Clonmel, Tipperary. One of his men knew the password, entered the gate, and let Ernie's men in. The garrison was forced into the guardroom while guns, ammunition and grenades were taken into vehicles and driven away. Winston Churchill immediately complained to Michael Collins that the Treaty was being violated.[13]

The leaders of the anti-Treaty group had asked Mulcahy, in January, to allow the IRA convention to vote as to whether to support the Treaty. The Free State government refused initially, then conceded, and then refused definitively. The anti-Treaty IRA proceeded to hold a convention in Dublin on 14 March 1922 to determine their position on developments since the Treaty had been approved. This resulted in the creation of an anti-Treaty IRA group that opposed the Free State. They elected Liam Lynch as their chief of staff and Ernie as director of organisation.

Ernie made another bold move early in March 1922 in Limerick City. Michael Collins had recognised Limerick City's strategic importance on the west coast, with its significant Castle and Strand barracks being vacated by the departing British. He asked Michael Brennan, the pro-Treaty commander of the 4th Western Division in adjoining County Clare, to take over the barracks from the British, even though they were located in the 2nd Southern district. When Ernie heard of this, he reacted immediately, asking his comrade Séumas Robinson to round up well-armed men in Crossley Tenders mounted with machine guns and to send them to infiltrate and surround key locations in Limerick. Ernie planned to take over the Castle and Strand barracks to secure all of their arms and ammunition. Fellow anti-Treaty commanders in adjoining counties sent him supporting troops from their units. He had them parade the streets of the city.

After this show of force, the Free State troops agreed to allow the British barracks to be turned over to Ernie's 2nd Southern. Richard Mulcahy, now the Free State minister for defence, had just made a special trip to Limerick City to assure his Free State forces that they would take over the key British barracks. He failed and was forced to return to Dublin in anger. Ernie had won without firing a shot, maintaining the accepted principle that the British would turn their facilities over to whoever was the local area commander. Ernie was left with one challenging aftermath. He had ordered the hotels to house and feed the numerous anti-Treaty troops who occupied the city, and now he had to find a way to pay their bills.[14]

This uncomfortable standoff between the two forces continued. Each pro- and anti-Treaty faction within a given command struggled to persuade colleagues who had gone the other way to join their side. The pro-Treaty group could not compromise since they were bound by the terms of the Treaty.

On 14 April 1922, the anti-Treaty Dublin No. 1 Brigade seized the large, symbolic Four Courts in central Dublin, as had been done by the Irish Volunteers in 1916. These buildings housed not only Ireland's national courts but also much of the nation's historic archives and legal documents. The anti-Treaty IRA group established their headquarters and garrison there, and several hundred of their officers and men, including Ernie, occupied the building. They had no plan at this point, but they were making a symbolic gesture that was not lost either on the British or the Free State leaders – they were also seeking to establish a permanent garrison in Dublin to rival the pro-Treaty Beggar's Bush barracks. Here was a large group of anti-Treaty forces occupying significant government buildings in defiance of the Free State forces controlling the city. This standoff continued from mid-April to late June with each side making gestures. Free State troops paraded their armoured cars by the entrances to the Four Courts while demanding that the occupants leave.

On the political front, the Treaty called for a constitution to be drafted and approved in London, and then put before the Irish people. National elections were called for on Sunday, 16 June, but the constitution had not been made available to the public until the evening before and so there was no time to read it thoroughly or debate. Collins and de Valera had made a political pact on 20 May that their factions would fight the general election jointly and form a coalition government, but Collins renounced the pact in Cork on the eve of the election, having given in to imperial pressures from London.

The result of the election – for 128 seats – provided the pro-Treaty side with 58 votes, the anti-Treaty Sinn Féin with 36 and Labour with 17; the remaining 17 votes went to Independents, the Farmers' Party and the Businessmen's Party. With Labour support, the pro-Treaty side were able to hold a majority – especially since the Sinn Féin members abstained from taking their seats, as they would have had to take an oath of allegiance to the King of the United Kingdom.

Liam Lynch had been elected chief of staff of the anti-Treaty IRA group. In that position, he could have declared war on the Free State and the remaining British forces. He did not do so; instead, he called another convention for the anti-Treaty group in Dublin. It was held on 18 June 1922 at the Mansion House in Dublin. A resolution to declare war on the Free State was proposed and voted on, but it was defeated by a narrow margin. Lynch and some of his 1st Southern Division officers opposed it.

Ernie was in favour of having the IRA, with support from some elements of the Free State army, attack the remaining British troops in Ireland or provoke the British to instigate an attack on them – and thus hopefully unify all the Irish elements against the British. In furtherance of this objective, Ernie, with a group led by Tom Barry and Rory O'Connor, persuaded soldiers at the Free State Curragh camp to hand over a convoy of tenders with rifles and ammunition. There were discussions at the IRA convention called by Liam Lynch on the subject of provocation.

Rory O'Connor, who was then a senior anti-Treaty leader in the Four Courts, and many men supporting the resolution to declare war immediately on the British left the meeting and returned to the Four Courts. Ernie remained until the end of the convention but returned there himself that evening. By the time Lynch returned to the Four Courts later that night, he was denied access. Joe McKelvey of Belfast had been elected as the new IRA chief of staff. Lynch left Dublin, returning to Cork and his 1st Southern.

The opportunity to end the stalemate in favour of reaching a compromise agreement with the Free State had been lost. The Irish Civil War was about to erupt.

CHAPTER 5

IRELAND'S CIVIL WAR, JUNE 1922–MAY 1923

Two events helped precipitate the intense military attack on the Four Courts in late June by the Free State army supported by armaments from Britain. On 22 June 1922, Sir Henry Wilson – a Unionist member of the British parliament, an advisor to the government of Northern Ireland and a former Chief of the Imperial General Staff – was shot and killed in front of his house in London by two Irishmen. Wilson was thought to be the leader of a small group of senior British military officers who believed the British government had been too lenient in its Treaty terms with Ireland. This unofficial group was also rumoured to be close to Winston Churchill, secretary of state for the colonies and one of the key British signatories to the Treaty. The question was: who had ordered Wilson killed and why?

Ernie believed Collins had ordered Wilson's assassination by two of his people in London in order to blame the anti-Treaty IRA and focus critical British attention on the Four Courts group.[1] This view was verified many years later when Ernie's interviews with 450 of his warring comrades were published in a series called *The Men Will Talk to Me*. One of the men was Commandant-General Joe Sweeney from Donegal, who had fought with the IRA in the War of Independence and went pro-Treaty in the Civil War. Joe eventually rose to be chief of staff of the Free State army, so he should have been a reliable informant in April–May 1949 when Ernie interviewed him. Sweeney told Ernie:

> I met [Michael] Collins in Dublin the day after [Henry] Wilson was shot. It was two men of ours did it, he said. He looked very pleased. The last time I had seen him so pleased at a shooting was when [the] District Inspector who had kicked Tom Clarke when a prisoner in 1916, and had ill-treated others, had been shot on his orders in Wexford.[2]

If Sweeney was correct, Collins could have had at least two motives, or a combination of both, for ordering Wilson's execution. One was to discontinue Wilson's urging Churchill to scrap the Treaty, which was opposed to what Collins was trying to achieve; the other was for the action to be blamed on the anti-Treaty IRA. In Frank O'Connor's 1937 biography of Collins, he made it clear that he believed Collins had ordered Reggie Dunne to kill Wilson because he was a leader of the Unionist British group urging Churchill and others to scrap the Treaty and bring war to Ireland again.[3]

The second event that helped precipitate the attack on the Four Courts occurred when Ernie suggested to Joe McKelvey, newly appointed as anti-Treaty commanding officer at the Four Courts, that they kidnap a senior Free State officer in retaliation for the recent arrest of their own Commandant-General Leo Henderson. They would hold him prisoner in the Four Courts until their general was released. Ernie not only suggested their target – Ginger O'Connell, a high-ranking Free State officer – but also went out with his assistant, Seán MacBride, and kidnapped O'Connell in Dublin. Later, in captivity, Ginger joked with Ernie and others he had known well from prior days. The kidnap did not secure the release of Henderson.

But this was no joking matter to the British. On 26 June 1922, Winston Churchill wrote a letter to Michael Collins signed by Lloyd George:

> The ambiguous position of the Irish Republican Army can no longer be ignored by the British Government. Still less can Rory O'Connor be permitted to remain with his followers and his arsenal in open rebellion in the heart of Dublin in possession of the Courts of Justice ... His Majesty's Government cannot consent to a continuance of this state of things, and they feel entitled to ask you formally to bring it to an end forthwith.[4]

Free State forces under pressure by the British then demanded the surrender of the Four Courts by notice delivered at 3.40 a.m. on 28 June 1922. The IRA command in the Four Courts refused to surrender and the attack began. The Four Courts complex was made up of separate buildings, many of which were not connected by underground tunnels. This made it dangerous for its occupiers to move from building to building without being hit by incoming rifle, machine gun or cannon fire. Buildings on one side of the complex looked down into it, creating ideal platforms for sniper fire into the complex. Adequate preparation had not been made to ensure that the complex was defensible, nor had adequate arms for its defence been collected.

The IRA now had over 180 men in its garrison there. Many were staff, not combat-tested men. Joe McKelvey and his senior officers, Rory O'Connor, Liam Mellows, Paddy O'Brien and Ernie, had known an attack was imminent. They had debated whether to stay to fight it out. If the senior anti-Treaty officers had had the foresight to realise they were facing long-term overwhelming odds, they could have chosen to leave. Lynch, who had been arrested but was released, had returned to rejoin his 1st Southern, hoping the standoff could be worked out. The pro-Treaty forces should never have released him. The IRA officers and garrison at the Four Courts could have quietly left in the dead of night, melting away into Dublin and its surrounding area. Calmer heads may have been able to negotiate a settlement between the anti- and pro-Treaty groups. The attack would not have happened, and peace might have been achieved. Instead, the IRA senior officers decided to stay. Several years later, in prison, Ernie asked himself this key question: 'Lying in bed, I had doubts about our course of action in resisting the attack of the Staters on the Four Courts; I wondered if any other solution could have been reached.'[5]

Paddy O'Brien was then instructed by the leadership to direct Ernie to become officer in charge of the defence of the Four Courts. Ernie objected that he was not the senior officer. Liam Mellows put his arm around Ernie's shoulder, saying, '"We'd all prefer to serve under you, don't you know that, for you have had the most experience of any of us." He patted his rifle barrel.'

The British had previously made artillery and heavy machine guns available to the Free State army surrounding the buildings and the attack began. Ernie did his best to defend the position and inspire his men. His command post was exposed to incoming fire. Returning to his room in the midst of battle, he described the books of his that had somehow survived his ordeal during the War of Independence against the British: 'I picked up ... Baudelaire, two *al fresco* prints, Tintoretto and Piero della Francesca, a portfolio of drawings. There were two bullet holes through a copy of Vasari's *Lives of the Italian Painters* ... A piece of artillery [had] gone through a John Synge book illustrated by Jack Yeats ... A volume of Montaigne had escaped shell and bullet. He would have been a good man to have here with us ... I put him in my pocket where he lay beside a thin copy of Shakespeare's *Sonnets*, which I had been reading last night.'

During the siege, Ernie had noted that his men were kind to each other when they were in danger. He observed that one would never expect that they could be so caring of comrades during the attack, often protecting others rather than themselves. But he also understood that they were in an untenable position with poor defences, communications and weaponry, surviving on food and ammunition smuggled in by members of Cumann na mBan who approached the gates at night. Ernie was fortunate not to be killed or seriously wounded. A bullet cut the strap of his field glasses throwing them to the courtyard floor, but no bullet claimed him.

A priest and doctors came to the Four Courts to take care of the dead and wounded. When a doctor asked who was in charge, Ernie replied, '"I'm in charge ... My name's O'Malley."' The doctor responded, '"I don't agree with you ... but you're a great crowd. Don't you think you have done your duty? Can't you surrender now?"' When Ernie replied in the negative, the priest tried to convince him otherwise, saying, '"Padraig Pearse had to surrender to save the people ... The movement went on when he was dead."' Ernie answered, '"Padraig Pearse fought a good fight ... We haven't done so. We're not men just now, we're a symbol, and I think we should hold this place to the last. No, Father, we won't surrender."'

Shortly thereafter, there was an enormous explosion and the block where munitions had been stored earlier under the Record Office blew up with a roar. It contained historic records that would never be recovered. The Record Office, on the exterior of the complex, had been evacuated; the Free State forces were in possession of it and were continuing to make inroads on the entire complex. A fire was started that ultimately spread and demolished the Record Office. Ernie and his men tried to avoid the pieces of metal, stone and wood crashing all around them as rifle grenades were fired through the open windows and into the courtyards. More and more men were being wounded.

Commander Joe McKelvey and Rory O'Connor insisted that the Four Courts garrison be surrendered to Free State forces. Ernie and Liam Mellows disagreed, but eventually Ernie accepted. They debated who should make the surrender; no one, including McKelvey, wished to take responsibility for this last step. Ernie was in charge of the battle group, so he decided to make the surrender himself. In front of the Four Courts complex, he met Brigadier-General Paddy Daly, who commanded the Free State forces surrounding it, and asked for conditions for the men he was surrendering. However, Daly had been ordered to accept nothing but an unconditional surrender.

After surrendering the Four Courts' garrison, Ernie walked over to a Free State officer he had known earlier, during the War of Independence – a Clare man, Captain Ignatius O'Neill. Ernie asked O'Neill to do something special for him. He had some valuable papers in his pocket that he wanted his former comrade to deliver secretly to an IRA source. In spite of the danger in so obviously assisting the senior enemy officer, the captain promised on his word of honour to do what Ernie asked him.

General Daly ordered Ernie to march his men along the quays of the River Liffey to the Jameson Distillery buildings a few blocks away. As they marched in columns of four, a curious crowd surrounded them. The women lamented the fate of the captured men: 'Look at the poor boys, God help them. Who'd ever think it would come to this.' They came to the distillery, which was surrounded by Free State soldiers with fixed bayonets. Daly ordered Ernie to lead his men inside the distillery, to a large courtyard surrounded by high walls. The ground-floor windows had iron bars facing the street.

Rory O'Connor had been urged by Ernie to leave the Four Courts and continue the fight. He refused and so was also captured in the distillery. When the armed Free State troops guarding them had lowered their rifles to the ground, Ernie immediately thought he saw an opportunity for his men to disarm them. He went to Rory and told him how they should rush their captors and overcome them. He noted that the Free State men could not use their rifles easily in the crowded space. This gave his men a chance to overcome their captors, hold the building, and continue their fight. Rory refused to make this attempt with Ernie. Ernie was severely disappointed. He could not understand why his comrade would not act.

The Free State soldiers left the yard, and Ernie was alone there for a moment with a few of his men. Seán Lemass came up to him with excitement. He pointed out a small gate in the corner of the yard that apparently led into the manager's house fronting on the outside street. He thought they might use it as an escape route. Ernie and a few men opened the gate and went into the house through the kitchen, where the manager and his wife were looking out into the street; upon entering they said to the couple, '"Good day. Please excuse us passing through your house, it's rather urgent," and walked past into the crowd.'

They went directly to Paddy O'Brien's house behind Dublin Castle. His sister opened the door and was amazed to see Seán Lemass. '"How on earth did you get here? We heard you were all prisoners in Jameson's." "Oh, we did not like the distillery, so we left it," said Seán.' Ernie had escaped again. As the officer responsible for the Four Courts defence, he would most likely have been executed in December 1922 with the four other senior IRA officers captured there.

Shortly after Liam Lynch, in Cork, received news of the surrender of the Four Courts, he resumed his prior role as chief of staff of the anti-Treaty IRA forces. Soon thereafter, he appointed Ernie to head the Northern and Eastern Commands. Ernie was later promoted to be Lynch's assistant chief of staff, the second most senior position in the anti-Treaty forces.

In July–August 1922, the pro-Treaty Free State army consolidated their military position, controlling most of Ireland. They continued to enlarge their forces, with many men responding to recruitment for salaried positions. Michael Collins was appointed commander of the Free State army. Their efforts to take control of the extensive anti-Treaty areas included a large operation in which ships landed troops in southern and western ports in Cork, Kerry and Mayo. These thrusts enabled them to capture many areas in these counties. The Cork–Kerry landings facilitated a pincer movement, which led to the capture of Limerick City and the Kilmallock-Bruff-Bruree triangle, three towns south of the city. The Mayo landing party gained control of barracks and towns not only in Mayo but also in the adjoining counties of Sligo and Roscommon. The Free State had also quickly established a national salaried police force, the Garda Síochána.

There was a short period, from the surrender of the Four Courts at the end of June 1922 until early August, when the IRA had a clear military advantage in the southern counties. These counties constituted the territory of Lynch's 1st Southern and Ernie's 2nd Southern. When the Civil War began and Lynch and Ernie achieved higher commands, these divisions were assigned to other commanders.

These IRA forces may not have had artillery like the Free State army, but they were armed with machine guns, a few armoured cars, trench mortars, rifle grenades, and modern rifles and handguns. They had more troops in the southern counties than the Free State, and their troops were better trained and motivated than the green, often undisciplined Free State forces. The Free State did have cadres of seasoned troops like the Dublin Guards, formerly good fighters in the original IRA who bolstered the newer recruits.

In early July 1922, had Ernie travelled south from Dublin to assist Lynch in bringing together their 1st and 2nd Southern Divisions, forming an army capable of marching on Dublin, the outcome of the Civil War could have ended differently. However, both young officers lacked the experience of leading a large consolidated army. Even if this strategic concept had occurred to them, they didn't have the command experience or the transportation capacity to execute it.

The divisions that they had led up until the truce had been staffed with Volunteers motivated by the concept that they were fighting Britain for their country's freedom. Now they would have to fight fellow Irishmen. During the dormant period between truce and Treaty, many Volunteers had returned to their farms and jobs. It would have been difficult for Ernie and Lynch to mobilise them quickly for a march on Dublin.

But Lynch did have the capacity to organise his southern command to successfully resist at least some of the Free State landings on the south-west coast and their subsequent moves to capture key locations while taking over local infrastructure. Why Lynch and his deputy in the Limerick area, Liam Deasy, were not able to overcome the Free State onslaught is demonstrated by the battles for Limerick City and the Kilmallock triangle, which went on from July until 6 August. John O'Callaghan's *The Battle for Kilmallock* provides a clear outline of how these encounters could serve to predict the outcome of the Civil War.

They began on 11 July with the Free State attack on Limerick City. Lynch first made a strategic mistake by allowing truce negotiations between anti- and pro-Treaty forces in Limerick City to go on for days in early July, giving the Free State commander, Michael Brennan, time to bring in needed reinforcements, including artillery pieces. Brennan began attacking IRA defence points using his artillery. By 21 July, Lynch withdrew his troops, leaving Limerick City to Brennan.

Instead of remaining in Limerick to lead his troops directly, Lynch shifted his headquarters to Clonmel in Tipperary before moving again to the Old Barracks, Fermoy, Cork. He was too far away during the key month of July to be the hands-on commander his men needed.[6]

The IRA initially had more seasoned troops in the south, but they lacked the leadership required to use them effectively against Free State forces strengthened daily by reinforcements. They had trouble feeding their men and lacked control of the local transportation systems required to move troops. In the battles that went on from mid-July to early August, Free State forces took Bruree in a decisive victory. Nearby, the IRA was about to capture Bruff, but withdrew at the last moment – a setback. After receiving reinforcements, including artillery, Free State forces finally captured Kilmallock on 5 August. Meanwhile the Free State was successfully landing troops by sea at Kerry and Cork on 2 and 8 August. By mid-August the IRA had lost most of the key areas in the southern stronghold counties they had previously controlled.

The Free State was now able to consolidate its control of infrastructure in the previous IRA strongholds in the south, and in the rest of the country. The Free State army had demonstrated that IRA forces could no longer offer meaningful resistance. The failure of the IRA to exploit their earlier military advantage was described bitterly by Tom Kelleher, Lynch's successor as commander of the 1st Southern: 'It is my personal opinion that Liam Lynch and Liam Deasy were simply not up to it, but neither was our headquarters staff in Dublin. We were allowed to fragment in the countryside when we should have throttled the Staters in the early months of 1922.'[7]

In a practical sense the Civil War was effectively over by mid-August 1922. At this point, the IRA no longer had the ability to effectively engage their enemy. If Liam Lynch, in Fermoy, and Ernie O'Malley, in Dublin, had had the experience, maturity and wisdom to understand this, they might have saved their country many months of conflict and grief. Ireland was subjected to war from 1919 to the late spring of 1923, broken only by the waiting period from July 1921 to June 1922.

Lynch, Ernie and their anti-Treaty division commanders in 1922 faced insurmountable challenges that did not exist during the War of Independence. Before, the Irish people had given the IRA effective support in fighting the British. Now they supported the Free State and informed on the IRA. Formerly, meaningful segments of the Catholic Church supported the IRA; now, almost the entire Church actively supported the Free State, and business interests had turned against them.

The people in the southern counties had been the centre of opposition to the British during the War of Independence, but they had also suffered the greatest damage to their local communities, to their farms, to their small businesses and to their creameries. They had lost their fathers, their sons, and many of their homes as well. Most of them were finally ready for peace.

Charles Townshend points out that when the Civil War began in the summer of 1922, Lynch made a grave mistake in assigning Ernie as head of the Eastern and Northern Commands, headquartered in Dublin, rather than returning him to a field command, where he would have direct contact with his troops. This had been his zone of greatest military effectiveness when fighting the British. While there were over 1,000 men in the anti-

Treaty Dublin Brigade, they were scattered throughout the city and so outnumbered by pro-Treaty forces there that they could not be brought together for meaningful actions. Ernie could not mount coordinated attacks with them. He was separated from the troops in his Eastern and Northern Commands. He ended up living alone in an upper-class safe house in Dublin; he played tennis on its court to keep in shape and was supported by his hosts, the Humphrey family. He had no meaningful support staff except for an adjutant, Todd Andrews, and his military secretary, Madge Clifford. He rarely travelled to visit his scattered units, who were constantly being captured or decimated by the aggressive Free State army controlling their territory.

Ernie's dispatches to Lynch continually point out the futility of his position. But either he did not protest forcefully enough to be moved by Lynch to a meaningful command in the south or west, or Lynch simply refused to recognise that he was wasting his most effective combat leader in a hopeless situation.[8]

Ernie had to establish his own headquarters staff from people not captured in the Four Courts surrender. This took several months. Even then, his staff were scattered around the city, sleeping and working out of unofficial safe houses or small businesses and shops. Dublin was controlled by Free State forces constantly looking to arrest them. These safe premises were owned by republican sympathisers. Many of these were known to Free State men, who constantly raided them hoping to capture Ernie and his people. The anti-Treaty men and women in Dublin were also known personally to Collins's troops patrolling the city, as they had worked beside them in their former IRA roles.

Almost every day saw the capture of one of Ernie's dedicated staff in Dublin. It was dangerous for more than two or three of them to meet together. Ernie himself had several narrow escapes as he moved about the city by bicycle at night. He was able to meet with his superior, Lynch, only once in the four months after the Four Courts surrender.

Madge Clifford provides insights as to his morale during what must have been for him a challenging period. When asked, 'How would you describe his state of being in terms of happiness ... Was he lonely?' Madge answered, 'He was quite happy – happy as could be. Oh, never lonely. He just thought of the men the whole time and their welfare.'[9]

This challenging period appeared to further develop Ernie's strong sentiments against those in Ireland who supported the Treaty. The passionate feelings he must have shared with many IRA comrades at the time were expressed in a letter he wrote to the editor of the *Freeman's Journal* on 24 August 1922:

> You ... condone the suffering of our prisoners ... the midnight assassination of Harry Boland. ... You would outlaw the Republicans, treat them like bandits and reduce this ghastly business to a war of extermination ... You cannot escape your share of responsibility for this disaster. Ever since December last, you have by misrepresenting the issue and by falsifying and suppressing the truth, helped to create an atmosphere which made civil war certain. And now ... you are wantonly and maliciously inflaming the minds of Free State soldiers against the men who are defending the Irish Republic ... You would lash these soldiers into a furious blood-lust against their fellow-Irishmen ... You say the people are overwhelmingly in favour of the Treaty. It is a lie ... The crime is at your own doors. When the Treaty was signed without the knowledge of the men who won the war ... We are following ... the traditional, historic and ascertained will of the Irish nation for absolute independence ... Therefore we go forward to ultimate victory.[10]

Ernie did not understand that his men had not 'won the war', nor did he appreciate that the will of the Irish nation had already voted to support the Treaty, which did not provide for 'absolute independence'.

The cruelty that the Free State practised against IRA prisoners in the Civil War was similar to the excesses perpetrated by both sides at the end of the recent War of Independence. Ernie's passionate reaction to the abuse and execution of his men, who had fought for Ireland's freedom, by the Free State army had a deep impact on his attitude as a senior anti-Treaty military leader. This passion appears to have equally affected Liam Lynch. Thereafter, neither IRA commander would look at the struggle in balanced military terms: they were outraged patriots who must somehow right the infamous wrongs being perpetrated against their men. Righting such wrongs included reprisals where opportune, and their feelings were so strong that peace efforts would not be entertained.

Ernie's Northern and Eastern Commands were hardly commands. He had scarcely any available forces to raise for meaningful military endeavours. His September 1922 military dispatches display the deep difficulties he faced. Ernie wrote to general headquarters on 18 September, 'Perhaps you do not realise that 90 [per cent] of officers in the Dublin Brigade have been arrested ... and about 89 [per cent] of the 1st Eastern Division ... Officers are arrested so frequently ... that it is extremely difficult to get any kind of a sustained report system.' The commander of the 1st Eastern Division wrote to Ernie on 20 September, 'We have not a single volunteer with us from the old 6th Brigade. They went "wrong", lock, stock and barrel ... There is one man in the town with us.'[11]

Frank Aiken, commander of the 4th Northern Division, wrote to Ernie on 16 September, 'I don't think you should risk coming down here yet awhile ... At present none of the officers know their resources exactly.' The 4th Northern had been a strong IRA division. The commander of the 1st Northern Division, Séan Lehane, wrote to Ernie on 19 September:

> This with the exception of a small section in [the] East and a few scattered riflemen in North Donegal is the only body of men operating in the [1st Northern] Division ... The population is for the most part hostile ... supporting a Column of any effective strength is out of the question ... The capture of Nos. 1 and 2 Brigade Columns ... had the effect of demoralising the few men left who regarded the game as practically up.

Ernie wrote to Liam Lynch on 22 September, 'The Boundaries of the 4th/5th Northern [Divisions] are to my mind a ridiculous military area. I think that all Divisional areas would want to be shaken up again.' Ernie wrote to Lynch again on 24 September, '3rd Northern; no contact with this area for some time past ... the Northern Government were examining correspondence.'[12]

Influential people from abroad, including the Irish College in Rome, sought Ernie out in Dublin, offering to broker a peace deal between the two warring Irish forces. Other senior military commanders might have grasped at these opportunities, considering the dire circumstances faced by the anti-Treaty forces. Ernie's dispatch to Lynch on 22 September shows how he handled these peace inquiries, 'I have turned down all people who have tried to get in touch with me concerning peace; I have referred them to you. It has a very bad effect on the morale of the troops to hear any peace negotiations are in progress.'[13] Ernie must have known that referring these foreign emissaries to his commander, Lynch – a man on the run somewhere in the south – was simply telling them to go away.

Ernie was deeply committed to Ireland's freedom, but it's hard to understand his refusal to face the reality that by the end of September 1922, IRA forces faced overwhelming odds and had become fugitive guerrillas. This had been their position in January 1919, but now they were not fighting occupying British forces; they were making war against Irish countrymen who had been their comrades in the earlier war. They were no longer willingly supported by the Irish people; the people now supported the Treaty, which removed British troops from the twenty-six counties. They were fighting the Free State, which had an effective, established government, and their Sinn Féin party abstained from participating in the Dáil.

Had the leading divisional commanders, O'Malley and Lynch, decided it was time to seek peace, other key anti-Treaty generals like Frank Aiken might have gone along with them. The Civil War could have ended in September 1922 instead of eight damaging months later in May 1923. Many unfortunate developments, including the executions of the prominent IRA leaders Erskine Childers, Rory O'Connor, Liam Mellows, Joe McKelvey and Dick Barrett in November–December 1922, would have been avoided. The continuing executions of IRA men held in prison and the imprisonment of so many other anti-Treaty men and women between October 1922 and July 1924 would not have occurred. Ireland could have managed a quicker recovery from Civil War.

Seán Lemass, a former IRA officer who had fought under Ernie's command, described the qualities that made Ernie an exceptional field combat leader, but when asked about Ernie's capacity as a senior leader at headquarters in charge of strategic planning, he gave Ernie very different marks:

I'm not quite sure he was as good a man in a Headquarters post deciding on strategies. I'd say he'd be no good at all.

This could be unfair to us because the time I saw him at his Headquarters office, then Officer in Charge of what was then the Eastern Command of the IRA. It was clear that we'd already lost the Civil War.[14]

In November 1922, four months after his escape from the Jameson Distillery, Ernie was alone in a spacious safe house in a suburb of Dublin owned by Mrs Ellen (O'Rahilly) Humphreys. The Humphreys family were strong anti-Treaty sympathisers and had a long multigenerational history of supporting the Irish republican movement. Several of their prominent acquaintances were among the sixteen men executed in 1916 as leaders of the Rising. The Humphreys and other opponents of the Treaty, at considerable risk, continued to support the anti-Treaty forces and its leaders.

The Humphreys' house had a secret room on the second floor where Ernie slept at night. The house had been raided in October when Ernie was on an inspection tour of his forces in the north, but the Free State troops had not found the entrance to his concealed room. This gave Sheila Humphreys, Ellen's daughter, who was also living in the house, the false security that they would not raid again. During her later anti-Treaty Cumann na mBan activities, Sheila would be imprisoned by the Free State and went on a hunger strike.

At 7.30 a.m. on Saturday, 4 November 1922, Sheila knocked at Ernie's door, '"Earnan, the house is surrounded; the Staters are coming in the gate." Excitement was mounting in her voice.' Ernie replied, '"Thank you, Sheila, I'm all right. It's come at last."' He knelt down to pray for courage and then sat on the bed with his revolver in hand and listened in the darkness. He thought, 'My will to fight seemed to me intact.'[15]

While waiting Ernie remembered the Táin, the legend Nannie had told him and his brother Frank as children – of the ancient

Irish warrior Ferdia who tragically died fighting his former comrade Cúchulainn. He heard a group of soldiers come to the second floor and crash their rifles against the walls searching for a hidden space. 'A rifle butt crashed against the wooden partition. A man's voice said, "It's hollow" … A heavy crash; the door swung open and a hand appeared. I fired twice; once at the hand, then below and to the right at what might have been the body, and there was a cry of pain.'

Ernie went on firing as he emerged from his room and chased the Free State soldiers down the stairs. During his gun battle with the soldiers, Ernie had inadvertently shot Sheila's aunt, Miss O'Rahilly, through the chin. Fortunately, the wound was not life-threatening and she was immediately taken care of by Sheila's mother, who assured Ernie she would be alright. Mrs Humphreys then smiled at him, and Miss O'Rahilly did her best to smile in spite of her pain. He felt terrible about hurting this innocent woman. The two ladies had been showing the soldiers around, trying to keep them away from Ernie's hiding place.

He then went into Sheila's room. '"They're hiding behind the walls outside," she said … Her bronze-gold hair was plaited around the back of her head. Her blue eyes shone with excitement; they matched the colour of her dress with its foamy white collar.'

When he went out of her room to the upstairs hall, there were more soldiers on the ground floor; Ernie threw his hand grenade down at them, and they ran out the front door. One of them had dropped his fully-loaded rifle upstairs, and another a pistol. Ernie picked them up to arm himself for the battle ahead. Ernie's superiors had ordered him to surrender the Four Courts, but no one could tell him to surrender now. Another group of soldiers rushed the house. Fire hit the house and windows as other soldiers behind fences covered their attacking comrades. Ernie heard some of them shouting that he should surrender.

Ernie fired at his attackers, 'As I fired I shouted, "No surrender here!" This was not going to be another Four Courts.'

He left the house to protect the three women. He stood on the lawn, firing at the soldiers behind walls surrounding it. 'Bullets whizzed around as I stood on the grass looking for a mark to fire at ... I could not see anyone ... I ... fired back at what might be the source of these wasp sounds. A heavy rock struck me full force in my back. I felt a cold twinge in my stomach and my knees bent forward, but I did not fall. I must not let them know I have been hit.'

With his rifle held against his thigh, Ernie went on firing. He was hit again in the shoulder 'with a sledgehammer' and fell heavily, but he staggered to his feet pretending he had merely stumbled. It was hard to fire because his rifle hand had become numb: '[my] fingers seemed thick and slow to move on the trigger. I was hit again in the back, I found myself on my knees ... My back felt wet. Blood was gluing my right hand to the rifle stock.' He reached the back door and collapsed on the floor. Sheila came to help him and found there was a huge gaping wound in his back. He was covered with blood. He lay helpless on the floor. He tried to ask her to destroy incriminating papers inside his tunic but could not speak.

Free State soldiers entered the house and stood looking down on him. He saw them dimly. One soldier picked up his rifle, ejected an empty cartridge case, put in a new one and pointed the muzzle at his body, moving the bolt down to receive a new cartridge. He was about to finish Ernie off. 'I saw the bolt move forward ... It was as though I was looking at a carp through a glass tank, the slow swish of tail, the dignified vacuous mouth and the blurred outline.'

But then another Free State soldier came to Ernie's aid. He pushed the rifle held by his fellow soldier towards the ceiling and took it away from him. '"That's O'Malley," he said, "and you'd better leave him alone while I'm here."' Ernie remembered that the soldier had stood astride his legs, rifle in hand, while more Free State soldiers crowded around him.

The medical report from the military hospital noted that there were nine bullet wounds in Ernie's body from this encounter; several of the bullets were still there when he died in 1957.[16] In his June 1934 application to the Irish Pensions Board, Ernie reported that, in addition to the rifle shots which hit him during the Humphreys' house attack, beginning in May 1918, he had been wounded by gunfire and grenade fragments in the wrist, ankle, shoulder, hip, face and clavicle.[17] This did not include the lasting injuries Ernie had received to his face, eyes and feet when tortured by the British at Inistioge and Dublin Castle in 1920.

They brought him on a stretcher to a hospital. At the main gate, when he was carried in, two soldiers came up. '"That's him," said one, and they raised their rifles to their shoulders as if they were a firing squad. "Shoot away," I said, "and waste lead." But the Red Cross men put me on the ground and stood between them and their target.' Ernie heard mention of a name, Portobello, and knew he was finally in the enemy headquarters.[18]

Ernie was barely conscious as he lay badly wounded in the Portobello prison hospital, but he could hear various doctors discussing his case as they stood beside his bed. He later recalled that he couldn't see the doctors, but their voices came through to him as if through a haze. He heard a precise, dry voice he recognised as being that of his former professor at the UCD Medical School, Surgeon Henry Barniville. The surgeon was bending over him in his hospital bed. 'The case is hopeless,' Ernie heard him say. He also recalled another doctor repeating 'Hopeless', while still another unknown voice apparently said, 'He'll live.'

Later, a hospital orderly sat beside Ernie and read him a 'Stop Press' article in the newspaper falsely reporting his death a few days before. Ernie also realised that a senior officer in uniform had been standing at the end of his bed one night, looking intently at him. He could not recognise him in his condition. The next day one of the orderlies reported to him in awe that the Free State army chief of staff, General Seán MacMahon, had come in the night before and stood looking down at Ernie for some time. The orderly reported that as he left, the general had said, 'I hope he won't die.'

Ernie, who now lay wounded in the Portobello prison hospital, was no ordinary prisoner. Jailers, Red Cross helpers and wounded British soldiers located there continued to offer to help him escape in spite of the danger to themselves. There was a sympathetic British soldier in the hospital bed next to Ernie. One day just before he was released, he brought in a Webley .45, a heavy British army pistol, and put it under his mattress. 'That's for you when you're able to use it,' he said. The soldier had been in charge of a sentry post, which could be a means of getting Ernie out of the prison. He mentioned that he might be able to get the guard at the sentry post to look the other way if Ernie could physically make his escape. Later a friendly Red Cross orderly slipped in to see Ernie, saying, 'We'll try to take you out of here some night on a stretcher, through the window. I have two men. If only I could get another.' This went on when he was still confined to his bed, could hardly sit up, and could not even stand. Yet he and those around him thought constantly of his escape.

On 8 December 1922, after a month in prison hospital, Ernie heard that four of his fellow senior officers captured in the Four Courts – McKelvey, O'Connor, Mellows and Barrett – had been executed without a trial. This was in retribution for an IRA attack the night before in which two members of the Dáil were shot at on their way to parliament; Seán Hales TD was killed in the attack.

International leaders decried these executions, protesting to the new Free State government. Many Irish leaders involved with international affairs acknowledged that the executions represented an international public relations disaster for their government.

Nothing better illustrates the tragic effect of the Civil War on former close IRA relationships than these executions. Rory O'Connor had been a schoolmate and good friend of his former IRA comrade Kevin O'Higgins. As minister for home affairs of the Free State, O'Higgins played a key role in the decision to execute the four men. A year before, Rory was best man at Kevin's wedding. These executions were reminiscent of the executions of the leaders of the Easter Rising by the British authorities. Through his prominence in these hated executions, O'Higgins signed his own death warrant. He was assassinated by apparently random republican gunmen without official IRA support on 10 July 1927.

As Ernie lay severely wounded in bed at the Portobello prison hospital, his deep love of art comforted him. He recalled his devotion for the Italian painters: 'Giotto, Masaccio, Andrea del Castagno, Mantegna, Pierro della Francesca, for I had known them for a longer time ... They had a classic formalism, a ceremonial grace, which enhanced their figures ... Holbein would intrude, with Cezanne and the glowing flame of Van Gogh, or the vigorous touch of Albrecht Durer.' Ernie recognised how unusual these interests were in the world he had inhabited for the past five years: 'I had met few people in my wanderings who were interested in painting.'

Ernie was told he would be shot. 'An orderly was rubbing my wound granulations with copper sulphate as he said, "I'm afraid it's healing too quickly, and I wish it was not, for they intend to shoot you as soon as we have patched you up."' Then he was moved to the Mountjoy Jail: 'One of the orderlies was crying as he helped to carry me out. "You're for it," he said. "They're taking you to the Mountjoy to shoot you. Oh, why are they doing this to you?" The guard outside the hospital saluted, as ... a last courtesy ... So this was the end ... I was to be shot sometime during the morning.'

Marion Malley, Ernie's mother, made valiant efforts to help her severely wounded son when he was transferred from the Portobello prison hospital to Mountjoy Jail. She badgered the authorities to give him the medical attention he needed to survive; she asked a doctor she knew, Surgeon Smith, to attend to his wounds. She wrote to Desmond Fitzgerald, the minister for external affairs, on 22 May 1923, 'The Military Governor ... assured me that my son was alright and *very comfortable*. How could he be comfortable lying on a mattress on the floor – with two painful wounds on his back? ... Ernie, I expect, would be very angry if he knew I had troubled anyone, but he always spoke so affectionately of you.'[19]

Fitzgerald, a fellow IRA prisoner with Ernie in Kilmainham Jail during the War of Independence, had given Ernie sixpence for his tram fare as he was about to escape. Marion went on to arrange for a priest, Father Paddy Brown, to visit her son in jail. Several of her younger sons were also imprisoned in Mountjoy Jail for a short time for their activities supporting the anti-Treaty IRA faction. At one point the governor of the prison, Patrick O'Keefe, mockingly asked young Kevin Malley on his arrival whether Mr and Mrs O'Malley would be joining their sons soon.[20]

Luke Malley, Ernie's father, was then an official in the Irish Land Commission under the Free State government. He had been adamantly opposed to the IRA fight against the British, and he now objected to the anti-Treaty resistance to the Free State. His oldest son, Frank, had been an officer in the British army, and his third son, Albert, had enlisted in the British army as well. Luke and Marion were now, however, in a most challenging position. Apart from Ernie, four of their younger sons had fought with the IRA in the War of Independence or were now fighting or working against Luke's employer, the Free State. The Malleys had already lost one of their younger sons, Charlie, when he was killed in July 1922 fighting the Free State army in Dublin. It is probable that Luke Malley's government agency career was adversely affected at that time because of his children's anti-Free State activities.

A delay occurred while a lawyer was brought in to defend Ernie at his coming trial. Ernie refused his services. He knew the trial would end in his execution. But there was no trial and no execution. American notables and others had been making inquiries to the new Irish Free State government about Ernie's situation. He still could not walk. The authorities did not wish to have their new government compared to the British, who were still being blamed for tying a severely wounded James Connolly to a chair to be executed after the Easter Rising. He, like Ernie, had been unable to stand.

Later, while recovering from a hunger strike in November 1923, Ernie wrote a letter from Kilmainham Jail to Molly Childers, whose husband had been executed by the Free State a year before. He was still so weak it took him six days to write it. He did not write with the spirit of a fearless combat commander but as a highly vulnerable man:

> I look upon you as my second mother and feel I can always open my heart to you. I am glad of the [hunger] strike

whatever the result. It has brought me nearer to God, to Mother and to you, and I hope I will prove worthy of you all ... I used often wonder why I had small hands for a boy. I found out when I was in Kilmainham in 1921 when it was the means of my being able to put my hand through a very small hole and slide back the bolt on the outside of my cell and so open the door. I often think what particular position am I destined to fit, and I am, as yet, in the dark.[21]

There was not a hint of self-pity for his condition as a badly wounded man being held indefinitely in horrible jails; he showed no regrets for his life, or for his continual setbacks. In prison he had been elected to the Dáil as an anti-Treaty Sinn Féin representative for North Dublin in the general election of 27 August 1923. He had not sought this political office – others had put his name in as a candidate. Ernie's election in 1923 was a continuance of the Irish republican practice of electing leaders to the Dáil who were in prison or in exile, including Jeremiah O'Donovan Rossa, John Mitchel or, much later, Bobby Sands.

When a summons to new members was sent to his home from the clerk of the Dáil, Ernie's mother sent it along to Mountjoy Jail. While in prison, later in 1923, Ernie managed to get letters out to his family asking for books. His younger brother Kevin would be sent to the Hodges Figgis bookstore to buy them; his mother then got them to her son in prison. The book store's clerks wondered why this young boy was buying such serious volumes on historical and classical subjects.[22]

During his imprisonment, Ernie continued to be personally threatened by some of his captors. In September 1923, a prison officer entered Ernie's cell and asked, '"What's your name?" ... I did not reply. We had been ordered not to answer any questions. "Get out of bed. There's nothing wrong with you."' Ernie refused and threatened to throw his wash basin at him. 'One of the police [guards] came near the bed. "It's O'Malley. Nobody is going to touch him while we are here." The officer turned quickly and walked out. The policeman who had spoken linked arms with the others and they stood outside the door ... and would not permit anybody to enter.'[23] While being threatened by some of his captors, Ernie was simultaneously being protected by others.

The assistance received from men who were his enemies is key to understanding why Ernie survived so many life-threatening situations. It is summed up by the Free State soldier who prevented him from summary execution earlier, 'That's O'Malley and you'd better leave him alone while I'm here.' Ernie had become a hero for many connected with the conflict in Ireland from 1918 to 1924. This included enlisted men and officers of the opposing armies. When given a chance, they took many personal risks to save him. Lady Luck alone didn't save Ernie.

Peadar O'Donnell and George Gilmore, two of his fellow prisoners in Mountjoy Jail, reported:

> People noticed how neatly he kept himself in jail ... They used to make fun of the fact that he always polished his shoes every day, a thing nobody else did ... He kept himself prepared for the day he'd go out in good shape ... We used to shout at him because he got into books of recipes calling them out to George Plunkett in another cell when we were tortured with hunger ... But that was typical of him, instead of playing away from the hunger he faced up to it.

During the hunger strike, O'Donnell reported, 'once he had made the decision [to go on hunger strike] his physical condition would not have mattered because he was a person always prepared to stake his life on any decision he made.'[24]

Late in 1923, to protest the conditions of their continued imprisonment, the anti-Treaty prisoners made one last effort to get their position better recognised by the authorities. They began a hunger strike in Mountjoy Jail on 13 October 1923. It spread to the other prison facilities and eventually included over 8,000 prisoners. Ernie, still bedridden, described what happened:

> Practically all volunteered; some were exempted, including myself, but I refused this concession. I wondered how long I could last; two weeks, I thought, since I had been sick for the past month, seldom out of bed. I had become thinner ... Jail had been a constant struggle, a determined effort to recover health ... Jail life is a slow poison even in the case of a healthy man.[25]

After forty-one days the strike collapsed without any definite promise to improve the conditions complained of by the prisoners or to secure their release.[26]

Before the hunger strike or even Ernie's imprisonment, the Civil War saw a casualty that shook both the opposing forces. Shortly after the surrender of the Four Courts on 30 June, Michael Collins had been made commander of the Free State army that Ernie and Lynch were now fighting. Late in August 1922 Collins decided to visit his own people in Cork. In July and early August, his Free State army had quickly defeated the IRA in the south, effectively taking over the area.

Collins was well remembered and admired by many Cork men and women as the 'Big Fellow' who loved children and older people. That day, 22 August 1922, they all came to see him as he drove through the West Cork towns of Bandon, Sam's Cross and Rosscarbery on the way to his fateful end at Béal na mBláth.

Collins had been strongly urged not to make this trip by his own intelligence chief in Dublin, and Corkmen along the way had also warned him that the possibility of an IRA ambush was simply too dangerous. The IRA still had the ability to muster effective fighting groups into action in the Cork area during Collins's visit. Collins did not heed these warnings. When returning to Cork City from the country that day, his convoy came to a curve in the road with high, wooded banks looking down on it. The advance guard on a motorcycle noticed a wire leading to a mine in the road. Collins's key adjutant, Emmet Dalton, immediately shouted, 'Drive like hell', but Collins overruled him, stopping the convoy. Instead of lying prone under the vehicles – the wise combat position when confronting snipers – Collins went out to stand in the middle of the road, firing his rifle up at the attackers. He was shot in the head from the high bank above by an IRA team member previously trained as a sniper while in the British army. He died shortly thereafter that evening.[27]

When Ernie was captured in early November, Liam Lynch was not in a strong position as commander of the anti-Treaty forces. He could not closely direct his far-flung forces, since the Free State controlled the communications systems, the roads and the railways. The morale of his troops was low, and outside the southern counties his forces were in relative disarray.

However, he continued to believe his forces should not negotiate for peace in spite of ongoing reversals. On 26 November, only weeks after Ernie's capture (which must have been a serious blow), he wrote a dispatch to his entire command. Lynch said, 'The National Position is now stronger than at any time since July 1921 and is improving rapidly every day.'[28] Lynch appeared to have lost his sense of reality. Before the Four Courts battle, he had favoured negotiating with the Free State rather than going to war. Since then, he had become adamantly opposed to peace.

Months later, in March 1923, the relative strength of the IRA versus the Free State army was as follows: the IRA southern command, including the 1st and 2nd Southern Divisions, amounted to 6,800 troops; on the other hand, there were 15,000 Free State troops in the south. Throughout Ireland, the IRA had 8,000 troops; the Free State had 38,000, a difference of 30,000 troops. Outside their southern commands, throughout the rest of Ireland, the IRA could only muster 1,200 troops.[29]

In early February 1923, IRA commander Liam Deasy tried to persuade his sixteen fellow commandant-generals in the field to accept a fair offer of amnesty just made by Richard Mulcahy, the Free State commander. The entrenched attitude of IRA leaders even this late in the conflict is indicated by the refusal of all sixteen men to accept this offer.

Their refusal to accept reality may have emanated from the same source motivating Ernie and Lynch to resist earlier offers of peace – that is, the brutal treatment their comrades received from the Free State army. Brigadier Frank Carty's reply to Deasy represented the feelings of his fifteen fellow IRA commanders:

> In reply to your appeal for an undertaking from me similar to that which you have signed ... I most emphatically refuse to be any party to such a shameful and cowardly surrender of the Republic, whose ultimate victory is assured ... Too many of our dear comrades have been murdered behind prison bars by the Imperial Free State Government to surrender now the ideals for which they died ... The murder of Republican prisoners only tends to make our Cause more sacred and to harden the determination of our men to carry on the fight.[30]

Between September 1922 and May 1923, seventy-seven IRA prisoners were officially executed by the Free State – some without trial – while another 157 were killed while prisoners; the latter were either assassinated or died in prison from various causes. Tom Malone, son of Tomás Malone and author of *Alias Seán Forde*, wrote, 'During the month of March [1923] twenty-five [IRA] prisoners were murdered by a new form of execution. On March 7 seven prisoners were brought from Tralee to Ballyseedy Cross; they were tied arm to arm on either side of a log and a mine was set off under them … Pieces of [their bodies] were scattered at the roadside and on the branches of trees and the crows had been picking at them.' Ernie O'Malley commented, 'The thundering pulpits were strangely silent about what the crows ate in Kerry.'[31]

In late March 1923, Lynch met his IRA executive group in a rural house in Tipperary to consider peace. They were on the run from superior Free State forces and acknowledged their desperate position. Eleven voting members of the IRA executive considered the following resolution: 'That in the opinion of the Executive further armed resistance and operations against Free State Government will not further the cause of independence of the country.' The resolution was proposed by Tom Barry. It was defeated six votes to five, with Liam Lynch, Frank Aiken and four others voting against it. Lynch's 'no' vote eliminated the possibility of seeking peace.[32]

Major-General John T. Prout was the Free State officer in charge of a command that included Tipperary. Shortly after Lynch's executive meeting, Prout became aware of the fact that senior anti-Treaty officers were travelling through his area. He ordered a thousand troops to search the countryside, day and night. The small Lynch party, armed only with revolvers, was being hunted by a large Free State force armed with modern high-powered rifles. On 10 April 1923, this force came across Lynch's party travelling by foot over the coverless Knockmealdown

Mountains. With their limited arms, Lynch's group could not return effective fire.

Lynch was shot and seriously wounded. He asked his men to leave him to die; they refused. Finally he ordered them to put him down and go on. Florence O'Donoghue, in *No Other Law*, reports on Lynch's death:

> 'I'm finished,' he said ... Frank Aiken took his papers and his automatic. They put a coat over his body, from which life was ebbing slowly, and they left him ... When a [Free State] Lieutenant Clancy reached ... Liam [he] said, 'I am Liam Lynch, Chief of Staff of the Irish Republican Army. Get me a priest and doctor. I'm dying.'[33]

Frank Aiken, who succeeded Lynch as chief of staff, wrote, 'It would be impossible ... to describe our agony of mind in thus parting with our comrade and chief.'[34]

In the Civil War, Ernie had lost two of his closest comrades and his brother Charlie. He described Charlie's death:

> My younger brother Charlie, aged seventeen, had been killed on the third day of the fighting (in Dublin) on O'Connell Street. He had refused to leave his post. I had not seen him during four years, throughout the Tan war, but I had seen him a few times in the Four Courts before we were attacked, all too few the times I now understood. I had been isolated from the family and had never gone home since I left the house in 1918.[35]

Commentators who note how this shows Ernie's lack of sentiment for his brother ignore that he had left his family completely for a cause. Most people would put their family first; he put his cause first. Happily, Ernie was able to recreate a close relationship with his surviving siblings when he returned to Dublin from America in 1935, thirteen years later.

But during the warring years, Ernie had substituted his cause for his family. His comrades in the cause, like Paddy Moran, became his new family. Paddy had been one of his close friends in Kilmainham Jail, and Ernie regretted that after Paddy refused to join his escaping party, he was soon executed. Ernie must have mourned Paddy's death even more than he did his brother Charlie's

Criticism is also made of Ernie's lack of sentiment when his key mentor, Michael Collins, was killed. Collins had been his early sponsor, first sending him out to be an organiser in the countryside in 1918–19 and then participating in his appointment to lead the 2nd Southern early in 1921. Ernie writes later of his reaction to Collins's death: '[I]n late August Michael Collins was killed in an ambush in County Cork. Those Free State people who had once glorified the ambush now spoke of it as a cowardly form of murder. The two men more than others responsible for the Treaty were now dead.'[36] (Arthur Griffith had just died a week before of a cerebral haemorrhage.) But Collins had now become the enemy – the enemy of what most mattered to Ernie: the IRA's cause to make Ireland completely free.

Lynch noted dispassionately in his military dispatch of 27 August 1922 to Ernie, 'There were only 9 men in party who ambushed Collins RIP and party. The main body had withdrawn only some minutes previously; we had no casualties.'[37]

However, in a letter to his comrade, Liam Deasy, written the next day, Lynch acknowledged the tragedy of Collins's death: 'Nothing could bring home more forcibly the awful unfortunate national situation at present than the fact that it has become necessary for Irishmen and former comrades to shoot such men as M. Collins who rendered such splendid service to the Republic in the last war against England.'[38] Todd Andrews, who was with Ernie the day Collins died, recalled Ernie saying simply, 'Terrible, Disgraceful!'[39] And Máire Comerford, who was with Ernie later on that day, reported that he had said, 'That's not good news. That's very bad news!'[40]

Ernie realised that Liam Lynch's death was equally tragic. In July 1923, while in Mountjoy Jail, he wrote a poem, 'To a Comrade Dead', about Lynch's death:

Dead comrade! You who were a living force
Are now a battle cry ...
You, who in life,
Have shown us how to live and now have
Taught us how to die, teach us still.
We children of unbeaten hope who oft have lacked
Courage and strength to further the cause
Of our endeavour—a nation free![41]

Twenty days after Lynch was killed by Free State forces, Frank Aiken issued an order to the IRA to cease all offensive operations, and on 23 May 1923, he ordered his troops to dump arms. The IRA never formally surrendered either their weapons or their men. They were still deemed to be at war, but in effect the Irish Civil War was now over – although sporadic fighting, raids and executions continued.

CHAPTER 6

POST-JAIL: IRELAND AND EUROPE, 1924–1928

In mid-July 1924, Ernie was released from the Curragh internment camp with the last few IRA officers held by the Free State government – more than one year after hostilities had ended. Free State authorities feared an earlier release might empower Ernie to raise his IRA comrades to continue fighting. He was still suffering from the many bullet wounds received when he was captured by overwhelming Free State forces in November 1922, and from the earlier British torture that crippled his feet and damaged his eyes. He had also survived a forty-one-day hunger strike before being released.

Gavin Foster's study of the Civil War explains what happened to many IRA veterans, like Ernie, who found themselves outliers after the Civil War. Imprisonment of IRA men had continued well after Frank Aiken's ceasefire and dump arms orders in May 1923. The Free State created a Special Branch investigative police unit to watch over and harass IRA veterans. Some were convicted of crimes they had committed while fighting in the Civil War. There were sixteen IRA men killed by the Free State after May 1923.[1] Significant political, social and economic discrimination, including exclusion from local employment opportunities, continued against republicans until the late 1920s. All this led to a significant exodus of IRA veterans to the United States and other countries in the mid-1920s.

Ernie had no money and no prospects in his native country. Although his mother had supported him in so many meaningful ways after he was wounded and then imprisoned by Free State forces, Ernie probably knew he would not be received kindly at home by his conservative father. Luke had refused to support either the IRA during the War of Independence or the anti-Treaty IRA forces during the Civil War. He could not have understood why IRA holdouts like his son Ernie continued to insist on a free republic rather than supporting the new Irish Free State.

When Ernie finally went home to visit his parents in 1924 after being released from prison, his younger brother Kevin was there and gave this account: 'He just walked in and went to his seat in the corner and had tea and bread and butter … [Our] parents were there. He didn't say very much. Behaved as though he had always been coming home.'[2] Ernie had come into a house where he was welcomed by every family member except his father.

He continued to be honoured as an Irish hero by the anti-Treaty republicans who admired the extreme courage he demonstrated under torture and under fire. Nevertheless, he now believed he was a man whose mission had failed. His insistence on complete freedom for Ireland was not embraced by most of the Irish men and women he had fought to free from the British yoke. The Irish majority had supported the new compromise Treaty rather than continuing the fight against Britain.

Where Ernie lived in Ireland for the seven months after his release and what he did is not completely known. It has been reported that he spent some time at home but also with friends such as Count George Plunkett and Robert Barton, a signer of the Treaty who later went anti-Treaty and had been Ernie's cell mate for a time. Plunkett had occasionally acted as an intellectual mentor for Ernie during the warring years, and Ernie later wrote to his wife Mary from Mexico. The Plunketts were a deeply republican family. Their son Joseph had been one of the sixteen leaders of the Easter Rising executed by the British.[3]

In 1924 Ernie did not anticipate that the fight he and his committed IRA comrades had waged against the British would eventually lead to Ireland gaining many of the freedoms for which he had fought, excepting freedom for the six northern counties. Treaty requirements such as pledging allegiance to the British Crown and maintaining Irish ports under British rule, which were so hated by republicans, were eliminated under the de Valera Fianna Fáil government in the 1930s. Michael Collins had made a better estimate than Ernie or Liam Lynch that the road to Irish freedom would gradually develop after the Treaty. When released, Ernie must have felt he was a failure. He was no longer acclaimed or even welcomed by many of the countrymen for whom he had fought.

Later, after arriving in Rome in December 1925, he wrote a letter to Kay Brady, a former Cumann na mBan member and friend, about how he had felt after being released from prison: 'Those months spent in my country before leaving were really terrible. You did not realise it. Mrs Childers did and only for her peculiar insight, through suffering, I don't suppose I would have become anyway normal, not that I am normal now.'[4]

Ernie had been a member of the IRA executive committee, and when he was released from the internment camp, he resumed his position. The executive committee met in August 1924 when he was also appointed to a new five-man committee for emergency consultative purposes.[5] If something drastic occurred in Ireland requiring the IRA to mobilise again, this committee would make the decision to do so. The IRA kept its governing body together after the Civil War ended in order to retain the capacity to act again should they deem it necessary to pick up arms against the government. Ernie's status in the IRA in the post-war period is signified by the fact that he was listed second, just after President Éamon de Valera, in the list of twenty-one senior officers who attended the meeting. In October he was made honorary secretary of the Sinn Féin party, but there is no record of any actions he took, either in the IRA or Sinn Féin positions, from then until he left for a sojourn in Europe in February 1925 to recuperate after his long, punishing imprisonment.

Peadar O'Donnell, who was present at that IRA meeting, later reported Ernie's counsel to the defeated IRA group:

> De Valera was in the chair. I remember Ernie saying there were two sides to the Irish people, that they were capable of great heroism when that side was up, and when they were in the mood of depression and defeat, they sank very low. And that the job of the IRA now was to restore the morale that had been endangered by all the confusion over the Treaty.[6]

This was a mature reflection from a man still in his twenties.

Ernie was a member of Sinn Féin. According to Sinn Féin's policy of abstention from any role requiring the pledge of allegiance to the King of the United Kingdom, he could not attend any meetings of the Dáil, to which he had been elected while in prison in August 1923. He also did not receive any compensation for his position.

In 1926 de Valera left Sinn Féin and created a new party, Fianna Fáil, promising to participate in the Dáil if and when the oath of allegiance to the British Crown was removed. Ernie refused to join them. In the June 1927 elections, when all persons running were required to take the oath if elected, Fianna Fáil agreed to take the oath. Ernie refused to run. In the new Dáil, Fianna Fáil became the principal opposition party; they would eventually take over political leadership in the Dáil in 1932. Ernie maintained this position for years, even when Fianna Fáil eventually became the ruling party and de Valera continued to want him to join. After his release, Ernie did not appear to express interest in serving in any political role despite being a member of the Dáil.

Ernie had decided to make a lengthy journey in Europe to restore his mental and physical health. He could climb in the Pyrenees and see the paintings he loved directly in museums and churches. He undertook a sustained campaign to finance his travels by raising almost £300 from the White Cross and a wide variety of friends in Ireland. Some of these were gifts, others were loans. The White Cross was an Irish charity that gave funds to former Irish Volunteers and their families who needed it for medical purposes.

A partial list of Ernie's donors and lenders includes: White Cross, £100; mother, £25; Johnny Raleigh, IRA comrade and friend, £30; Mary Anne, his early Nannie, £5; Frank Gallagher, friend, £70; Msgr John Hagan, £40; Cecil Malley, brother, £5.15.0; Miss Florence, for teeth, £3.3.0; Miss P., for glasses, £1. Many of the advances he received were loans. When he returned to Ireland in the autumn of 1926, he was £200 in debt to friends and family.[7]

When setting out on his journey to Europe in early 1925, Ernie decided not to get a passport from the Irish Free State. Instead, he went to England to obtain a false British passport under an assumed name. He may have had help from an undercover IRA group in London. He became Cecil Edward Smyth-Howard of Winchester, England; he was a medical student and 27 years of age, one year younger than Ernie was at that time. This unusual effort demonstrated that he had lost none of his concern about continued Irish Free State and British scrutiny of his life years after his battles with them had ended. He had become a famous revolutionary who merited observance.

During his time in Europe, Ernie asked many correspondents, like Msgr John Hagan, Rector of the Irish College in Rome, to use his alias when writing to him at various addresses in France, Spain and Italy. He also stayed in small pensions to avoid the police identity scrutiny that hotels required. He noted several times in correspondence that he believed British diplomats and its military stationed in Europe might be following him and spying on his activities there.

Challenges dogged Ernie throughout his solitary travels in Europe. During much of the time he lived hand to mouth, hoping a meagre loan or gift from friend or family might be waiting at his next destination. The condition of his damaged feet led him to seek someone who could design boots that would alleviate the pain and awkwardness of climbing in the Pyrenees.

His trip began with a flight in February 1925 from London to Abbeville, a small city in the north of France; it ended with his return from Dieppe to London by boat and then on to Dublin in September 1926. In between, Ernie visited well over one hundred cities, villages, mountain retreats, museums, churches and historic sites in France, Spain, Italy, Switzerland, Germany, Belgium and Holland. He kept scrupulous, detailed lists of places he visited, paintings he saw, books he read and people he met, as well as his itinerary while trekking in the Pyrenees mountains between France and Spain. Although he met old friends and made new ones along his many byways, he travelled alone. During the warring years, he had fought side by side with many IRA comrades, but because of his role as an organiser he had often operated individually, without support.

He reported in his diaries on scenes in Barcelona after his train trip from France: 'Police with swords and helmets, blue cloaks lined with red, civil guards with ... greenish uniforms and cloaks armed with rifles ... Girls mostly do not wear hats and dress their hair in many fashions; men in the poorer quarters wear a kind of canvas shoe which is very cheap and lasts only two months.'[8]

In the spring of 1925, Ernie went to the small village of Bourg-Madame in France. There he finally discovered a shoemaker who managed to build special boots for him that balanced the distorted, injured features of his feet. He could now walk almost naturally – and of equal importance, given his interest in the mountains, he could climb in the Pyrenees. He remarked, 'Finally I am the master of my foot.'[9]

One of his deepest satisfactions during the trip was climbing high in the Pyrenees and the people he encountered there:

> I reached the foot of the Cascade, up which I had to climb, the mist came down heavily, and after an hour keeping my direction as best I could by the paint splashes on the rock ... The mist lifted for a moment to show me a steep precipitous descent on my right ... I reached as far as I could go ... I made a fire of rhododendron roots and ferns, boiled some water, made tea and ate some bread and cheese ... I discovered a rough stone [shepherd's] hut ... I decided to sleep there ... Later two shepherds, a man and boy came in sight ... I asked the elderly man if I might sleep in the hut, and he said it was small, but that they might be able to make room. He made a fire, and we sat down on the bed of boughs of trees and warmed ourselves.[10]

At the end of his climbing, Ernie philosophised on what he learned from the mountains:

My mountain tramp had ended … The mountains which take one out of this world and make one pure like themselves … Their majesty makes one feel … one's smallness and one searches in one's heart for the superficialities of life which in their midst must be cast away … Memories of kindly faces and simple men leading their lives more kindly than we do, the pleasant camaraderie of the climbers, remain with me. The hardships now fit into their due perspective and are to be commented on gaily, and the peace remains above all, for 'God is very near to you in the mountains.'[11]

His European travels enabled him to indulge his passion for the arts, visiting museums to view the masters whose works were so inspiring to him. During the shelling of the Four Courts, he had returned to his command room only to find his treasured volume of Vasari's *Lives of the Italian Painters* and his reproductions of Piero della Francesca and Botticelli riddled by bullets and shell fragments. Now he had the opportunity to view these masterpieces directly. He went to Florence to see his beloved early Italian Renaissance painters at the Uffizi Museum. In the winter of 1925–6 he spent time with Msgr Hagan at the Irish College in Rome while visiting the Vatican and the museums there. Later he even worked for a time at an archaeological site in Sicily. In Paris he visited the Louvre, staying until closing time.

During his journeys in Europe, Ernie continued to correspond with Kay Brady, whom he had met in Rome while she travelled with her family. He described the little Italian girls who captivated him, earnestly telling him their stories in Italian, which he could not understand. He went on to describe the children running the service in a local Roman church he visited while it was holding a children's Mass.

His love for the early Italian painters was reinforced by his visit to Italian churches and museums. He wrote to Kay about how he could now view their work directly: 'Recently I saw that Raphael's 'Transfiguration' was left unfinished at his death ... Do you remember the two figures on the left on the mountain top? They represent St Julian and St Laurence, personified by Guilio and Lorenzo di Medici. I think it would be useful if I made up notes on good pictures for myself.'[12]

His letters illustrate Ernie's deep loneliness and need to communicate with an understanding woman. Like Molly Childers, Kay became one of his muses. 'I'm glad you sent such a long letter ... I really did feel quite miserable when the train steamed out almost as much as the day you all left for Naples when I wandered around like a lost soul ... I don't belong anywhere, but I am at home there [with Mrs Childers].'[13]

During Ernie's stay in Paris in 1926, he went to see his old friend from the IRA Seán MacBride, who had just moved there. He must have learned from Seán that his own efforts to hide his presence in Europe from British surveillance had not been just a paranoiac reaction. Seán had been befriended by a French army colonel, Lacassi. The colonel was assigned to the Deuxième Bureau, the highly efficient intelligence department of the French army. Lacassi warned Seán that British intelligence was watching him in France, accessing his apartment and opening his letters. Seán was aware that the British had asked for his own extradition back to Ireland. The colonel assured Seán that he was safe, because the French knew he was an anti-Treaty IRA officer who had escaped from a Free State prison. The French would protect him as a political refugee. Upon leaving, the colonel told Seán, 'We also regard Mr. O'Malley as an Irish political refugee.' The colonel was warning Seán that his friend Ernie was under close surveillance from both British and French intelligence in Europe.[14]

Former General O'Malley had become a well-known revolutionary leader to the world at large. He was sought out by others fighting for their independence. Two separatist groups in Europe, the Basques and Catalans in Spain, had previously contacted him. In a 1935 letter to Harriet Moore, editor of *Poetry*, Ernie mentioned that he 'went to Catalonia to help the Catalan movement for independence'. He also made a reference to working with these groups in his European diaries: 'I had to go to St-Jean-de-Luz in the Basque country to meet a Spanish Basque, one of the leaders for Basque independence. I mentioned his name. Jose Maria's face lit up, yes he knew him. I produced his card with his *nom de guerre*.'[15]

Ernie's failure to specify anything further in writing probably stemmed from his caution in not exposing either himself or the Basques and Catalans he met. One does not randomly carry around the secret war name of a separatist Basque leader unless a meeting with him was previously planned. The French were well aware of Ernie's activities. In a subsequent meeting with Seán MacBride in 1926, Colonel Lacassi said, '"You know your friend, Mr O'Malley, a nice man, but what is he doing?"' Seán replied that he didn't know. Lacassi went on to say, '"We are a little bit worried, because he is now acting as chief military adviser to Colonel Macia, the leader of the Catalan separatist government here in Paris ... Unfortunately, however, they are planning an invasion of Spain next Saturday afternoon ... Perhaps you could talk to your friend Mr. O'Malley. ... Perhaps you might dissuade them from this expedition."'[16]

Ernie had never mentioned any of his contacts with the Spanish groups to Seán, but when Seán soon thereafter met Colonel Macia, the Catalan leader immediately informed him that his group was working with 'our good friend General O'Malley'. Eventually, Colonel Macia took his group of thirty to forty men to the Spanish border by train from Paris. They were gently arrested and sent back to Paris by French police just before they could enter the country.[17] Ernie's contacts with the separatists had been endorsed by the IRA army council, which, according to Peadar O'Donnell, had nominated him to be their contact with the Catalonian independence movements.[18]

His relationship with the republican elements in Spain continued for years. A decade later, on 5 November 1936, Ernie presided at a public meeting held in Dublin on the question of Irish republican support for the Spanish Republic resisting Franco's forces in the Spanish Civil War. The Basque government sent a representative to the meeting. He faced resistance from conservative Irish groups in Dublin who opposed supporting the elected Spanish republican government, viewed by them as both communistic and anti-clerical.

He was inherently shy in spite of his demonstrated prowess as a leader of men in combat. This meant he had difficulty addressing large groups. Ernie never became a confident, effective public speaker. During the Dublin meeting in 1936, Peadar had to rescue him by taking over Ernie's role and presiding over the meeting himself.

Ernie's deep passion for literature and the arts increased during his travels in Europe. His growing interest in the theatre, from Sophocles to the moderns, developed: and he read Lady Gregory, Edgar Wallace, George B. Shaw, Ibsen, Strindberg, George Russell (Æ), Pirandello and Eugene O'Neill. It must have taken great effort for him to obtain these books while travelling hand to mouth all over Europe, often far from cities and libraries. Earlier, during his organiser training missions all over Ireland, he had overcome similar challenges to keep his books with him, when a bicycle was his only means of transportation.

He had also used his enormous drive and energy to satisfy his intellectual curiosity from various sources during his formative years. At this time, he only had an occasional mentor, like Count Plunkett. The books Ernie began reading as a young man demonstrate how he later became an intellectual with such a broad range of interests even though his formal schooling in the humanities was lacking. His first authors included Plutarch, Shakespeare, Montaigne, Vasari, Melville, Dostoyevsky and Baudelaire. By 1919 he had also developed an interest in Irish writers from ancient times to the present, including the contemporary Irish poet and mystic Ella Young, who, as an anti-Treaty republican, was aware of Ernie's military career.

His appreciation of painting, literature, theatre, cinema and music had been fuelled further by his opportunity to read widely in all of these subjects during his recent years in prison. Ernie's life had now shifted in Europe – from being the fighter and prisoner of 1918–24 to being an intellectual.

Returning to Ireland in September 1926 after his travels in Europe, Ernie lived at home with his parents and resumed his medical studies at University College Dublin. His medical studies continued to suffer from his lack of concentration. He took walking trips in the nearby Dublin mountains and helped found the Dramatic Society as a part of the UCD's Literary & Historical Society. He was assisted in this effort by his friend William Fay, who later became ambassador to the United States. He served as the best man at the wedding of his friend Johnny Raleigh to Beatrice Mooney in Limerick, becoming godfather to their first child. Johnny had accompanied Ernie to London in November 1921, during the truce negotiations, to purchase arms for his 2nd Southern Division. Ernie also found solace in writing poetry for friends and family.

In early 1927, while in Ireland, Ernie wrote his fictional *San Mareno Letters*, demonstrating his potential to develop into the future renowned author of two stimulating books on Ireland's warring period. These to-date unpublished letters present a fictional, highly satirical report on political events in an imaginary tiny European republic of eight thousand souls called San Mareno. The letters were designed to mock the political situation in Ireland at that time, and Ernie introduced many parallels between San Mareno officials and contemporary Irish government figures. He made it clear he despised politics.

In these letters Ernie presented the president of the San Mareno Republic, a conservative who hated to spend public monies on anything but the basics, writing to the chairman of its senate, a liberal who believed in spending public monies for culture: 'I fail to perceive why the people of a small state, San Mareno, should be so penalised as to bear the burden of heavy taxes which maintains the members of an unnecessary House.' To this the chairman replies, 'Dear Mr. President, I resent the impertinence of your last letter and laugh at its absurdity. Are the traditions of this nation, the oldest republic in Europe, to be set at naught to suit your petty whim of economy? Why not suppress the output of literature ... pull down the monastic buildings of architectural beauty?'[19]

By the late summer of 1928, Ernie still had not passed his final medical exams at UCD, nor had he found a meaningful focus for his life in Ireland after his travels in Europe. In September he was asked by Frank Aiken, his former senior IRA comrade, to join him in making a tour of the United States. Their purpose was to raise funds from the large Irish American community to establish an Irish newspaper in Dublin capable of representing independent Irish interests without any interference from Britain or conservative Irish commercial interests. This was the idea of

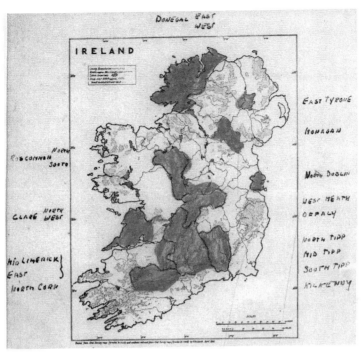

Map of Ernie O'Malley's areas of responsibility as an IRA organiser, 1918–21.
(Courtesy of O'Malley Papers P17c, UCD Archives)

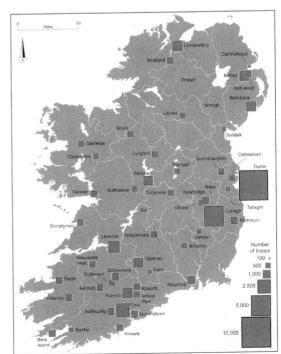

Map of British troops in Ireland,
1921. (Map by Mike Murphy,
courtesy of the editors, *Atlas of
the Irish Revolution* (2017) and
Cork University Press)

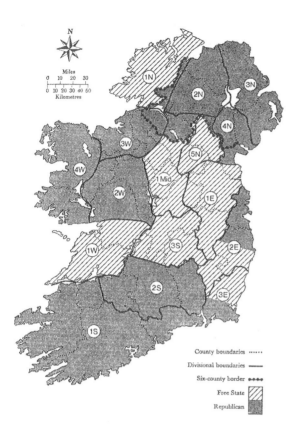

Map of pro-Treaty and anti-Treaty IRA forces in mid-1922. (Courtesy of Michael Hopkinson, *Green against Green* (Dublin: Gill & Macmillan, 1988))

Ernie O'Malley on a mountain ledge overlooking the Pyrenees, early 1926.

Ernie O'Malley driving Helen Golden's car from California to New Mexico,
September 1929.

Mabel Dodge Luhan at
her 'Los Gallos' home,
Taos, New Mexico,
autumn 1929.

A Native American dance festival, New Mexico, 1930.

Sketch from page of Ernie O'Malley's
Mexican Diary, February 1931.
(EOM Papers, NYU Library,
AIA#060)

American poet Hart Crane in Mexico City,
spring 1931. The picture has a note to Ernie
on the back: 'for Ernest O'Malley with much
affection and devotion from Hart Crane'.

Russian film director Sergei Eisenstein (*right*) and film photographer, Eduard Tissé (*left*) in Mexico, spring 1931.

Helen Hooker standing by her bronze-cast fawn, made and exhibited in Greenwich, CT, 1930, photographed by de Witt Ward.

Helen Hooker, New York City, 1930.

Ernie O'Malley sitting in Helen Hooker's New York City studio, February 1934, photographed by Helen Hooker.

Right:
Helen Hooker and Ernie
O'Malley sitting in Helen's New
York City studio, February
1934, photographed by Helen
Hooker.

Below:
Ernie O'Malley at the
gravestones of Diarmuid and
Grainne, near Burrishoole
Lodge, Newport, Co. Mayo,
1938, photographed by Helen
Hooker.

Ernie O'Malley being lifted into a boat by a man at Burrishoole Lodge in the summer of 1939, watched by Cathal O'Malley and a nurse.

Cathal, Etain, Helen, Ernie and Cormac O'Malley, in their garden at Clonskeagh, Dublin, summer 1946.

Jack B. Yeats (*left*) and Ernie O'Malley at an art exhibition of Richard King in Dublin, 1947. (From *The Capuchin Annual* 1948; source: COM Papers; courtesy of Cormac O'Malley)

Catherine (Bobs) and Harry Walston at Burrishoole Lodge, March 1939.

Ernie O'Malley, John Wayne and Cormac O'Malley at the door of Isle of Morn cottage, on the set of *The Quiet Man*.

Back row, left to right: Ernie O'Malley, Maureen O'Hara, Tom Maguire; *front row, left to right*: John Wayne, Meta Stern, John Ford. Taken with Maureen O'Hara's camera during the filming of *The Quiet Man*, in June 1951.

Left:
Cormac and Ernie O'Malley at the Galway Races, July 1951. (From *The Irish Press*; source: COM Papers; courtesy of Cormac O'Malley)

Below:
Ernie and Cormac O'Malley, with guard dog Rommel and horse Sheila at Burrishoole Lodge, Newport, Co. Mayo. (From *The Irish Press*; source: COM Papers; courtesy of Cormac O'Malley)

Ernie at Kilmurvey, on Inishmore, Aran Islands, Co. Galway, August 1954, taken by Jean McGrail.

John Ford (*left*) and Ernie O'Malley, after filming *The Rising of the Moon* in Co. Clare, May 1956. (From *The Irish Press*; source: COM Papers; courtesy of Cormac O'Malley)

Ernie O'Malley (*left*) with Lord Michael Killanin (*middle*), and John Ford, during the filming of *The Rising of the Moon* in Co. Clare, May 1956. (From *The Irish Press*; source: COM Papers; courtesy of Cormac O'Malley)

Left to right: Minister Seán Lemass, Taoiseach Éamon de Valera and Minister Frank Aiken attending the start of Ernie O'Malley's state funeral procession in Howth, Co. Dublin, 27 March 1957. (From *The Irish Press*; source: COM Papers; courtesy of Cormac O'Malley)

Funeral oration by Seán Moylan TD (*right*) at Ernie O'Malley's graveside, Glasnevin Cemetery, Dublin, 27 March 1957. (From *The Irish Press*; source: COM Papers; courtesy of Cormac O'Malley)

de Valera, who believed that this paper, the *Irish Press*, would be one of the bulwarks required to eventually create a free Irish republic. Irish Americans had been financially supportive of the IRA's struggle against Britain in the 1918–21 period, and Aiken had a list of American cities and individuals they would visit to stage meetings and raise needed funds.

De Valera was sending two of his IRA former generals, Aiken and O'Malley, to America's Irish community. He also believed Ernie's reputation as a military hero would make him a good rallying point for their effort in the United States. The Irish American public enjoyed using the term 'General' to designate Ernie and Frank during their fundraising efforts.

When Ernie left Ireland for America in October 1928, he was also trying to leave behind the mystique that had developed around him as an IRA warrior. During the warring years he had been dismayed to find, attending dances in the countryside, that his name was featured in songs written about the IRA episodes. Years later he wrote a letter to Harriet Monroe indicating his feelings about growing into the role of an Irish hero: 'Here in America I have been cut away from my own country where I was developing into a symbol. This country has helped me to live my life apart from all the associative memories that intrude too much at home; its impersonality and detachment have helped me find something of myself.'[20]

CHAPTER 7

CREATIVE JOURNEY: AMERICA AND MEXICO, 1928–1935

Just before dawn on 12 October 1928, their ship, *George Washington,* docked in New York Harbour. Ernie's American diary begins with his observant, caustic humour: 'Our taxi man stated his fare was $5.50. My companions assured him we did not wish to buy the taxi.' They walked to the subway instead. 'I watched the people. The men wore rather striking ties, but they did not seem to be good ones. The women had close fitting hats ... not many chewed gum, about 6 [per cent]. On other subways one finds 90 [per cent] chewing ... The fine for spitting was $500.'[1]

At the beginning of their tour, Frank Aiken and Ernie kept up exhausting and usually separate schedules, speaking to Irish groups in American cities to raise funds for the *Irish Press.* Ernie's demanding travel schedule in the autumn of 1928 involved moving from the east coast to the mid-west and back: New York–New Jersey, Philadelphia, Boston (and adjoining cities), Connecticut, Rhode Island, Pittsburgh, Cleveland, Detroit, Chicago, Cincinnati, and then returning to Washington and New York to finish out the year.

Ernie also took time to continue his intellectual pursuits during the tour. He had already begun to write his memoirs, which would develop into his two books on the warring period. His new creative life would constitute the meaningful theme for the remainder of his years. While in New York City, he visited its libraries to research Irish themes; throughout the tour, he attended presentations of theatre and music whenever he could.

Frank and Ernie continued their separate campaigns across America until the spring of 1929. Ernie visited Minneapolis, St Paul and St Louis in the Midwest, continuing on through Butte, Montana to the West Coast, covering cities in Washington, Oregon and California. He gave interviews to various newspapers along the way. Occasionally he set a newspaper straight when it called him General O'Malley, noting that he was no longer a man with a military title. Both of their campaigns had many disappointments with small crowds or scant financial support, but Ernie and Frank had successes in some cities as well. While travelling, Ernie continued to expand his interests by visiting artists and authors in large metropolitan centres like New York, Chicago and San Francisco.

There were even occasional moments of glory for Ernie. A newspaper reported his presence at the annual meeting of an Irish group gathered in New York City at the Knights of Columbus Club Hotel on 21 October 1928:

> [This] was one of the most fashionable social Irish events ever held in New York City. The grand march was led by Ernie O'Malley, the Irish Republican leader, was participated in by all the prominent Irish Republicans in the city. When Mr. O'Malley entered the hall, the band played 'The Soldiers' Song' and all the audience joined in the singing. The young Republican leader got a splendid reception. Addresses were given by him.[2]

In April 1929, Frank was in New York City. He wrote to Ernie, then in California, that he was about to head home to Ireland and hoped Ernie would complete their campaign over the next few months. Together they had raised enough funds to establish the *Irish Press*. It would speak for those who still wanted Ireland to become a free republic. Ernie's friend Frank Gallagher became the editor.

At the end of their campaign Ernie remained in California. He expanded his interests in early 1929, spending more time with artistic people like Edward Weston, the photographer; Robinson Jeffers, the poet; and John Ford, the movie director. They recognised that Ernie was a creative person who could intuitively appreciate their work. He established immediate, close, lasting relationships with many of these new friends. During his visits with Weston in Carmel, California, the modernist took his photograph, later remarking that Ernie had led one of the most exciting, fascinating lives he had ever known. Weston mentioned to Ernie how much he had enjoyed developments in the arts now occurring in Mexico City. He had recently spent time there with the photographer Tina Modotti, and their chats together stimulated Ernie's interest to eventually make a visit of his own to Mexico.[3] In a later letter to Ernie, Weston illustrates the strong bond that had been created between the two men, closing his message, 'With many happy memories–my love dear friend–Edward.'[4]

Were the many supportive Anglo-Irish and American friends from the creative-intellectual world Ernie would make in America and Mexico from 1928 to 1935 drawn to him because of his reputation as a 'gunman' and young commandant-general in the Irish warring years? That may initially have created a means of introduction, but all of these eminent people report how they were immediately drawn to Ernie by his lively, creative, intellectual side. This was true for Jeffers, Ford and Weston. It was also later true for Helen Golden, Dorothy Brett, Dorothy Stewart and Paul Strand in the American West and Southwest; for Hart Crane in Mexico; for Harriet Moore in Chicago; for fellows at the Yaddo Retreat in Upstate New York; and for James Johnson Sweeney in New York City. His relationships were not restricted to this period; they continued personally and by correspondence when he returned to Ireland in 1935, lasting for the rest of his life.

At this time Ernie also began giving talks on Irish history and literature to groups on the Pacific Coast. He gave an interview to the *Seattle Daily Times* in March 1929 where he signalled his shift from a military life to being a creative intellectual: 'My soul lies with the arts. In them lies happiness. I hope to be able to restore Ireland's interest in them.'[5]

In August 1929, he met a former New York actress, Helen Merriam Golden, in Pasadena, California, where she lived with her three children, Terence, Deirdre and Eithne. Her recently deceased Irish husband, Peter, who was originally from Cork, had been a leading Irish Shakespearian actor before immigrating to New York, where he became an ardent supporter of the IRA cause during the 1916–21 era of the struggle for Irish independence.

Ernie's modest compensation and travel expenses from the *Irish Press* fundraising campaign had been spent, the tour was over, and he was almost destitute. He found himself living from hand to mouth, as he often had in Europe. He was adopted and partially supported by Helen Golden in exchange for his duties on a trip she wished to make to the Grand Canyon in Arizona. Ernie would help her with the various challenges that arose as they maneuvered over the rough roads covering the Southwest in 1929. There was constant bickering as to what direction to take and where to spend the night between Helen and her friend, Mariana Howe, a furniture maker from Boston who joined the trip. Ernie was constantly called on to intervene between these two strong-minded women.

Helen's original idea had merely been to take her son Terence to visit the Grand Canyon. When Ernie heard of Helen's plan, he had suggested that the group drive on to Taos so he could spend time with Ella Young, the Irish poet and mystic who was visiting there. Helen knew Ella well and agreed to extend their trip. Ella's lyrical poetry and her interest in the folklore of ancient Ireland had resonated with Ernie's own fascination with the 'fairy' people whose tales had been told to him as a child by his nurse Nannie.

They drove from Pasadena to Santa Fe, a short distance from their eventual destination, Taos. The road went over mountains and through deserts that were often barely passable in their old car. Rocks damaged their vehicle and they had trouble crossing some streams and rivers. They slept in crude accommodations in, beside and sometimes under the automobile.

This was Ernie's first introduction to the beautiful, rugged country of the American Southwest, still inhabited by American Indian tribes. He fell in love with the wonders of the Grand Canyon:

> the sheer cliff, grey and red at intervals ... lower a strata of cliff then a slope, blue black, extensive, running to a plateau on the cliff, may be prolonged purple-red and the slope beneath has close to Bright Angle Canyon streaks of salmon pink and salmon red running in little waves to the edge of the canyon proper. There a cliff edge, then puce black walls jutting out startlingly and running into the river.[6]

When he left post-war Ireland for Europe in 1925, Ernie had been able to combine visits to cities like Paris, Barcelona, Florence and Rome with treks in the French–Spanish Pyrenees, where he encountered its remote, simple mountain people. It had not been his plan to repeat this theme, but a similar contrast in experiences occurred during his visit to America in 1928–30. First, he visited its metropolitan cities, New York, Boston, Chicago, St Louis, Seattle, San Francisco and Los Angeles, while raising funds for the *Irish Press*. Helen Golden then helped him to travel through the beautiful American Southwest's sparsely inhabited countryside; he stayed there for over a year, from September 1929 until December 1930, in the artistic communities of Taos and Santa Fe, before he went on to Mexico. The town of Taos was located right next to the large, historic, still-active Taos Indian pueblo.

Taos was an old New Mexican town with a picturesque hotel. It became enhanced as an artists' colony in the early 1920s when D.H. Lawrence, the controversial English novelist, and his German wife Frieda came from England with Dorothy Brett to live there. The Lawrences had left Taos in 1924, before Ernie arrived with Helen Golden's group, but many colourful characters from the artists' colony were still there. When they first arrived in Taos, Ernie, Helen, Mariana Howe and Terence stayed in the Adams Auto Camp. They were regularly invited to meals, outings by automobile and visits to American Indian ceremonies by the 'regulars' in the artistic community. Helen, Mariana and Terence returned to Pasadena for a while, but Ernie remained there by himself as Ella extended her visit.

Helen Golden came back to Taos with her young daughter Eithne, and they took a cabin next to Ernie's in the auto camp. Helen had told Eithne's teacher in Pasadena that the trip was an 'educational experience', justifying her leaving school. Eithne remembered later that Ernie would come over and read to Helen and Mariana; she recalled that he was reading draft chapters of what were the working manuscripts for his two books on the warring period, *On Another Man's Wound*, covering the War of

Independence against Britain, and *The Singing Flame*, describing the Irish Civil War.

By May 1930, he had written three chapters of *On Another Man's Wound* and had them posted to a friend in New York to be typed.[7] A major part of Ernie's time during his entire period in America and Mexico, from 1929 to his departure for Ireland from New York City in 1935, was spent on writing and rewriting these memoirs. His friends and physical surroundings may have been vastly different in Taos and Santa Fe than they were in New York, but this writing was his constant focus and preoccupation throughout the period.

Ernie's new friends in Taos included Dorothy Brett, an English aristocratic expatriate who had worked with D.H. and Frieda Lawrence. She often entertained Helen and Ernie at informal meals in her house. Another friend was Mabel Dodge Luhan, a rich woman who originally had given the Lawrences the ranch where they had lived. It was she who brought Dorothy to Taos, and she continued to invite American intellectuals and artists to her home. These included the married couple Hutchins Hapgood and Neith Boyce, who came from upper-class Eastern families but were now part of the radical journalist group in the Southwest. Mabel's fourth husband, Tony Lujan, was an American Indian from the Taos Pueblo. 'Spud' Johnson was an older writer who edited a fringe magazine, *The Laughing Horse*. Ernie later house-sat for Spud and read the library he had in his house.

Ella Young, who resided in California, visited Mabel in the summer and autumn of 1929. She and Ernie shared their interests in lyrical writing, which celebrated the charm of ancient Irish legends and the beauty of the Irish countryside.

Hutchins' and Neith's daughter, Miriam Hapgood, was a pretty girl in her early twenties. In 1929, she was visiting Mabel in Taos with her mother, searching for meaning in her life. Ernie became smitten with Miriam when they shared rides around the countryside. Although Ernie had been a brave young general, he was not a bold or confident suitor. He pined away in his diary after Miriam, worrying why she didn't come on some of the local car trips with him and asking himself why she always seemed to be interested in everything but him. He often ended a daily entry by asking himself where Miriam was that evening. Ernie's life as an ascetic revolutionary had not prepared him for courting the young lady effectively. He summed up his feelings: 'I wish I had seen [Miriam] before I left. Again I'm a little boy lost. Will I ever get over this strange feeling of having my heart in my mouth.'[8]

Ella Young later summed up the unequal nature of their relationship: '[Miriam] doesn't see him much, for half the time she is mad at him for something and not speaking to him – but that amuses her as much as seeing him so it's useful.'[9] Miriam, urged on by her parents, eventually married a man from an establishment East Coast family. She wrote an autobiography where she acknowledged Ernie's courage and military accomplishments, but clearly she did not return his romantic interest.[10]

When Helen Golden and Ernie came to Taos in September 1929, the Great Depression was just about to begin – a month later the stock market would crash in New York City. Ernie did not record any discussion of this major event. It was as if the Taos community was living in a cocoon isolated from the rest of the world. With a few exceptions, such as Mabel Dodge Luhan, many were living on little money and had gone to Taos not only because the artists' colony provided people of similar interests but also because life was less expensive there.

Helen Golden later commented on Ernie's time in Taos from 1929 to 1932:

He made himself walk, even with very weak feet and ankles …
I could circle his ankles with my thumb and finger they seem
so thin … Ella said he suffered great pain when he first rode
a horse here at Brett's in 1929, but he made himself ride and
finally conquered that too … His three years in California,
New Mexico and Old Mexico have done wonders for him
physically … I think he will always be erratic probably and
capable of intense irritability, at times, but I always felt he
had been heroic enough to justify his peculiarities.[11]

In spite of his continuing precarious health, Ernie tried to climb
a difficult peak in the area. He fell badly, lay unconscious for
a time, and injured both legs, which required a recuperative
period. He downplayed such happenings, pretending they had
never occurred. Early in 1930, Dorothy Brett had given him a
temporary job supervising the construction of a cabin by a few
American Indians in the mountains near the Lawrence ranch. It
was typical for Brett to be generous, providing Ernie with a job
to earn needed money.[12]

Although Ernie tried to put his warring period behind him
while visiting the peaceful, beautiful country of the American
Southwest, it kept returning to haunt him. In March 1930,
Ernie was staying in Brett's cabin while she made a trip to New
York City. He had grown close to Brett and wrote to her of
Taos happenings during her absence, sending her a piece of sage
from Taos Mountain. In his letter to her in New York, Ernie
mentioned D.H. Lawrence's recent death. This reminded him of
the deaths he had experienced as an IRA fighter in the early
1920s. He wrote:

I have seen so many of my comrades die that death seems
as much a part of life as life itself. Yet I know there were

some deaths that I never recovered from. They left a strange void which has always remained, a gap, yet a communion as well for I can feel the dead, nor would I be surprised to find someday they walked in to resume an interrupted conversation. I found it easier to get over losses in my own family than I did of my friends.[13]

Many members of the Taos community were fascinated by the various American Indian tribes living in New Mexico and neighbouring Arizona and Colorado, visiting their reservations where ancient tribal ceremonies were still held. Ernie became intrigued by the effort of the native peoples to hold on to their distinct cultural traditions in spite of the overwhelming United States army and government forces, who had taken their lands and independence away from them. He compared the history of the American Indian to that of the Irish people whose freedom and culture had been suppressed by their British conquerors. Ernie made detailed observations of two Southwest Indian tribes and their rituals:

Laguna Indians congregating from all quarters, colours very varied ... War Dance, six facing six, women hold hands outstretched palms upwards, men carry rattle in right hand, women have feathers on top of head, hair streaming down their backs, coloured ribbons reaching to heels, attached on one ear – a coloured plaque ... women have a slower step than the men, another group, eight by seven, led by a man in front started off with a bark and sang or intoned a continuous chant of varying notes ... The whites looked a poor crowd in comparison.

The Navajo ... were the fine looking Indians, deep brown women wearing the long billowed dresses with kiddies following them around ... Cowboys in ten gallon hats ... shirts edged with leather ... shirts tucked with plaited shirt bands and short leather boots ... Men with heavy necklaces of turquoise ... The elder women had finer colouring in their clothes, in fact, the Navajo colours were always pure as were their features.[14]

By November 1930, Ernie had moved to Santa Fe from Taos and gave two talks at the home of Mr and Mrs Raymond Otis. In Santa Fe he stayed at the house of his cousin Sylvia Laithwaite, who was a head librarian there. Santa Fe was only a short ride from Taos, and his friends had introduced him to the intellectual leaders of Santa Fe, who were interested in hearing the Irish rebel-intellectual speak. A newspaper report read:

> Mr O'Malley read first from the works of the earliest Irish bards, beginning with a vigorous poem of the fifth century. He told of a thousand poets who roamed the countryside until, upon the production of a certain number of lines, they obtained the rank of Bards ... At the final talk of the series tomorrow evening, at the Raymond Otis house, Mr O'Malley will discuss modern Irish novels and novelists, and has promised a reading from the much talked of *Ulysses*, of James Joyce.[15]

In December 1930 Ernie was invited by an American artist, Dorothy Stewart, to drive her and her friend Theodora Goddard, an artist from New York, from Santa Fe to Mexico City in Dorothy's car. Dorothy had lived and painted in Mexico before and wanted to return, but she felt more comfortable having a man along. Ernie had heard from Edward Weston that Mexico City was an ideal place to witness the modernist developments in the arts. He was delighted to be able to make the trip. The Mexican Revolution presented an example of how a more inward-looking government could help to counter the traditional influences of Europe and America while establishing more indigenous-orientated art forms. This movement reminded him of the challenges the Irish people had had with the suppression of their native culture by the British conquerors. Many international creative artists were either in Mexico City or about to arrive there in the spring of 1931.

On the trip to Mexico, Ernie drove his two passengers from Santa Fe to Laredo, Texas, across the Mexican border, through Saltillo and down to Mexico City, arriving there on 6 January 1931. Their trip by car took eight days, a journey that could now be accomplished in two or three. The roads were often almost impassable.

To someone fascinated by local colour, exotic food, deep native cultural identity, expressive architecture and painting, striking local people and a riot of bright sensual surroundings, going to Mexico for Ernie must have been highly stimulating. The first impressions in his Mexican diaries illustrate how he could hardly manage to write all of his observations down, there was so much to see. He was intrigued by the people in Mexico City:

> A woman knocked down by a tram, a man jumped off a passing tram, picked her up, jumped back again. Swiftly, perfectly in accord [with] his actions. I saw cyclists swerve nearly at right angles yet keeping their speed when a motor [car] backed out suddenly across their line ... Their reactions are immediate, they are all alive ... A pretty girl with jet black hair was being seized by the police ... She sat firm and refused to move, setting her face square with intensity

and hate while she shouted at them … [A man] with a thin
scraggly neck, like an ostrich, and a small hat turned up
at the brim on top of a heap of curls. He threw a card on
the ground, clapped his hands over it [and] dropped some
imaginary dust … After a long oration he produced fountain
pens and sold some.[16]

He suffered from his customary challenge during all of his
travels – a continual lack of money. Dorothy and Theodora
were fond of Ernie and helped him, letting him stay with them
in various lodgings while contributing to buying food so he
could eat, but he was constantly the dependent man. For years,
every American visitor to Mexico City had gone to Sanborns,
the famous restaurant – at one time a drugstore and breakfast
spot – with Orozco murals on their walls. His travel companions
went to Sanborns regularly to meet the other American expats
who congregated there, but Ernie simply couldn't because he
didn't have the money and didn't wish to depend on Dorothy
and Theodora to pay his way.

Through letters of introduction, Ernie contacted various
Mexican officials in the ministries of culture and education,
asking them for a job to teach English to support himself. They
replied graciously but never offered him the paying jobs he
needed. Apparently, he was able to work in the training schools
for rural teachers in two Mexican states, but he probably did not
receive much, if any, compensation.[17] Parts of Mexico could be
dangerous. His friend Carleton Beals, the American author, was
held up in the countryside outside Mexico City; the thieves took
everything he had, including his clothes. When he protested, they
gave him back his socks so he could walk back to the city.[18]

Late in the spring of 1931, Ernie met the poet Hart Crane in
Mexico City. Crane was there on a Guggenheim Fellowship. They

hit it off immediately in spite of Crane's heavy drinking and wild behaviour. In a note to Ernie, Crane wrote, 'Hope apologies for last night are acceptable ... Please! ... Katherine Anne [Porter] is leaving me her extra bed for your use here.'[19] Two of America's most notable writers from the period – Crane, author of the poem 'The Bridge', and Porter, author of short story collections including *Pale Horse, Pale Rider* – sharing a place together in Mexico City and inviting Ernie to 'crash' in their pad. Crane later gave Ernie his flat for several weeks when he returned to his home in Ohio.

In a letter to Malcolm Cowley, a leading American literary critic of the 1930s, Crane described how much Ernie meant to him as a friend: 'I have my most pleasant literary moments with an Irish revolutionary, red haired friend of Liam O'Flaherty, shot (and not missed) seventeen times in one conflict and another; the most quietly sincere and appreciative person, in many ways, whom I've ever met ... Ernest O'Malley by name. And we drink a lot together – look at frescos – and agree!'[20]

Ernie had spent much of his time in Italy studying its painters and sculptors. He was at his best in Mexico when studying and comparing the frescos of Diego Rivera and José Clemente Orozco, which could be found all over Mexico City. Whereas many people of that period recognised Rivera, who was given assignments to do major frescos in large public buildings in the United States, as the more significant artist, Ernie preferred Orozco. He gave both artists his keen critical eye:

The man Diego is not so deep; he has not the same cool, quiet passion, is not so sorrowful, so sincere as Orozco, nor has he his vision. Orozco ... must feel the sufferings of the people terribly and his depiction of them is awe inspiring ... The mobility and dignity of his figures ... have no parallel in Diego's work. He paints with gusto, with a sensitive meticulousness or rush ... with an exuberance, a joy in life ... Orozco paints sadly, he sees the ultimate end of things, the turmoil, the truth of life.[21]

Ernie returned from Mexico with autographed photographs from Sergei Eisenstein, the great Russian film director of the 1930–40s, and his assistant Eduard Tissé; he visited them in June while they were making a film in an old estate in Teflaque, Mexico. He returned from Mexico with hundreds of photographs, drawings and prints by local and visiting artists. These cover a wide variety of subjects, including people working in the country, horsemen, women in their colourful costumes, landscapes, village life, and urban and country architecture.

When Dorothy and Ernie returned to Santa Fe, they decided they would publish a book together on the American Indians of New Mexico using her prints and his text, but it never materialised. Some of Dorothy's vivid prints of Mexico ended up years later on the walls of Ernie's country house, Burrishoole, in Mayo.

In a letter he wrote from Mexico City in March 1930 to Countess Plunkett in Dublin, Ernie summed up his feelings about Mexico: 'This country is in many ways like home and I like it very much. The United States seems pale and anaemic compared to it, yet I did like parts of the States, especially the Southwest.'[22]

In the summer of 1931, Ernie drove Dorothy and Theodora back to Santa Fe. They had had a fine time in Mexico, but as Ernie observed, they had never been able to really penetrate its culture. He realised how his lack of fluency in Spanish had limited his ability to completely understand Mexico or its people. He had not gone as deep as he would have wished. They were still tourists, although they had been able to key into the vital life that international intellectuals enjoyed there.

There is a much-repeated tale about Ernie's return to the United States that has never been fully verified. The story has it that since Ernie's visa to the United States had expired, he could no longer enter the country legally – so Ernie swam across the Rio Grande holding his clothes above his head in the middle of a pack of sheep to avoid detection. Dorothy Stewart, who had crossed legally in her car, was waiting for him on the American shore.

By 1931 the Depression had hit all of America hard. Public schools had been closed in the Taos area for lack of funds. Helen Golden had moved there from Pasadena with her three children in 1930. Upon his return from Mexico, Ernie moved from Santa Fe to Chimayo, a village south of Taos where he continued to write. When Helen asked him to tutor her three children, he agreed and returned to Taos. In early 1932 she developed pneumonia and was hospitalised in Santa Fe, leaving Ernie in charge of her family. He set up a military regime where each child had specific duties to perform each day and was rated accordingly. He gave them daily lessons in mathematics, English and geography. The three children were taught to cook and take care of themselves.

Ernie sometimes became exasperated with the children, telling them they had to improve their behaviours. When a pony that the children loved died right outside the cabin and their little dog insisted on sleeping by his dead friend to protect him, Ernie praised the dog, covered him with a blanket, and pointed out to the children that they needed to demonstrate the character the dog had shown them all. When Helen returned from the hospital, Ernie extended his disciplined requirements to her and Mariana, insisting that the children take a more active part in cooking and other domestic chores they had previously often ignored.

Eithne recalled that the most valuable part of her entire life's education had been Ernie's teachings as their tutor in the little cabin in Taos where they had all lived together. When working many years later as a translator at the United Nations in New York City, she realised that Ernie's insistence that she fully learn the principles of English grammar and sentence structure had enabled her to become a skilful translator of other languages.[23]

His contacts increased with the American Indians he had become so fond of, noting that they often spoke Spanish together. What he did not mention was that neither they nor he knew much Spanish.

He was fortunate that the modernist photographer Paul Strand had come to Taos to do some work there. The two struck up a friendship in the spring of 1932, and Strand made a profile photograph of Ernie that became the image many have come to know him by. They took walks over the mountains, and Ernie read portions of his memoirs to his new friend. Strand became invaluable to Ernie, giving him references to many artists and intellectuals he later met in New York. The men became lifelong friends and corresponded for years to come.

Ernie's days in the American Southwest and Mexico were finally coming to a close. It was time for him to return to New York to prepare for the rest of his life. He was aware he still had little money and limited prospects. He reminded himself that now, more than ten years after he had been a commandant-general at 23 years of age, he had let several opportunities in Ireland go. These included his medical studies in Dublin and the possibility of his serving in the Dáil. Either of these paths would have led to a professional position and dependable income for him in his native country. Nor did he have any interest in becoming an officer in the Irish Free State army that he had fought against in the Civil War, and by whom he had been imprisoned. This could have offered him yet another professional career alternative.[24]

He was still winging it with few, if any, definite professional opportunities. He had finally decided that he was destined for the artistic, creative, intellectual life. Ernie had no clear career prospects, but he had the makings of two books.

At her request, in June 1932 Ernie drove Dorothy Stewart's car from Santa Fe to New York via Indianapolis. Ernie's letter to Paul Strand back in Taos gives an account of both his long drive from Santa Fe and his first visits to New York's artistic communities. He admired the beauty of the rural Midwest; he spent nights sleeping in Dorothy's car beside the road while passing through the farm country of Kansas and Ohio. The car needed constant repairs that Ernie could barely afford, but he finally arrived in New York City in early July.[25]

Following a recommendation from Strand, he first visited the Yaddo Foundation, a retreat for creative people located in Saratoga Springs, New York. Ted Stevenson, author, playwright, screenwriter and a long-time friend of Paul Strand, was at Yaddo. Ted acted as Strand's surrogate for Ernie there, and later, in New York City, he introduced Ernie to the Yaddo group and supported him in other ways. Elisabeth Ames, Yaddo's executive director, had rarely shown interest in its individual fellows, but she appeared to be impressed by Ernie during his initial visit.[26]

In New York City, courtesy of Strand, Ernie was welcomed at the Group Theatre run by Howard Clurman and Lee Strasberg. Marlon Brando would get his start as an actor there years later when he was trained by Strasberg. One of America's leading playwrights, Clifford Odets, was present and Strand wrote to Ernie, 'A letter came from Clifford Odets, one of the actors of the Group, saying you had been there for three days and "made a great hit with the people." That you told some "excellent dirty stories."'[27] Ernie enjoyed the communal spirit of the Group Theatre. He had already begun to be accepted by some of the most important modernist circles existing then in New

York. However, he bemoaned the fact that due to his difficulty in finding work, he could not pay his fair share of the group's communal expenses, which was expected of every participant.

Shortly thereafter Ernie received a letter from Ames inviting him to be a guest at Yaddo in order to complete his memoirs from mid-August through mid-September 1932. He was overwhelmed by the 'palatial bed' in his room at Yaddo and grateful for the opportunity to mix with other writers and artists. The experience at Yaddo also gave Ernie a new status in the American creative world. Many aspiring writers and artists of all kinds were taken in as fellows at Yaddo before and after Ernie received his invitation. The distinguished list included Leonard Bernstein, Truman Capote, Saul Bellow, James Baldwin, Carson McCullers and Sylvia Plath. The philosopher Sidney Hook and composer Israel Citkowitz were there when Ernie came, and later Citkowitz and his sister Rebecca befriended Ernie in New York City. He had joined the major league of American creative artists.

Ernie began to meet other leading people in the New York artistic world. This included the composer Aaron Copland, the painter Georgia O'Keeffe and her husband, the photographer Alfred Stieglitz, who maintained a salon for modernist artists in the city. Ernie became a friend of James Johnson Sweeney, then a lecturer at the Metropolitan Museum of Art who later became director of the Solomon R. Guggenheim Museum in New York City. He also met Mariquita Villard, who would later arrange Ernie's introduction to his future wife.

Nevertheless, none of these distinguished people helped Ernie overcome his financial challenges. He lived constantly with the limitation of being broke as he fraternised with both struggling artists and wealthy people. He moved around from place to place in New York City with temporary lodgings provided by friends and acquaintances. He reported to Helen Golden that he was saved for a while by finding two gold sovereigns he had left in a house in New York years before when raising money for the *Irish Press*.[28]

In his own relatively impoverished position, Ernie felt compassion for the victims of the Depression begging on the streets of New York in 1932. He described their pleas and condition with his usual acuity:

> 'Can you give me 5 cents for a meal?' ... 'Spare a cigarette, mister?' Some faces tough and lined, others, but few, with pathetic gentleness, many shifty and cunning. It's hard to live there and not be affected by the terrible want ... A shirted crowd mostly, waiting eagerly for a few honest, direct words; instead they get isms. It's brutal and selfish.[29]

At one point he painted the interior walls of an old building in exchange for living in its basement and meals. Ernie had found this job by becoming for a time 'a Transient on Federal Relief', a federal programme that established work opportunities in cities for those in need. The paint fumes bothered him, but he soldiered on with his manual jobs.[30] At this point in 1934, he was also hoping to get a job in a restaurant as a busboy. He spent a lot of time in the New York Public Library, where he continued to study ancient and medieval Irish history and literature. He also worked on his poetry, short stories and essays, and submitted some for publication.

A few of Ernie's poems appeared in Harriet Moore's magazine *Poetry* in early 1935 and 1936, but his other work wasn't published at that time. He was delighted to be invited to give four lectures on modern art in a Metropolitan Museum of Art course at New York University for James Johnson Sweeney, but he was not paid for them. Many jobs in the city were promised to

Ernie, but they always fell through. He began to think someone or something was jinxing his efforts to support himself. During this period, he was completing the manuscript of his book, *On Another Man's Wound*, which described his activities in the War of Independence.[31]

In late 1934, he finally finished his book and began to send it to publishers in New York and Boston, often with a helpful introduction from one of his friends. Ernie then started to receive rejections from these publishers. Given his known background, the turndowns were always polite and sometimes deferential, as when he was addressed as 'General', but no one would publish the work. He was furious when a publishing house would hold his submission for months before sending him a rejection notice. In April 1935, Ernie wrote to Helen Golden, 'Writing has been very bad ... The book is now at the 9th publisher, but I have had a few decent letters from publishers; however, that is no consolation.'[32]

He described how he dealt with the continual prospect of being hungry in New York City: 'Last year being so hard I organised New York so that I could be invited out to dinners about 4 nights a week, but they became ... mostly society or semi-society functions and in the end I decided it was much better to be hungry.'[33]

By 1935 Ernie had now lived in New York for almost three years, with the exception of visits to Boston and a summer spent in Chicago in 1933 to work at Ireland's pavilion in the World's Fair, and he had little to show for it. He could not find suitable work; he could not get his book published; he often had trouble finding a place to live; and he had to depend on the charity of friends, which hurt his pride. In a letter to Strand, he demonstrated the courage that had taken him through the terrible challenges of his military life: 'This last year I went through several kinds of hell, and only last month was I able to realise that I was above defeat. That may sound presumptuous, but it's true. I touched bottom and found that at any rate.'[34]

However, there were two rays of light that emerged for Ernie during these daunting years in New York from 1932 to 1935. One was the military and disability pensions, for his service and wounds, that in 1934 he learned he was about to be granted from de Valera's new Fianna Fáil government. The other was a young woman he met in Greenwich, Connecticut in June 1933.

In 1932 de Valera became taoiseach. After the January 1933 election, Fianna Fáil held a majority in the Dáil; it had become Ireland's controlling political party six years after its founding. De Valera's compromise approach to dealing with the Treaty had worked, and he proceeded gradually to undo most of its objectionable features, such as the oath of allegiance to the British Crown, British access to Ireland's ports, the office of the British governor general to Ireland, and the 1922 constitution's limit on Ireland's territorial sovereignty to only twenty-six counties.

Many leading figures of the Fianna Fáil party were men who had been Ernie's comrades in the War of Independence. They began to take care of their early comrades, who had suffered so much during and after both wars. Wartime pensions for those who had fought in both wars were made available to former IRA men like Ernie. He was informed by Frank Aiken, then minister of defence, that he would become eligible for both a substantial military service pension and a disability award. He was advised to make an application for this by citing the many wounds from combat and torture he had received during the 1918–22 period. It was finally determined that he would receive £335 annually, a decent sum at that time.

Frank Aiken urged Ernie to return to Ireland. Others in Ireland had suggested that he become editor of the *Irish Press*, which he had helped to found through his fund raising, but that never developed. Ernie was ready to go home, and he finally did so in mid-June 1935. He had outstayed his visa, but his brother Desmond, who was then in the British Merchant Navy, helped him – he was taken as a stowaway on a British ship in Boston harbour bound for Dublin.

Before he finally left the United States, Ernie visited the home of John T. Hughes in Boston. Hughes was a successful lawyer who had accumulated an enormous library of Irish volumes in his home. Ernie had been holing up there since he first came to the United States, and he paid one more satisfying visit in order to continue work on his memoirs. John was one of the many American friends who did so much to sustain Ernie while he was in America.

The promise of a service pension and disability award must have meant a great deal to Ernie. For the first time, his distinguished service to Ireland was being publicly recognised, and he could live with the financial security that had evaded him so dramatically up to this point. He was now 38 years old – about time to be able to live without facing the continual challenge of poverty; without having to borrow from friends in order to merely survive. But there was another deep significance to these payments. He was now a man with a secure future income and could offer marriage. Over the past two years, he had fallen in love with an American artist; he would eventually ask her to marry him.

It all began in June 1933, when Ernie was invited to lunch in the Greenwich, Connecticut home of the American industrialist who had founded Hooker Electrochemical Company. Elon Hooker and his wife Blanche were both from distinguished families; Blanche's father, Dexter Mason Ferry, had built the successful Ferry Morse Seed Company in Detroit. Elon had also created enormous wealth on his own, and he was descended from Thomas Hooker, one of the founders of the state of Connecticut.

The couple had four daughters and used their traditional Sunday lunches to invite friends, among them young men, to meet their three unmarried daughters. Their youngest daughter Blanchette had already married a man who must have been one of the most eligible bachelors of his time, John D. Rockefeller 3rd – tall, austere and the oldest of the five Rockefeller brothers. With the assistance of his wife Blanchette, who became a mover in New York society, John 3rd sustained the powerful philanthropic legacy begun by his grandfather, creator of the family fortune, and continued by his father. Mariquita Villard, a girl from an American publishing family who was a friend of two of the three Hooker daughters, had suggested that the parents invite Ernie, and she brought him to their house that day.

At the table that Sunday were three Hooker daughters: Barbara, an English major at Vassar who had visited Ireland; Adelaide, who majored in music at Vassar and later married John P. Marquand, one of the best-selling American novelists of his time; and Helen, who was 28 years old. Helen was known to be independent-minded and had already travelled extensively in Europe. She had been the maid of honour for Blanchette when she married John D. Rockefeller 3rd. It's difficult to imagine two men as different as John and Ernie, but later Ernie remembered kindly that when they met, Johnny, as he called him, 'did his best to put me at ease by asking me questions on Irish production'. Ernie also reported, 'Adelaide was very … sceptical about me … It was an insult in her eyes for a Hooker to marry a European, but particularly an Irishman and a Catholic.'[35]

The lunch began well but ran into trouble when Helen's father, realising that Ernie had had contact with the American Indians in the Southwest, asked him about his experiences with them.

Ernie launched into an attack on the US government's treatment of the American Indians, noting that it had taken their lands, broken many treaty promises and forced other indignities upon them. Mr Hooker became annoyed and afterwards declared that Ernie was never to set foot in their house again. Helen may never have witnessed a man who would stand up to her father in this manner. She took Ernie away from the lunch to show him her sculpture studio on the Hooker grounds.

Helen had had some unusual experiences for a girl of her background. She had won the National Junior Girls Singles Tennis Championship in 1923, and the Junior Doubles as well – playing with Helen Mills in 1922 and with another partner in 1923. After this she gave up the competitive tennis circuit to become an artist. She refused to go to Vassar like her sisters and instead studied art, first at the Art Students League of New York and later in Paris and Spain. She became something of a rebel in her own family.

In 1928 Helen and her sister Adelaide travelled through Europe. She went to Oberammergau in Germany (the village where the famous Passion Play is performed every ten years) to study woodcarving. They then passed through Sweden to Finland, where they could obtain visas to visit the Soviet Union. They entered Russia in November 1928. In St Petersburg Helen met and spent time with a bright young American scientist, Dr William (Vassily) Horsley Gantt. He was working with the distinguished Russian researcher Ivan Pavlov, who had pioneered the development of behavioural psychology. His studies demonstrated that the effect of positive and negative reinforcement on animals might show that human behaviour could be influenced by positive and negative stimuli. Helen also studied painting with Pavel Filonov – founder of his own Russian system of Analytical Art – met other modernist Russian painters, took photographs and visited several Russian cities, which she captured in her watercolour paintings.

At that time, there were only several hundred foreigners travelling in Russia. Her father Elon was not happy with his daughters' trip and cited financial restraints as a reason for the sisters to return home in March 1929. Later Helen visited France and Venice, and went on to Greece to study dance at the Kanellos School of Hellenic Choral Drama. Ernie had met a remarkably independent American woman.

Early in 1931, while travelling in France, Helen wrote to her father:

> If we really want to be of any value to each other, it must be that of friendship – and not the commanding parent. Many girls have left home and made it very difficult for everyone because of the feeling that they were mere puppets for the parents to make dance. I believe you do want to help me, and I very much desire your advice on many things, but friends must be very sure not to interfere with the natural development of an individual even if it really is a disappointment to them as you have made me believe I am to you. That may be but I have a definite and constructive path to follow, and I long for us to share what we can of it as friends together.[36]

The relationship between Helen and Ernie did not develop into a meaningful romance for more than a year after their first meeting in Greenwich in mid-1933. Ernie went to work at the World's Fair in Chicago for several months shortly after their notable Sunday lunch, and Helen followed her instincts and went to meet him there. They met again in New York City when he returned later in 1933, but his letters to Helen showed that they had still not really connected. Ernie was definitely interested in her but feared she really loved Vassily Gantt, whom she had met in St Petersburg.

Vassily had returned to America from Russia in 1930 to join the faculty at Johns Hopkins University, where he later became a full professor. He continued seeing Helen in the early 1930s. There is a photograph of Vassily, Pavlov, Helen and her father Elon together at his Greenwich estate in 1931. That year Helen had also made a sculpture of Vassily's head. Ernie heard from a friend in Taos, Dr Gertrude Light, that Helen had stayed for a night or two in Rio Chiquita, near Taos, with Vassily early in 1933. She was travelling with him but could not make up her mind whether to marry him or not. There were rumours that they might elope, since the Hooker family did not approve of their marrying. Helen wrote to her mother early in February 1934, 'I didn't ask Vassily to come up [to her mother's family farm in upstate New York] and the Rochester crowd didn't care for him if you remember.'[37]

Later, in February 1934, eight months after she first met Ernie at lunch in Greenwich, Helen wrote to her mother again: 'Ernie O'Malley is posing for me for a portrait head and I wish I could catch something of his Irish charm and courageous spirit. I read one chapter of his novel of the experience in prison in Dublin and it was thrilling.'[38]

Nevertheless, five months later, in July 1934, Ernie still felt that their relationship had not come together. He expressed his anguish to Paul Strand: 'I was keen on a girl but found when spring was over that she was living vicariously through me in the memory of a man with whom she was really in love. That hurt a great deal, the shock of it. A very fine girl indeed ... I am very inexperienced in the ways of women.'[39] Ernie was vulnerable, and he must have been afraid he was being rejected again by a young American woman.

Helen was about to choose between two compelling suitors. Neither one, Ernie or Vassily, would probably ever know exactly what was going through Helen's mind when she decided which of them would be her husband. Perhaps she could not have articulated precisely why she picked one man over the other, but Helen believed she had made the right choice.

By the spring of 1935, Ernie realised he was the lucky fellow. Before that, his letters to Helen had been signed 'Very sincerely', were addressed to 'Helen Hooker', or were left with no signature, likely to express how upset he was that she was interested in another man.[40] On discovering Helen loved him in return, Ernie must have been elated. He was a different man in April 1935 when his letter to her began, 'Dear Pussy Cat' and ended, 'With all my love'. His letters became interspersed with affectionate declarations: 'I feel quite warm inside when I think of you'; 'That is all the news … except to tell you how much I love you. Is that news?'[41] The fighter and intellectual had finally become a lover whose feelings were reciprocated. They began to discuss where and how they would marry.

They ended up marrying in London in September 1935, after Ernie had returned to Ireland. He had experienced deep feelings for Helen that he had probably never known before, and she had finally chosen a man after a young life filled with colourful experiences and suitors. Their relationship had begun with a mutual attraction that took some time to develop and was then enhanced by their appreciation of the vivid qualities that each had demonstrated up to that point in their lives. However, they were unaware of the depth of the character differences that would severely challenge their marriage as the years went on.

CHAPTER 8

DUBLIN: HUSBAND, AUTHOR, LIBEL DEFENDANT, 1935–1939

Before getting married, Ernie had asked Helen to visit Dublin to be sure she would enjoy living in Ireland. He later recalled that when he met the Hooker family and courted Helen, his heart was in Ireland, but he hoped that Ireland would suit Helen.[1] First, she visited Japan with her sister Adelaide and her mother on a trip sponsored by the Garden Club of America. The sisters then travelled by themselves to Korea and China, leaving China on a train that would take them across Asia to Europe. Somewhere in Western China when Helen was climbing into the top bunk of their cabin clutching her passport, it flew out of the open transom window. Fortunately, they were not far from the next stop. Helen and Adelaide got off with their luggage and hired two railroad hands, who propelled Helen back by a railroad handcar on the tracks to find Helen's passport – a virtual needle in the haystack. With her artistic eye, she could remember the landscape scene where she had lost it, stopped the handcar, and then miraculously spotted her passport beside the track. She picked it up and went back to Adelaide, who had been guarding their luggage, to wait for the next train.

After he returned from America in mid-June 1935, Ernie made a five-week trip to the south and west of Ireland with

Paul Strand, who was returning from Moscow to New York. They drove around the countryside in Johnny Raleigh's Ford car, visiting the historical sites, churches, monuments and ancient ruins that Ernie would later photograph with Helen. Paul was obviously impressed with Ernie's passion for the aesthetic aspects of Ireland's culture, and he later proposed they do a book together on an Irish village or group of villages where he would do the photography and Ernie the text.[2] They never managed to do the book.

In the summer of 1935, Helen's mother had sent a close friend, Mrs Sarah Sheridan, to Dublin unannounced to inspect the Malley family before the marriage. She reported to Helen's parents that three of Ernie's brothers were doctors, two sisters were nurses, and his father Luke had retired as a respected senior civil servant. Ernie's mother, Marion Kearney Malley, was also an aunt to Sir Gilbert Laithwaite, later the private secretary to Lord Curzon, British Viceroy of India; Laithwaite would also become the first British ambassador to Ireland in 1949.[3] The Malley family had at least passed muster with Helen's parents. Ernie was about to become a husband whose father-in-law was concerned with his future prospects but who became somewhat mollified when he believed Ernie would follow in his brothers' footsteps and become a doctor.

Helen and Adelaide arrived in London after their train trip across Asia, and Helen then went on to Dublin alone. She decided she liked Dublin and would be happy there, but she could not be married in a Roman Catholic church in Dublin because she had not been baptised.

To solve the problem, Helen and Ernie were married on 27 September 1935 in the St James's Roman Catholic Church in London. It was a small wedding. Kevin, one of Ernie's younger brothers, was best man, and Adelaide was Helen's maid of honour. Mrs Sheridan attended, as did four of Ernie's other siblings: Cecil, Marion, Kathleen ('Kaye') and Brendan. The British press had been alerted from a New York source that a daughter of the American industrialist Elon Hooker was getting married in the city. To fool them, Kevin and Kathleen Malley pretended to be the bridal couple while Helen and Ernie slipped out for a small reception followed by a brief honeymoon in London. The reception was held at the Cheshire Cheese in Fleet Street, a famous old tavern. Ernie chose this site because it had been a meeting place in the eighteenth century of one of his favourite authors, Dr Samuel Johnson. On returning to Dublin, they spent time in a hotel before moving to 229 Upper Rathmines Road, a comfortable south Dublin suburb. The couple had little money, later recalling, 'We began with butter boxes for furniture.'[4]

Several months after the wedding, on 24 December, Helen's father Elon shared his thoughts with Ernie about their marriage:

> I have been interested in the plans for the new home in Dublin and your university work to complete preparation for the profession of medicine ... It has not been easy to write – your letter is appreciative of that – but my only interest is in Helen's long term happiness and the worthwhile success of those dear to her. Even so it is difficult to be reconciled to a life for her and her children so far away from her home traditions ... She is a wonderful girl – gifted and worthy of personal achievement. She has chosen – and I hope wisely – to trust her future to you. May God bless you both and make the hard places easier. I send you every good Christmas wish.[5]

Ernie felt he had to show himself, his wife and her family that he could become a professional. He went back to UCD medical school for two years, from 1935 until 1937, but had trouble preparing for his exams with the focus they required. He was then 39 years old, far more mature than his fellow students and still suffering from his wounds. His much younger classmates knew of his military background and must have looked at him as if he were a man from another world, which, indeed, he was. His efforts to be an effective medical student were not successful; he ended up not even taking his final exams over the next two years. The use of X-rays had been introduced into the training for medical students. Occasionally a professor at UCD, aware of Ernie's background, would ask him if he could use an X-ray of his body to show the bullets remaining there, illustrating the use of this new device to Ernie's fellow students.

His deep involvement in Ireland's warring period and the ten years he spent travelling in Europe, America and Mexico had taken him far away from his previous medical training. His transition from revolutionary to intellectual during this last decade led him to write two memoirs, to focus on the culture of the American Southwest and Mexico, and to make new friends in the creative, artistic worlds of the Americas. Ernie had travelled too far from the world of medicine in Ireland to be able to return effectively to it now.

Ernie was now back in Dublin, with access to his large family of eleven Malley siblings. His eight brothers and two sisters lived compelling lives. Two of his brothers, Frank and Albert, had joined the Dublin Fusiliers in the British army, fought in the First World War and then died of blackwater fever while serving in the King's African Rifles in Africa during the early 1920s. His brother Charlie, a veterinary student, 18 years old, was killed in a Dublin shoot-out against Free State forces at the beginning of the Civil War.

Cecil, Kevin and Paddy served in the IRA during the War of Independence and the Civil War. Cecil broke both legs jumping from the roof of Dublin's Custom House, which his group had attacked on 25 May 1921. Kevin, who had the bottom of his leg amputated due to infantile paralysis as a child, carried secret messages in his wooden leg stump as a courier for the anti-Treaty IRA in 1922, when he was only 15 years old. Paddy was arrested by Free State forces and participated in the forty-one-day hunger strike in Mountjoy Jail when he was 17 years old; he later became a banker in Ireland.

Brendan, too young to be involved in the IRA, became a captain in the British Medical Corps in the Second World War. He had several important assignments, including protecting Rome's water supply from being poisoned by the retreating German army. Desmond, the youngest brother, joined the British Merchant Navy. While serving in the British navy during the Second World War, he twice survived when his ship was sunk by German U-boats. Later, while assigned to the Indian navy, he was severely wounded near Sri Lanka during a Japanese attack and spent five years recovering in a British military hospital in Australia.

Three of Ernie's brothers, Cecil, Kevin and Brendan, became distinguished doctors. All three were first in their class at the University College Dublin Medical School. Cecil, a leading surgeon, became the first Roman Catholic to be a fellow of the Royal College of Surgeons in London. He developed a highly successful practice in London. Kevin did postgraduate work at Johns Hopkins in Baltimore and became one of the most prominent heart specialists in Dublin. During Ernie's final years, Kevin carefully watched over his brother's frail heart condition.

Ernie's two sisters, Marion and Kaye, had interesting careers as nurses in London and Dublin. Marion later died, in 1948, when her Irish-born husband crashed their small plane on the French coast after going over the English Channel. He had previously lost an arm flying for the Royal Air Force against Germany. Marion had a lively, endearing personality, and everyone in the family called her 'Sweetie'. Kaye was a captain in the Irish Nursing Corps during the Second World War. She later became treasurer of the Irish Countrywomen's Association and was awarded their highest honour – the Buan Cairde. She and her husband bought a lovely house in Howth, the Dublin suburb where Ernie's state funeral began. Kaye had taken her brother into her home to nurse him during the final months of his life.

The children supported each other throughout their lives. Their parents had sent deeply motivated, hard-working young people out into the world. Several were blessed by outstanding success, and several survived serious wounds from the wars that consumed Ireland and Britain from 1914 until 1945.

From his arrival in New York harbour in October 1928 until his return to Ireland in June 1935, Ernie had been writing his memoirs. He had already submitted his first memoir, *On Another Man's Wound*, to about fifteen publishers in the United States in the mid-1930s.[6]

The Macmillan Company, a noted international publisher, had written to him in October 1933:

> It is with very genuine regret that we must write you of our decision in regard to your autobiography. It has been read by an unusual number of our advisors, and they all agree on the inherent interest and importance of the work. Unfortunately, we can see no place where the book would fit in with our plans for the coming seasons, and we have regretfully decided we cannot make you an offer for the book despite its undoubted originality and importance. In these difficult days we are frequently obliged to decline

unusual manuscripts which might otherwise have found a place on our list. We are all, however, keenly interested in you and your work and would always be most happy to consider any books which you may write in the future. Very truly yours, Lois Dwight Cole.[7]

This was in the depths of the Great Depression. Macmillan was telling Ernie that this could have been a determining reason for declining his book.

Two years later, in 1936, and then in 1937, Ernie's book *Wound* was published in England and America to critical acclaim. Why did so many publishers originally turn it down? Other more acclaimed authors experienced similar early rejections of their leading works. Marcel Proust and James Joyce, Ernie's countryman, were the two most acclaimed novelists of the twentieth century. Proust suffered when two major French publishers originally rejected his book, *Swann's Way*, in 1912. It was later published by Proust himself, and then by others, and became perhaps the most translated and commented upon novel of its time. On receiving his early rejections, Proust wrote, expressing Ernie's sentiments, 'It was so easy to write these volumes ... But how difficult it will be to get them published ... trying to get them into print, dealing with publishers, seem to be overwhelming tasks.'[8]

In July 1935, Ernie had shown both books to a friend in Dublin, Peadar O'Donnell, a fellow anti-Treaty republican who found them so engrossing that he stayed up all night to finish them. Peadar immediately had the manuscript delivered to a friend who was a literary agent in Dublin. Apparently, the agent also spent the night reading them. He then sent the manuscript off to a highly recommended London publisher, Rich & Cowen. The editor there shared the previous two readers' enthusiasm for the book. Soon after this, the publishing house gave Ernie a contract for his first memoir, and *On Another Man's Wound* was finally published in London and Dublin in the spring of 1936. The contract gave Ernie suitable advances and ten per cent royalties on sales, to increase as more copies were sold.

Rich & Cowen had a relationship with Houghton Mifflin, an American publishing house based in Boston, and in February 1937 they published an American edition of Ernie's book under a different title for marketing purposes: *Army Without Banners*. The London publisher had insisted that Ernie delete the pages in *Wound* which described Major King and Captain Hardy torturing him in Dublin Castle with a hot poker, a revolver and their fists. Houghton Mifflin reinserted these six pages in its publication.[9] Ernie's memoir was also translated into German and published there in 1937, with reprints in 1942 and 1943.[10]

Personal, colourful accounts of the War of Independence had been written by other IRA members; these included Dan Breen's *My Fight for Irish Freedom* and Tom Barry's *Guerilla Days in Ireland*. Both books were received well and enjoyed good sales in Ireland and America. However, neither had quite the literary quality, imagination and universal appeal of Ernie's book. He coupled vivid descriptions of his battle experiences, like his assault on Hollyford Barracks, with lyrical descriptions of the flora and fauna: 'chestnut flowers, the dripping mustard of locust trees shared the flaxen or gold hue with ragweed and the heavy gold of meadowsweet. Lilac scented blue near tufted clusters of mauve rhododendron, oak leaves in a now startling green twisted their paler-backed powder, tall avenues of beeches.'[11]

Ernie's book *Wound* provided a unique story of the struggle for Irish freedom. It was more than a work reporting a war; it became the passionate testimony of a young patriot fighting for his country's right to express itself against an oppressor that he believed had smothered its ability to express its own culture. His love for Ireland and its people resounds from every page.

Wound took readers into the life of the people living in the Irish countryside. In describing the departure from a farmhouse before an attack, Ernie uses words in Irish and allusions to history to give the reader an authentic view of the organic speech of the Irish people that he often encountered:

> Sometimes an old woman as I left a house would say, 'Goodbye. God save you and guard you, *a mhic*, and may you have the strength to fight well,' and press a strong, firm kiss on my mouth. For the moment I was her son whom she loved and was proud of. I could see the peaceful, quiet strength of her worn, serene face when I was on the road. It was as if Ireland herself, *An Shan Van Vocht*, the Poor Old Woman, had saluted one who was fighting for her. There was a strange, passionate love of the land amongst the people ... the arts were a broken tradition, the ideal of beauty had gone into the soil and the physical body.[12]

Before *Wound* was published in London, and in Dublin by Three Candles Press, Ernie wrote an introductory article on it for the *Irish Press*, and the newspaper serialised the book, running it daily for several months. This gave *Wound* publicity before publication, but it may have undermined its sales on publication. The prime motivation for serialisation was to get his book out to the rural Irish public, who might not be able to afford the book or be otherwise aware of its message. Ernie wanted to honour the heroic role his countrymen had played in the War of Independence.

The memoir achieved international acclaim. The *New York Times* described it as 'a stirring and beautiful book'.[13] The

New York Herald Tribune acclaimed it as 'a stirring tale of heroic adventure ... told without Rancour or Rhetoric.'[14] The Irish writer Seán Ó Faoláin applauded the book in the October 1936 edition of *Ireland Today*: 'his success depended largely on integrity ... Life must be respected. O'Malley has accomplished this difficult task finely ... He has given us a book as heroic as *Revolt in the Desert* [by Lawrence of Arabia].' Ó Faoláin also made a critique: 'As to the absence of pity ... this is, in the main, a soldier's record and ... there was then little room for that unmasculine (but not unmanly) emotion.' However, he concluded by saying, 'it has added another name to the permanent list of Irish men of letters.'[15]

Ernie's second memoir, *The Singing Flame*, covering the Irish Civil War, was not finished and presented inherent problems. The Civil War had left unresolved bitter feelings among men and families who had been on either side of that tragic conflict. There was a good possibility that libel charges might be brought against Ernie or its publisher if it were published. Twelve years had passed since the ceasefire and dump arms orders of 1923, but the issues raised in *Flame* were still sensitive. Ernie made no attempts to publish it during his lifetime. Forty-three years would pass before it was published.

After Ernie's death in 1957, his son Cormac eventually became the keeper of Ernie's legacy. From 1970 to 1973, Cormac submitted the unfinished manuscript of *Flame* to several Irish publishers, trying to interest them. No one would accept it in its unfinished form. When Cormac approached Frances-Mary Blake, an English admirer of Ernie's life story, she agreed to complete the book using Ernie's notes and undertaking further research. Anvil Press finally published the book in 1978. Blake wrote in her introduction, 'O'Malley was not simply an intransigent military man; he was fighting for a better Ireland, socially and politically and economically.'[16] Now, Ireland and the world had two books that covered both of the key conflicts which convulsed Ireland and its people from 1916 to 1923.

Some of Ernie's poems had been published early in 1936 in the *Dublin Magazine*, and with the publication of his first memoir, *Wound*, he established a new identity for himself as an author in Ireland. In August 1937 Ernie was invited to become a member of the distinguished Irish Academy of Letters. He had been proposed for this honour by two noted Irish authors and republican comrades, Seán Ó Faoláin and Frank O'Connor. O'Connor later described in his autobiography what had happened when he and Ó Faoláin went to the home of the Nobel laureate W.B. Yeats to get his needed support for Ernie's nomination. Yeats responded with humour by saying, 'What do you two young rascals mean by trying to fill my Academy with gunmen?'[17] Yeats then approved Ernie, who was accepted for membership.

Ernie and his fellow IRA comrades were often called 'gunmen', but as a young soldier Ernie used a gun only when necessary and began his military career by letting the other fellow shoot at him first, attempting to avoid killing wherever possible. Later he became a more avid fighter in his attacks on barracks, and he was also willing, as commander of the 2nd Southern in early 1921, to order the execution of three captured British officers according to the agreement he had made with his fellow commandant-general Liam Lynch. When Desmond Ryan, in his book *Remembering Scion*, referred to Ernie as a 'gunman', Ernie read the book and wrote to Ryan, 'I don't mind being called a gunman; we were, I suppose, though we didn't use that term ourselves. And as you are a pacifist, and I respect you for your beliefs, I don't see why you shouldn't use the term.'[18]

Unfortunately, the publication of *Wound* occasioned an unexpected negative response in October 1936 that plagued Ernie until he died. It was resolved in a Dublin court the next year. At that point, it became a serious financial liability for him. Two actions for libel were taken: first, against Ernie, Three Candles Press and the book's Irish printers and distributors; second, against Ernie and the *Irish Press*, which serialised the book. The libel actions were brought by Joseph O'Doherty, a barrister from Donegal who had served with the Irish Volunteers and then with the IRA. There had been a raid for arms carried out by the IRA in Moville, Donegal on 1 October 1919 during the War of Independence. The raid had been suggested by Michael Collins in Dublin and planned locally by the then-staff captain from Dublin, Ernie. In *Wound* he had described a situation where a member of the Irish Volunteers' executive had refused to go on the raid.

Ernie's lawyer presented two defences: first, that since O'Doherty had not been specifically named in the book, he was not libelled; second, that Ernie had accurately presented the facts of the matter as they occurred, and that he had written them in good faith without intent to injure anyone. O'Doherty's lawyer prevailed on the first point, showing that his client could clearly be identified as the person who had refused to go on the raid. Replying to Ernie's second defence, O'Doherty's lawyer argued that his client had been a member of the Dáil at the time of the raid. Therefore, the IRA group about to mount the raid to secure British rifles that night had unanimously agreed, without O'Doherty's involvement in their decision, that because of his elected political position he should not participate in the raid. He claimed Ernie had misrepresented the facts, published a book that made his client out to be a coward, and damaged his reputation, constituting a libel.[19]

In the report on the raid in *Wound* that formed the basis of the libel claim, Ernie had written a different story from the facts presented by O'Doherty's counsel:

An incident that most disconcerted me was the attitude of a member of the Volunteer executive on the night of the raid. The men were willing to take their chance, although I thought we would have to fight our way through on our return to Derry. 'I'm not going with you,' he said, as we were ready to move off, 'I have a wife to think about.' His withdrawal made a future doubt in my mind about the quality of a member of the executive.[20]

When lawyers bring a libel action, the case turns on what facts are believable. For Ernie to make a credible defence, he had to bring forward witnesses present at the event who would corroborate that his written version fairly represented what actually happened. Otherwise, it was just Ernie's word against O'Doherty's in the court proceeding, and O'Doherty had produced witnesses from Donegal who corroborated his version of the raid.

As Ernie wrote later, 'I knew there was little chance, if any, of winning the case. I found it hard to obtain evidence. People who could verify facts and incidents in talk were reluctant to appear in court.' On 18 November 1937, the court decided against Ernie. The court assigned damages of £250 against him and Three Candles Press, and £300 against him and the *Irish Press*. Ernie's share of the two judgements eventually came to £400, which was more than his annual pension and disability payments of £335. Helen's father offered to help Ernie with this large sum, but he insisted on paying it himself. He borrowed the £400, paid the Dublin High Court, and received certification from it in May 1938 that he had satisfied his obligation in full.[21]

There were at least two ways to consider the libel case. One was to consider it as one more terribly unfair turn of events against Ernie. He had been a hero fighting for Ireland's right to be free, continually risking his life and undergoing any and every hardship without complaint. He no doubt believed that his version of the raid was the truth as he remembered it. It was manifestly unfair that no men from Donegal present that night came to Dublin to testify for him. Once again, Ernie had failed.

The second way presented a different approach. Ernie had been aware that his version of the raid might have led to a libel suit. He said so himself when responding to Helen's urging before the trial that he settle the libel action out of court: 'I had to stand over what I had honestly remembered and had sincerely written. Also I knew that a series of libel actions could result.' However, if he had thought through the risks of libel, he could have merely omitted the section from *Wound* or written it differently. It was well known that the libel laws of England and Ireland were severe, and that an author had to be particularly careful not to breach them.[22]

Ernie's weaknesses as a rebel-intellectual were the obverse sides of his strengths. He would never hesitate to take risks, to fight for his principles; but occasionally if he had considered the consequences of his actions with more far-seeing judgement, he might not have taken some of the risks he did.

The consequences of the libel suit went beyond the severe financial and psychological reversals Ernie experienced at the time. It adversely impacted his relationship with his wife just two years into their marriage. Helen had been constantly reminding Ernie in the year before the trial occurred in November 1937 that he had the wrong lawyer, and that he should settle the case. She was concerned about the publicity a public defeat in court could cause for the Hooker and Rockefeller families. After the judgement, but before Ernie could resolve issues with his publishers as to how the judgement should be shared between them, bailiffs came to the house rented by Helen and Ernie, seizing its contents for payment. Some of the furniture, paintings and books were Helen's possessions. Ernie finally agreed to his share of the judgement, paid it in May 1938, and ended the difficult situation.[23]

Helen was an artist: a dedicated sculptor, painter and photographer. She was pleased that Ernie had become a respected author and intellectual in Dublin – she probably found this preferable to being the wife of a doctor. Over the next ten years, working together in Ireland, Helen and Ernie would undertake a variety of creative projects focusing on recognising and restoring the country's cultural heritage. Helen's taste and varied artistic skills became invaluable as they traversed Ireland endeavouring to preserve its cultural symbols.

In the spring of 1936, the couple had shared happier experiences while focusing on their mutual interest in the arts. They toured the south-west of Ireland, visiting and photographing various abbeys, historic ruins and religious relics. They focused on early Irish sculpture, examining it from the view of aesthetics rather than archaeology. They were beginning to develop their vision of making a record of medieval Irish history that could be presented to the Irish people as an example of their heritage. They would also visit with Ernie's friends Johnny and Bea Raleigh in Limerick.

Helen was pregnant with their first child, and on 10 July 1936, their son Cathal was born in Dublin after a difficult Caesarean operation. She had a challenging time, both in the weeks before and after the birth. She was shocked to hear from the doctor who delivered her baby that under Irish law he would have to save the baby's life before hers if a challenging situation developed. Cathal had arrived nine and a half months after their marriage. Helen hadn't expected to have a child that soon, and she had difficulty relating to her new role as a mother. Her mother Blanche and sister Adelaide came to Dublin for Cathal's birth.

Helen was a new bride with her first child. She wrote to her father, 'The fact that I have made the house liveable for myself and the baby could create a sense of imbalance ... But Ernie does far more to balance our home life and keep me from flying off at a tangent and steadies us all down regularly. We simply couldn't be happier.'[24]

In the autumn of 1936, the couple went to Paris and bought paintings reflecting their good taste. They continued their second honeymoon by travelling to Corsica, seeking the sun. In a letter from Corsica to Eithne Golden, the teenage girl he had taught four years before in Taos, Ernie demonstrated a rare instance of his sense of humour and humanity. Eithne had asked what Helen was like and Ernie obliged: 'she has neither bow legs or a squint. She is not platinum blonde nor does she talk through her nose. She is not smaller than 4' 1½". And she likes Ireland and the people like her.' He ended with, 'and here's a special hug for you. Love, Ernie.'[25]

Helen's love of the arts, her good taste in colour and paintings when decorating their own and other people's houses in Dublin, and her enthusiastic career as a sculptor who began doing busts of Irish friends and artists, opened Dublin's creative community to her. She developed close friendships with people in its artistic-theatrical community. Ernie's diaries and letters from 1936 to 1938 illustrate the couple's continual visits to the Abbey Theatre, art exhibitions, lectures and classical music concerts presenting Bach, Mozart and Beethoven, as well as modern composers.

The couple's fulfilling life in Dublin during this period is exemplified by the distinguished people who attended a dinner party they gave in August 1937. Their guests included diplomat William Fay; artist Maurice MacGonigal; poets Denis Devlin and Niall Sheridan; suffragette Hanna Sheehy-Skeffington; barrister Donagh MacDonagh; Dublin City's chief librarian, Róisín Walsh;

businessman Aodogán O'Rahilly, son of the O'Rahilly who had been killed in Easter 1916; and Irish Film Society founder Liam Ó Laoghaire.[26]

During this period Ernie and Helen developed a long-term friendship with Catherine 'Bobs' and Harry Walston, meeting them in both Dublin and London. Bobs was a vivacious young American woman and the granddaughter of Mrs Sheridan, the lady who had been sent to Dublin by the Hookers to check on Ernie's family. Harry was an English landowner, eventually Lord Walston, who later owned a large country house, Newton Hall, and an estate with 5,000 acres of farm land in Cambridgeshire. He also had a town house in London where Ernie and Helen could stay. Bobs and Harry had met and married in America in 1935, when he was studying at Harvard University. They shared Helen and Ernie's interest in the arts, and the couples found they had much in common. The Walstons would become particularly supportive of Ernie during the declining years of his life from 1953 to 1957.

In 1937 Helen began a pattern of individual travel. Baby Cathal was left with his father and a nurse in Dublin when she visited her family in America in early February. Helen then went from New York to London at the end of February, staying there throughout March and early April. In London she went to the theatre and visited friends. Her absences were not easy for Ernie.

In the spring of 1937, he wrote her a series of letters from their Dublin house while she was away:

> I played with the baby and he now knows somehow what to expect from me ... The baby is doing well and will soon be able to stand up ... I have taken him into my room a few times and now he is almost used to it ... The house is very lonely without you; The baby has another tooth. I

don't know when you'll be back, not when you say, I think, as I'm taking the car away to-morrow to wander about the country. I'm going away for a while. I have left a file of bills and letters in the table drawer of the Library ... Will you also if you leave again take the keys of your closets ... When you go away I am thinking of ... leaving the baby with mother. I can look after myself.[27]

Late in 1937, Ernie made a decision to finally give up his medical studies at UCD. Starting in October 1937, he enrolled in a UCD art history course directed by Françoise Henry, and he received a diploma in European painting in spring 1938. That spring Ernie and Helen visited Paris, where they spent time with Samuel Beckett, the Irish playwright author of *Waiting for Godot*. They bought more paintings and began putting together a significant art collection; she and Ernie acquired paintings individually with their own money. These included purchases of modern European artists, including works by Modigliani, Vlaminck, Rouault and Dufy.

Helen also began to receive a substantial allowance from her father. The financial assistance from her family was helpful for the couple and included shares of stock in the Hooker Company. Elon Hooker died without a will in May 1938. Under Connecticut law, Helen received one-eighth of her father's considerable estate. While much of her wealth would be held in various trusts, Helen would be able to access it indirectly. She had become an heiress in her own right, and this would affect the marriage in the years to come. Following her father's death, she went to America with Cathal and a nurse to be with her family for four months.

Upon her return, Helen and Ernie continued their trips from Dublin to London, buying paintings and books. Much of their compatibility as a couple was based on their well-developed, similar artistic tastes. A major theme of their letters to each other, particularly when Helen was away in America for spring and early summer 1938, focused on these purchases. Ernie noted:

> I wrote to the International bookshop [in Paris], but the books arrived this month; he had not sent the magazines we had paid him for ... The pictures came to Dublin, but for the past week I have been trying to get them, not having your prices of the frames ... I then had an exhibition of your work on the walls ... You should frame at least 6 when you get back and hang some up decently.[28]

These were not casual purchases. Helen and Ernie had an eye for Post-Impressionist painters who were selling at reasonable prices but would become valuable later.

Even though they were spending more and more time apart, their love affair still consisted of more than just their similar tastes in art. Ernie noted:

> It has been raining hard for nearly three weeks ... Finally, last week I bought some whiskey so the staying in doesn't matter so much ... I miss you very much, and the baby. It makes you feel as if you had lost something in some room and you keep searching for it. Anyhow I love you very much and wish you were here if only to fight with you.[29]

Helen returned to Dublin with Cathal and the nurse after her four-month American visit in 1938. She and Ernie had already decided to move from Dublin to Mayo. They found a house to lease – Old Head Lodge, Louisburgh – and Ernie went there in August 1938. Helen followed him to Mayo, keeping the lease on their Dublin house until they found a permanent home. This was

O'Malley country. Ernie was born and brought up in Castlebar. There is an old local Mayo saying, 'If you throw a stone here, you'll hit an O'Malley.' From Louisburgh, they began looking for a home on Mayo's beautiful west coast facing the Atlantic Ocean.

They came upon Burrishoole Lodge and began a long-term rental in November 1938, ultimately purchasing the property in Helen's name several years later. It was a large stone house on a river, with two boat piers with access to Clew Bay. Across the Burrishoole River, they could see Burrishoole Abbey, a fifteenth-century Dominican priory, the ruined skeleton of which loomed over the landscape. Their house had been built on property originally owned by one of the local O'Malley families, which was meaningful to Ernie. It was set on a beautiful piece of land and symbolised the romantic theme of ancient Ireland that they had been pursuing together since Helen arrived. Burrishoole would play a significant part in the years to come for Helen and Ernie's family.

Ernie's diaries demonstrate how much they enjoyed the countryside and ocean during their first year there:

> Out to the islands with Helen. Badly burnt. Sea swallows occupy one piece of an island … came back on mountainous waves. Primroses, blue bells and ferns on an island. Brought back four seagulls. Moyne Abbey. Potatoes in drills, ferns thick and painters green high on the mountains, yellow flaggers begin to fade … Island Mór. In to the quay … But the weather makes us put in at Inishguill. Later arrive at Burrishoole. Molly Gill and Rona for Cathal's birthday … Out in MacIntyre's boat to Island Mór.[30]

Friends and family were invited to Burrishoole during their first full year of residence in 1939. Bobs and Harry Walston were among the first guests. Another visitor was Helen's mother, Blanche Hooker. She had come to spend time with Helen, Ernie and her grandson Cathal, whom she had gotten to know during the child's visit to America the year prior.

Blanche was still in Ireland when the Second World War broke out in September 1939. There is a celebrated story in which Helen, demonstrating her sometimes unrealistic, entitled characteristics, demanded that Ernie contact the taoiseach, Éamon de Valera, to have him procure either a British or a United States navy destroyer specifically to take her mother safely back to America. Ernie did no such thing. De Valera certainly would never have entertained such an outrageous request. Happily, grandmother Hooker managed to return safely to America by other means.

CHAPTER 9

MAYO: IRISH ARTS SPONSOR, MARRIAGE DiFFICULTIES, KIDNAPPING, 1940–1950

Europe was now involved in another world war, but this conflict would only have a limited impact on Helen's and Ernie's lives at Burrishoole. The Irish government adopted a neutral stance, which was reluctantly accepted by Britain and the United States. This period in Ireland was called 'the Emergency'. Though the twenty-six counties were spared much of the violence and horror experienced elsewhere, the Second World War did not pass without incident or trial – there was a stray German bombing of Dublin in 1941 and rationing of imported items like tea, fuel and many domestic goods. However, the Irish had suffered a long, violent history with various invaders going back to the Vikings. They were taking no chances and created home defence units all over the country, particularly in coastal areas. None of these forces had to be called into action.

There were also no major attempts by groups to run German weapons secretly into Ireland for present or future battles against British forces, as had occurred before and during the First World War. By now resistance against the Free State had been minimised, and de Valera's party, Fianna Fáil, was clearly the controlling party in the Dáil. Limited pro-German activity was being carried out by a weakened IRA, many of whom found themselves interned in the Curragh prison camp by their former comrades turned Fianna Fáil politicians.

Having left his IRA activities behind, Ernie volunteered for the home defence unit in Mayo but was turned down, probably for medical reasons. He was then receiving the highest level of disability payments and carried numerous bullet fragments in his body. He may have participated in limited training for the local Irish defence forces, but his warring days were basically over. He was hopeful that the home defence programme's joint involvement of one-time opponents in the Irish civil war and former socially isolated sons of the Anglo-Irish and large landowners would serve to bring these Irishmen closer together in their country's future.

Helen and Ernie spent all of 1939 in Burrishoole. Many guests visited them, including Ernie's mother Marion, his brother Cecil, his sister Marion ('Sweetie'), Johnny and Bea Raleigh from Limerick, the Irish painter and stained-glass artist Evie Hone, the Irish writer Liam O'Flaherty and his wife, and the American playwright Gerald Sykes. Most visitors came from Dublin, and travelling to Burrishoole was not an easy trip in those days. Helen and Ernie must have enjoyed welcoming those family members born in Mayo back to their old haunts while demonstrating the beauty of Clew Bay to newcomers.[1] They also used Burrishoole as a base to travel the countryside, taking photographs of local country people in their rural communities as well as ancient historical sites and relics.

Two other important events affected the couple's lives during the early 1940s. This was the birth of their next two children, a girl and then a boy. Helen, having gone through a difficult Caesarean birth with Cathal, delivered both children in the Leinster Maternity Nursing Home on Upper Pembroke Street in

Dublin. Etain, a girl, was born there on 8 August 1940, followed by a boy, Cormac, on 20 July 1942. Meanwhile, Ernie was running the farm at Burrishoole. He missed Helen when she was giving birth in Dublin, writing, 'I wish you were back here. The place is lonely without you.'[2]

Cathal was only 4 years old when Etain was born. However, he was able to write, no doubt with his father's considerable help, a letter to his mother in the Dublin maternity home shortly before his sister arrived. It illustrated not only what it was like for a child to grow up on a farm in the west of Ireland but also how the first child feels when a new baby is about to arrive:

> Dear Mammy, Bricriu [the donkey] bit me ... He's very naughty, and he kicked Nanna two times, one and two, and bit Nanna too in the arm, I think. I don't like him at all 'cause he's bold ... Nora is alright, going on with the cows ... The hens are good (all of them?) Yes all of them ... The old cockerel fights with the white cockerel, and the white cockerel got blood on the head ... The bees are going on. I know I seed [sic] them. The other bees hive alright in the drawing room.
>
> Say please Mamma would you bring the baby. I'll spank the baby if he wouldn't talk to me and I'll send him away to Dublin and he wouldn't come back ... I love the baby ... Please Mummy I like you very much and that all now. Cathal.[3]

In addition to these stays in the city, Helen began to make visits to Dublin regularly in order to reaffirm her artistic interests and meet with friends. After the romance of beautiful Mayo had worn off, Helen and Ernie began to realise how isolated they were in the rugged countryside compared to the stimulating environment in Dublin that they had thrived on and contributed to with their artistic friends. In February 1942 Ernie reflected, 'Helen and I have to go [to Dublin] every now and then to meet people who speak our own language. Here, nobody is interested in creative work ... I have nobody to speak the language of books, literature or criticism. One is driven back in on oneself too much.'[4]

Wartime restrictions only reinforced their intent to build a meaningful farm at Burrishoole. Many items were either rationed or unavailable in Ireland during the Emergency – particularly imported goods. Ernie and Helen undertook the formidable task of creating a self-sufficient farm with their customary energy and optimism. They needed both qualities, since neither had previous experience as rural landowners or as farmers. First, they began to buy or lease land adjacent to Burrishoole, following the natural inclination to increase land-holdings in the country and, more importantly, to enhance their ability to develop a broader range of crops and livestock.

The couple immediately ran into trouble. They had not anticipated that well-entrenched adjoining landholders would resent having people with money from Dublin become purchasers of land around their holdings. One neighbour, Willie Walsh, actually threatened to hit Helen in 1940, when she was pregnant, saying he would drive her out of Burrishoole. He and his brother Sean continued their verbal abuse of both Helen and Ernie, drove cattle onto their land, broke gates and menaced them. They were men capable of violence, with sudden tempers, who apparently weren't afraid to threaten Ernie, a known war hero. Ernie later recalled how the Walsh brothers often said they would shoot him. He wrote:

I had no intention of appealing to law or to police. I was studying hard at the farm, and I meant to hold the land which had been O'Malley land from early times. The house had been burned in 1798, the land confiscated, the [O'Malley] brothers who had lived there had been hanged, killed or exiled … Helen was fearful, but after four years I won out. Eighty per cent of the people were then on my side, but previously no one had given me any help.[5]

Ernie's remarkable patience and persistence led to a resolution of the disputes with the Walsh brothers without anyone getting killed or recourse to legal or police action. But one wonders how his American wife felt about this. Helen had come from another country to marry a military hero known for his courage in battle in her newly adopted country. Now pregnant with his second child, she was confronted by an angry male neighbour who threatened to hit her and drive her off her property. This had occurred near to where her husband had grown up; where he was known and respected. Yet he had taken no direct action to protect her, either on his own or with help from local police or legal authorities. She had no alternative but to live through the long siege with their threatening neighbours.

Ernie and Helen gradually bought more land around Burrishoole, fenced it, and built sea barriers. By the end of 1942 they had about seventy acres. They worked with locals who supported their farming efforts and land acquisition. Local farm employees could also be difficult and demanding. They were not used to a martinet former general who required military-type schedules. Ernie often complained about them. Many part-time workers also had their own farm holdings requiring their attention. Throughout this period Ernie's greatest challenge was to find and keep a farm manager who would work under his direction. He had to advertise for one in local papers, interview around the county without results, and seek one out in trips to

184 • ERNIE O'MALLEY

Dublin. He could wait weeks before one might arrive, knowing they might fade away as easily as they had come.[6]

Ernie attacked the challenge of becoming an effective farmer the same way he had approached the need for expertise as an organiser in 1918. At that time, he began to study British army military manuals; now, he began to study government farming manuals and brochures with similar dedication. He maintained five farm notebooks for running Burrishoole. They are full of detailed information on preparing the land; planting, harvesting and rotating the various crops; and keeping the bees. There are thorough records of the duties, hours and expenses of farm workers, and of other information needed to further develop their farm. They note the names of the men, the days worked and the work assigned. The farm manager was also required to keep a record of work done, which was reviewed by Ernie.[7]

After two years of farming at Burrishoole, Ernie wrote a long letter to his cousin Sylvia Laithwaite, now a Dominican nun going by the name of Sister Malachi in Grand Rapids, Michigan; in the letter he details the progress they had made with the farm. He noted that Helen's garden produced everything from Indian corn to artichokes. They had two cows named 'Strawberry' and 'Ruadh'; a heifer, which was Strawberry's, named 'Bawneen'; an as-yet-unnamed horse; a donkey named 'Bricriu'; a pedigree duck named 'Pekins'; a drake, which was Pekins's, named 'Ferdiah'; and a number of hens. There were also beehives, three breeds of hen in what Ernie deemed were scientific houses, and a dog with a dubious name, 'Hitler'. The name 'Hitler' apparently caused reverberations in their local parish.[8]

Helen believed in buying only high-quality equipment, which was not the usual practice in rural Mayo. They brought in a wind machine to generate electricity that later broke down. They built a wooden dairy, painted it blue, and equipped it with a separator from Sweden and a butter-making machine. Reflecting the uncertainty of the times, Ernie also had a protective shelter dug for the family that was fully supplied with food, should invasion threaten them. He acquired a lugsail boat capable of taking them across Clew Bay in all weathers. He deliberately had not equipped it with a petrol engine, since he knew petrol would not be available during the Second World War. Ernie even practised rowing the boat across the bay, although he had been told not to do so because of his medical condition.[9]

By the end of 1942, they had accomplished a great deal with their farm. Nine acres were ploughed for crops, although it was difficult to get proper seed in wartime. They still had to lease land to grow all the food they needed for themselves and staff. They soon expected to be self-sufficient, except for a few luxuries like tea. Honey from local bees could be substituted for sugar, and they used candles for lighting to reduce the demand for electricity.

In addition, Helen improved the aesthetics of Burrishoole by hanging their paintings and using local fabrics for curtains. Guests would later say she was creating a new country taste by decorating with natural materials, such as using Irish tweeds for napkins and bedcovers.

Ernie was totally dedicated to making the farm work for them, but he was also wearing himself out, given that his war wounds were a continual problem. At times he worked with the men in the fields in all weather conditions, often coming back to the house exhausted. There was a war on, and he believed they had a duty to produce as much food as they could. He continued to take ambitious steps, later creating the first tuberculin-tested herd of cattle west of the Shannon River, hiring a special bull as a stud.

By mid-1944 the couple was beginning to show increasingly severe signs of strain while living in their country house in Mayo.

Helen did not understand farming and continually asked Ernie about its detailed issues, but he grew tired of explaining them to her. Later he wrote, 'She knew nothing of farming, nor could she understand the complexities of farming.' Helen must have been frustrated when her husband refused to discuss these matters so that she could understand what was going on. They were beginning to lead separate lives. She became increasingly lonely without the lively companionship she had enjoyed in Dublin, and didn't always receive the support from her husband that she felt she needed. He understood this growing issue between them in their marriage, recalling, 'She suffered from isolation for she did not read. That drove her back on me for company, but a good deal of my time was spent in study. And this made her dissatisfied.'[10]

Ernie kept himself busy with a variety of projects outside of the farm. One of these was to research and write a history of Mayo, which he never completed. Another project of his was to write the story of an Irish hero from the seventeenth century, the great Hugh O'Neill, Earl of Tyrone, but this never came to fruition. Yet a third was to collect folklore stories before they were lost to posterity. He collected over three hundred from local storytellers.

Ernie and Helen also had different views about managing and spending money. Helen had been spoiled as a girl from a wealthy family whose children could look upon money as something that would always be available to them. If a young woman from her background didn't pay a bill, someone eventually paid it for her. Helen avoided paying bills and made numerous purchases without worrying about how much money they actually had and what they could afford at the time. Helen had no interest in keeping accounts; Ernie had dwelled on keeping detailed spending accounts ever since his military days, when he accounted for every penny. Working as an organiser, he had even resisted accepting funds he needed from Michael Collins.

He came from a different world. His father and mother had struggled to keep their many children housed, clothed, fed and in appropriate schools. Ernie now worried about how they would pay local accounts at Burrishoole, which were either his accounts or those he had to take responsibility for. He had gone into personal debt, both to pay off the libel suit and also to buy the land he had acquired at Burrishoole. Much of their holdings there, including the house, had been bought by Helen in her name. This would cause problems for him later. The couple continued to buy land separately, much as they had bought paintings separately with their own money. Given his limited resources, Ernie continually asked Helen for financial help to pay their mutual bills, but she resisted. Money became an increasing irritant between them. Helen not only began to borrow money from Ernie but also insisted on borrowing it from their friends. This deeply upset him.

Another vital marital issue had also begun to go wrong. Ernie had habits that could be maddening to his wife. Earlier, when he insisted on reading late at night in bed, keeping her awake, Helen asked him to sleep in another room. He became accustomed to sleeping there. Helen's sexuality was an important part of her life. She believed they could solve their problems by making love, and she would often go to Ernie in his room when they had a disagreement. Ernie felt they should only make love when he felt relaxed and they had verbally resolved the differences between them. Lingering pain and discomfort from his severe wounds could also have inhibited his sexual desire. When his wife came to comfort him, he would sometimes send her away.

By mid-1944 Helen told Ernie that she would not stay on the land any longer, and Ernie, who had broken his leg badly at the beginning of the year, had had enough of farming as well. For him, the farm was finally in order and a good manager was in place. He was satisfied with the results of his efforts in spite of the difficulties encountered. Ernie realised he had become an intense labourer on the farm, as well as its ultimate manager. His leg injury took months to heal in 1944 and the farm work had also strained his heart. His heart issues dated back to his birth.

In fairness to Helen and Ernie, their five years of farming at Burrishoole had taken each of them away from their deeper passions: their creativity and their dedication to the arts. In 1942 Helen had rented a studio flat on Upper Pembroke Street, Dublin, which served both as a sculpting studio and a *pied-à-terre* that she could stay in during visits there. In May 1944, she took a big step back into her former artistic social life in Dublin by leasing a new house at 15 Whitebeam Avenue in Clonskeagh, an attractive Dublin suburb. This was to be a family home, for Ernie and the children as well. Cathal had started at the Xavier School near Dublin, while the two younger children were still with Ernie at Burrishoole until September 1944, when the entire O'Malley family relocated to Dublin.

That autumn Helen became directly involved in the Dublin theatre world. She was so moved by the aspirations of some leading Abbey Theatre actors to form a new group called 'The Players Theatre' that she provided some of the capital, at least £1,000, to establish the enterprise. This would develop into a meaningful future commitment for her, as she designed the stage sets and costumes. The most important person in this group was Gerald Healy, a noted actor and playwright. Liam Redmond, also an Abbey actor, was another key player. Since actors in those days were not paid a proper salary, their group insisted on paying each performing actor at least £1 a day, which was a good living wage.

Liam and his family lived in their home only two houses away from Helen's new house on Whitebeam Avenue. Liam's wife Barbara was the daughter of Thomas MacDonagh, one of the sixteen martyrs of the Easter Rising. Their children became friends, and the Redmonds' son, Dara, was Cathal's age and a schoolmate. In 1942 Helen had asked Liam Redmond to become Cormac's godfather, an offer he was happy to accept.

Helen encouraged the group to use her house, not only for some of their rehearsals but also for their board meetings. They soon began writing their own plays. Their first performance opened in Cork, followed by their first Dublin opening on 6 March 1945 at the Gate Theatre. This play about the famine written by Gerald Healy, *The Black Stranger*, received great acclaim. Helen had designed the stage sets and the costumes.

She asked Ernie to join the Players Theatre's board of directors. He refused on the basis of his general dislike for actors, whom he thought were too extroverted. He also didn't believe they should be trying to write their own plays. Ernie didn't hesitate to deliver his often-severe criticism on deficiencies he observed in the plays Liam Redmond was writing. He also objected strenuously to Helen having the actors continually in their new house. She ignored his concerns. This had become an exciting new project in her artistic and personal life. Helen and Liam began spending more and more time together. Ernie's jealousy of their relationship only increased with time as Helen continued to dedicate her energy to this lively theatrical group.

Ernie pleaded in vain with his wife to forget all of her theatre nonsense and concentrate on her core artistic ability, sculpture. Despite Ernie's concern, Helen had never really abandoned her dedication to sculpture, continuing to do heads of various important Irish subjects from time to time. She had wanted to meet de Valera and perhaps sculpt his head when she married and came to Ireland, but Ernie did not let this happen. She could never understand why he had refused to honour her special request.[11]

Helen had also built a sculpture studio at Burrishoole so she could continue her work while staying there. After sculpting her heads in either studio, she would send them to London to be cast in plaster. Among the distinguished Irish characters she sculpted were Siobhan McKenna, the actress, and noted writers Liam O'Flaherty and Frank O'Connor. In July 1946 she did a sculpture of Kurt Jooss, the German ballet master, when his ballet troop came to Dublin. Later, in America, she sculpted John P. Marquand, the American novelist who had married her sister Adelaide.[12]

Helen and Ernie were two highly independent, creative, spirited characters. They shared an unbridled energy and drive that enabled them to carry on several distinct activities at the same time. Helen had become engrossed with the theatre, but she never ceased being a sculptor. Ernie became a farmer from 1940 to 1944 but that had not stopped him from continuing many of his artistic and intellectual interests in both Mayo and Dublin.

At this time, Ernie began to engage seriously with groups in Dublin involved in modern painting, literature, Irish historical and international culture, and music. This would become the primary focus of his life for at least the next five years, even though during this period he also continued to write and interview former comrades on their warring years against British and Free State forces. He had previously developed a friendship with Evie Hone and became one of her leading supporters. He continued his friendships with two of Ireland's leading modernist painters, Jack B. Yeats and Louis le Brocquy.

He also became a commentator on various subjects for the British Broadcasting Company (BBC) and Raidió Éireann, the Irish radio network. Except for his authorship of *On Another*

Man's Wound and *The Singing Flame*, the years from 1945 through 1950 would become the most productive period of Ernie's life as a creative intellectual.

Ernie had always been fascinated by painters and their works. As a young man one of his most treasured books had been Vasari's *Lives of the Italian Painters*. During his warring period, from 1918 to 1921, when everything had to be carried on his person over the countryside, he managed to retain reproductions of Durer and the early Renaissance painters. When he visited museums in Europe in 1925–26, it was to see these masters' works in person. He travelled to Mexico with Dorothy Stewart, an American artist whose works he later hung in Burrishoole. While in Mexico he made acute comparisons of the works of Mexico's leading painters, Jose Orozco and Diego Rivera. In New York in 1934, he had given four Metropolitan Museum of Art lectures at New York University. It is hardly surprising that when back in Ireland he would seek out, befriend and support Ireland's leading modernist painters and artists.

He had returned to Ireland determined to encourage Irish artists inspired by modernist trends; artists whom he believed personified the nascent artistic ability that had been discouraged for so long during Ireland's time under its British overlords. He admired Evie Hone, who had been trained in London and Paris and was deeply influenced by Albert Gleizes as well as Braque, Matisse and Picasso. Ernie described Evie as 'the best [stained] glass worker in Western Europe. Her importance will increase in time.'[13] He bought several paintings by her, including *May Morning*, *The Crucifixion* and *Still Life*, and Helen also bought many of her paintings. He and Helen got to know her so well in their early days in Dublin and later during her visits to Burrishoole that when Etain was born in 1940, Evie became her godmother.

On 23 October 1945, Ernie opened an exhibition of Evie's paintings and stained-glass windows at the Dawson Gallery, Dublin. His remarks were covered in the *Irish Times* and *Irish Press* on 26 October; they noted that he had spoken on the traditions of Irish sculpture.

The deepest, most satisfying, long-lasting relationship that Ernie established with any modern Irish painter was with Jack B. Yeats, brother of W.B. Yeats. The younger Yeats became the most renowned Irish painter from the 1940s to the 1960s, but Ernie had admired his work well before that. He described Yeats as 'the most important painter this country has yet produced', observing that 'he has brought a fresh vision and a creative palette.' He went on to write, 'With Jack Yeats, the landscape is as real as the figures ... A new element is added to the humanity of the figures.'[14]

The relationship between Ernie and Jack was based on mutual affection, respect and a common vision for Ireland's need for political and artistic freedom. The two men also realised that as much as Ireland needed to create a fertile platform for its artists, for a time these artists would need the stimulation of other more culturally advanced influences like Paris and London to develop their native talent. Jack and Ernie also shared a passion for Ireland's cultural background. Their friendship began in the late 1930s, when Ernie returned from America. From 1939 to 1945, Jack sold a number of paintings to his friend. In 1939 Ernie fell in love with Jack's painting *Death for Only One*. He wrote to Thomas MacGreevy, 'I saw Jack Yeats, fell clear in love with a picture and felt I must have it. I was able to arrange payments over a long period.'[15] Since he didn't have the money to buy it immediately, he paid Jack for it in five instalments. In various periods, the men would frequently see each other in Dublin.

Ernie's relationship with Yeats was not restricted to their personal friendship and the occasional purchases of Yeats's paintings. For years Ernie acted as a promoter of Jack's work. He strove with others to create exhibitions of his paintings in Dublin and abroad; he also lent his growing collection of Yeats's paintings to exhibitions, like the one in London's National Gallery, as early as 1942. Beginning in 1944 Ernie worked to organise the 1945 Jack B. Yeats National Loan Exhibition, which provided a history of his development as a painter. He not only acted as a driving member of the organising committee sponsoring this project but also wrote the introduction to the exhibition catalogue. Yeats responded by giving Ernie a series of his early sketch books, including a special note of thanks.

Ernie also introduced Yeats to international influential leaders in the art world like his new friend John Rothenstein, director of the Tate Gallery in London, and his old friend from New York City days James Johnson Sweeney. Ernie had become an expert on Yeats's work and observed to Sweeney that about 80 per cent of Yeats's pictures were in private hands in Ireland, and most of them were held by Irishmen rather than the Anglo-Irish.[16] Yeats appreciated Ernie's offers of introductions for him. He wrote to Ernie, 'I have just got your note and I will be delighted to see you and [John] Rothenstein ... I thank you for bringing him along and introducing him to the picture.'[17]

Many people had supported Ernie when he needed their help: Michael Collins, during his warring years; soldiers of both his own ranks and those of the opposing armies when he was captured or wounded; his mother Marion and Molly Childers during his terrible time in prison; Count Plunkett, who put him up in Dublin after he was released from internment camp; Msgr Hagan of the Irish College in Rome; Kay Brady, during his travels in Europe; his supporters in America, Helen Golden, Paul

Strand and John Hughes the Boston lawyer; and IRA comrades like Peadar O'Donnell, who helped him to finally publish *On Another Man's Wound*. Towards the end of his life, his sister Kaye and brother Kevin, as well as many old friends like John Ford, would rally to his support.

But as Jack Yeats discovered, there could be no better friend than Ernie when a friend needed help. There was nothing superficial or short-lived about Ernie's backing; he provided lasting, meaningful support for his friends that continued for years. Ironically, Jack and Ernie would pass away the same week in March 1957.

Ernie also became a friend and an active supporter of another Irish modernist painter, Louis le Brocquy. Louis was a self-taught painter twenty years younger than Ernie. He first got to know Ernie in Dublin and was a guest at Burrishoole often when still in his twenties. Ernie became a mentor to Louis. After the Emergency ended, he urged Louis to move to London to paint full time. This would advance his techniques and standing, as London had become a more receptive world for Irish painters. Le Brocquy followed his advice, moving there in mid-1946. Ernie went to London himself in October, staying at the Walstons' house there until the end of December. Helen was also in London during the late autumn working on her theatrical productions, but by this time the marriage was beginning to fall apart. The couple saw less and less of each other, even when they both happened to be in London at the same time.[18]

In 1946 Ernie wrote a comprehensive, appreciative study on Louis le Brocquy and his paintings for the important London magazine *Horizon: A Review of Literature and Art*. The monthly magazine was then edited by the noted English critic Cyril Connolly, who published articles by the leading creative personages of the time. They included Irish literary figures and political commentators such as M.J. MacManus, Seán Ó Faoláin and Frank O'Connor. Connolly himself had an interest in, and wrote commentaries on, contemporary Irish matters. Ernie's review on le Brocquy's work was a most helpful step towards market recognition for this developing Irish modern painter.[19]

In his comprehensive study of le Brocquy's life and work, Ernie emphasised how the Irish landscape and people had influenced this painter who was stuck in Ireland during the Emergency period. He wrote how this isolation had helped him develop his own individuality in a painting style seasoned by wanderings through bleak country areas, 'Connemara, a gaunt, ragged district of mountain form, freckled lakes, broken boldered slopes bedazzled with light and serrated with an edge of sea.'

Ernie went on to show how le Brocquy had been entranced by the traveller community of Ireland, commonly referred to as 'tinkers' during that period. With them, 'primitive emotions, are easily aroused and expressed; their women drink and fight as readily as their men, and bear children without halting the day's journey ... They become a symbol of the individual as opposed to organised society.' Ernie then described how le Brocquy's latest paintings, featuring groups of these travellers, represented the development of his vivid style when he was directed inward to his country's deepest elements.[20]

Le Brocquy appreciated that Ernie had helped him to discover the west of Ireland as a base for much of his work. He was grateful for Ernie's deep understanding of his paintings, for his continual mentoring encouragement and for his public support of his own work, as in the *Horizon* article. Le Brocquy wrote, 'He taught me much, in Burrishoole, in Dublin in the Forties through his gentle but passionate ideas on art, on life.'[21]

Another friend of Ernie's who was involved in the development of modern painting in Ireland was Thomas MacGreevy. The two men had originally met in a flat rented by Lennox Robinson in Dublin on the night of 13 November 1920, later known as Bloody Sunday. MacGreevy had been a 1st lieutenant in the British army during the First World War, but on returning to Ireland he was sympathetic to Irish cultural nationalism. He later became director of the National Gallery of Ireland in Dublin.

The men developed a relationship of mutual respect that enabled them to act as partners in the development of Irish painters and the local market's appreciation of their work. They were also fellow intellectuals who corresponded about the work of international authors and painters. In February 1940, MacGreevy wrote to Ernie, 'You didn't think we had any pictures at the National Gallery now? I helped take them all down the ten days before the war ... I've been reading Arthur Waley's translations of the Chinese poets and loving them for their sensitively sympathetic detachment.'[22]

Both men were also dedicated to promoting the work of Jack Yeats. MacGreevy wrote a book in appreciation of Yeats's work that Ernie reviewed in the January 1946 edition of *The Bell*. Ernie wrote, 'It seems strange that Thomas MacGreevy's book is the first volume to be published on the paintings of Jack Yeats. Yeats's full stature as the most important painter in this country is now recognised but it is well to have that understanding clinched in print.' Ernie's stature as an informed supporter of modern painters and their works is demonstrated by his ability to hold meaningful dialogues with senior people in the art world, including Sweeney, Rothenstein and MacGreevy.

In 1947 Ernie became books editor of *The Bell*, where his old friend Peadar O'Donnell was now the editor. It was the leading intellectual magazine in Ireland. He continued to demonstrate his wide range of interests by writing the following essays for *The Bell* and other cultural sources from 1940 to 1947: a review of

Françoise Henry's *Irish Art in the Early Christian Period*, in *The Bell*, October 1940; the introduction to the Jack Yeats National Loan Exhibition Catalogue, National College of Art and Design, Dublin, June 1945; a book review of MacGreevy's *Appreciation and Interpretation of Jack B. Yeats*, in *The Bell*, January 1946; 'Louis le Brocquy', in *Horizon*, July 1946; 'Painting, The School of London', in *The Bell*, July 1947; and 'The Background of the Arts in Mexico', in *The Bell*, August 1947. In addition, he gave a lecture in 1946 at the Limerick City Library on 'The State of Painting in Ireland' and then wrote an essay on Ireland for London's *Architectural Digest* in July 1947.[23]

One of Ernie's best-known essays was written for *La France Libre*, a publication in London that supported the Free French government's resistance to Nazi rule during the Second World War. He named it 'Renaissance', and it was published in the December 1946–January 1947 edition. In it, Ernie provided his version of what Ireland had experienced from 1916 until the present. He helped the reader understand how the War of Independence against Britain, the Civil War between the IRA and Free State forces, and then the struggle between the Germans and British during the Second World War had impacted Ireland's attempt to maintain its independence by its neutrality. This was a complex period, and he explained what the Irish people were left with now that the conflicts had ended.

One of the most fascinating radio talks Ernie made was his discussion on worldwide music for Raidió Éireann. He took his Irish audience on an unexpected journey: 'Tonight, we are going from Japan to Tunis on a music trip. Oriental music will probably sound strange to many listeners. Some will think the music out of tune and discordant, the singing from voices will appear strident or harsh, and the instruments will seem to be making sounds at random.' He then explained to his listeners that they had been brought up to understand and appreciate European music, which sounded familiar to their ears, but that they were probably totally unfamiliar with the Asian and African songs representing these distinct cultures.[24]

He mentioned how Western music must sound to people from other cultures: 'Orientals listen in amused amazement to our Western songs and became indignant about our orchestras. When the well-known opera *Madame Butterfly* was first played in the theatre in Tokyo the staid, impassive Japanese faces changed from astonishment to laughter. Some of the audience had to be carried out of the theatre.'

Ernie demonstrated how Chinese music had influenced music developed in the adjoining countries of Japan and Bali. Then he described Chinese music: 'The Chinese chant even when they read aloud from their classics. They use a different speech intonation for old poetry, new poetry and one for prose. In their drama, which is really closer to our opera than to our theatre, the words are chanted, and the same musical accompaniment is common to a whole series of plays.'

The listener was then taken to the Near East and North Africa: 'Persia, Egypt and Tunis, all of which have been strongly influenced from Arab music and civilisation. Indeed, amongst the Arabs, poets retain some of the honour which they held in Ireland up [to] the suppression of the Bardic Schools here in the beginning of the seventeenth century.' He continued, 'In the Orient there is a great contrast between songs popular in towns and cities, and the primitive music of the Bedouin. Between these two extremes there is another type of song ... which may be sung in a coffee house with an accompaniment of violin and lute.'

Helen and Ernie's marriage continued to deteriorate after Ernie moved from Burrishoole to Dublin with the two younger children in the autumn of 1944, living in the house Helen had leased. She spent more and more of her time with the Players Theatre, travelling frequently to London to work with them in preparation for a performance of Paul Vincent's play *The White Steed* in October 1946. She rented a place there from September 1947 to January 1948 and considered buying a house later that year. Meanwhile, she arranged to have the two younger children brought to America to be with their grandmother, Blanche, at her house in Greenwich, Connecticut from July to December 1947. Cathal was with them only for the summer months.

Helen expressed her feelings to Ernie about their failing marriage in a moving letter from 22 October 1946: 'Perhaps you need to be alone the rest of your life, but I have already had to spend much of my life with you alone and without companionship of heart or act.' Her letter to Ernie was a cry for help, but it was too late for him to respond to it.[25]

In late 1946 Helen had tried to negotiate a settlement and divorce with Ernie, who opposed the idea. First, she asked him to meet her at Brown's Hotel in London with Seebohm Rowntree. He was a Quaker reformer and industrialist who had agreed to act as a neutral third party in helping them reach an agreement on issues concerning the children, such as custody and schooling. Apparently not much was accomplished at this meeting; shortly thereafter, Helen informed Ernie that he was supposed to contact her only through her lawyers. In January 1947 Helen instructed Ernie to be in contact with Thomas B. Gilchrist, a partner in a Wall Street law firm. Ernie ended up liking and respecting Gilchrist, with whom he was able to confide about his situation with Helen. Gilchrist would send sweets to the children and showed sympathy for Ernie's position.

Ernie wrote to Gilchrist that Helen was going around Dublin and London complaining that he was carrying on with three women: Bobs Walston; Barbara Rothchild, recently divorced from Baron Rothchild; and Libby Eden. Helen denied this, although Ernie had witnesses who were present when she made these accusations.

Around this time, he also wrote to his sister Sweetie: 'It would be a relief if Helen would go away for a while, for as long as Redmond is two doors away she is a cause of trouble, though his wife and children are in Aran [on vacation].' He explained that while it might be hard for the children to live with him in Burrishoole, 'I feel since Helen will not look after them ... as she has become more involved with Redmond, she will spend more time in London.' (Redmond was often in London for his film and theatre work at this time.) No progress was made on either a settlement agreement or a divorce. Ernie was still writing to Gilchrist years later about how the children at Burrishoole were doing under his care, and how Helen was continuing to borrow money and not pay bills incurred at Burrishoole, most notably the local taxes.

From the end of 1946 through the intervening years to 1950, the couple essentially led separate lives. The children were put in various schools, or were primarily cared for by nurses and household staff. Ernie wrote to his mother-in-law Blanche that during the Christmas holidays of 1946 neither he nor Helen was with the three children. Sometimes Ernie did not even know where Helen or the children might be. They spent six months in the United States in 1947 with their mother's family but did not write to him. In a letter to Cathal at his school in Limerick in September 1947, Ernie noted, 'I have not heard from Etain or Cormac but I sent them letters yesterday. I do not know where they are but I expect they may be at their grandmother's house.'[26]

Cathal was asked about his mother's presence in his life when he was 8 to 10 years old. He replied, 'When we moved to Dublin my mother got her own studio where she spent a lot of time. Later she became involved with the Players Theatre and no longer lived at home with us. I only saw my mother every six months or sometimes once a year during that period.'[27]

Cathal was attending Glenstal Abbey, a Benedictine boarding school in Limerick; Ernie was then living with the two younger children in their Dublin house while they attended the Sacred Heart Convent day school. In May 1948, Etain received her First Holy Communion in Dublin, but her mother was not present.

A health setback occurred in May 1948 when Cathal and Cormac were diagnosed with tuberculosis. They had caught it from the maid. Total rest was recommended. Helen argued that the children should be sent to America or Switzerland for treatment, while Ernie insisted that they should stay in Ireland where others were being treated. He hired a special nurse to take care of the boys and sent his daughter to live with friends like Sunniva Clarke in Killiney while she also went to school there.

Ernie continued to be concerned about the amount of time Helen spent with the actor Liam Redmond. The couple's deteriorating relationship is exemplified by these July–August 1948 entries from Ernie's diary:

Helen arrived back with Redmond at 1:15 by private car then drives him downtown ... Refuses Etain permission to go to Kay [Ernie's sister]. I refused her Etain for Aran [she had been invited to accompany Liam Redmond's family there] ... Helen leaves home with R ... Helen to be in London 1st week August with Redmond ... Helen left this morning with Redmond without giving me word ... Helen tried to create trouble with nurse and with governess. Said she was going to use Burrishoole for her English friends soon. I told her I was going away on 15th for a month. 'Where?' 'You'll know when I have made up my mind, unlike yourself, you

202 ❖ ERNIE O'MALLEY

leave no word when you leave sick children' … Helen not
in at night.[28]

Many of his daily entries from August begin simply with the
words, 'H away.'

In the autumn of 1948, when Ernie heard Helen was going
to give up the lease on the Dublin house where he was living
with the children, he drove the two boys and their nurse to
Burrishoole. The boys would spend time recuperating in bed. He
would tutor them. He became worried about where he could
get the funds required to sustain himself and the children there.
Helen's previous financial support for Burrishoole was no longer
available. Years later, in a 1953 letter to Paul Strand, Ernie
described the desperate financial situation he faced when he was
alone with the children at Burrishoole: 'She went off by herself
for two years whilst I brought up the 3 children in Burrishoole.
I had to teach the 3 of them as Cathal and Cormac had primary
tuberculosis, and they had to remain in bed for over a year. I had
little money, but I had fine books. I sold most of my valuable
books there.'[29]

To raise needed funds, Ernie had an auction held in December
1949 in London for selected items from his book collection, which
then totalled several thousand volumes. He had some first editions
(special presses) of the works of many leading contemporary
Irish, English and American authors, including W.B. Yeats, Lady
Gregory, Liam O'Flaherty, D.H. Lawrence and Elizabeth Bowen;
he also had works from classic authors, including John Donne,
John Milton, Miguel de Cervantes, Homer and Shakespeare, and
some art books as well. Sotheby's of London auctioned more than
420 of his books at its New Bond Street gallery in London. He
did not attend. Unfortunately, the auction made only £486.5.0
for Ernie – less than he had expected.[30]

He commented on the book sale in a January 1950 letter to Professor John Kelleher at Harvard: 'The Yeats books sold well, but the art books and the special presses did not at all realise what I once paid for them.' Ernie was a fanatic book collector, and it's not surprising he was somewhat dissatisfied by the results of the sale of his books.[31]

Ernie made another important decision concerning his large collection of paintings. He had moved to Burrishoole, which did not provide the wall or storage space to adequately hang or store them. He also feared that during his travels to interview former comrades, Helen could send someone to remove them. Finally, he wanted the Irish public to enjoy them – particularly the paintings of the contemporary Irish artists he so admired, Jack Yeats, Evie Hone and Louis le Brocquy. In October 1948, he made an anonymous loan of about thirty-five of his best art works to the Limerick City Library. These included several important works by Yeats, Hone and le Brocquy, and paintings and drawings by famous European artists like Maurice de Vlaminck and Amedeo Modigliani.[32]

On 31 March 1950, a dramatic event occurred that would alter the lives of everyone in the family. Helen had been growing increasingly concerned about the health of the children so long as they remained in Ireland. She had been spending her time without them in America. Ernie would not agree that they should go to America, even for a visit, for fear Helen would not return them to Ireland. Under Irish law she could not take the children out of the country without their father's written permission. Some family members and friends urged her to do something about her frustrating situation.

Apparently, she had kept in contact with Liam Redmond and his wife Barbara, who was particularly sympathetic to Helen's concerns as a mother. Cormac, the youngest child, then 7 years old, was still living with Ernie at Burrishoole. His two older siblings had been sent to an Irish-speaking boarding school, Ring College, which was located in County Waterford. Ernie left instructions with the headmaster that they should not be allowed to leave the school for any reason without their father's permission.

Unbeknownst to Ernie, in late March 1950 Helen returned to Dublin; she met up with Liam Redmond, who drove her to Ring College. She told the headmaster she merely wished to take the children to tea in the nearby Hotel Dungarvan. Because of Ernie's instructions, the headmaster insisted on going with them, but when he briefly left the dining room, Helen and Liam spirited the two children off to their car. They then made the long drive to Belfast in Northern Ireland, where Helen had arranged for a private plane to fly them to France. They had an emergency landing at Le Havre, were picked up by a private car, and were taken to a station where they boarded a train – first for Paris and then on to Marseilles. From there, they flew to Boston and travelled by train to New York City. Liam Redmond said goodbye to them in Marseilles and returned to Dublin.

When Ernie was informed of what had occurred at the children's school, he alerted the Irish police to keep them in Ireland, but it was too late. The French police were also notified but were not able to intercept the party. Helen and Liam had taken a clever route by train to Marseilles, avoiding the airports in Paris where police might be waiting for them. The world press had been alerted, and when Helen and the children finally arrived at her New York City apartment, local reporters were waiting at the front entrance. She evaded them by entering through a back door with the two children.

When Cathal was asked sixty-seven years later if he remembered this experience, he replied, '[Mother's] explanation was that we were going to the United States for health reasons, to recover fully from primary TB. Memories of the journey are still very vivid in my mind. The emergency landing at Le Havre was very memorable as was the gun under the French chauffeur's pillow.' Asked about the shock of being taken from Ireland, Cathal said, 'It is seared in my memory. It was a very profound loss. However, the opportunities in the United States, as compared to Ireland, propelled me to focus on my future.'[33]

In 1950, when they were taken from Ireland to America by their mother, Cathal was 13 years old and Etain was 9. The prime caregiver over the past several years had been their father, Ernie. Given her theatrical commitments, their mother had not been able to give them much personal attention, even when they lived together as a family in Dublin from 1945 to 1948. When the two boys contracted tuberculosis from the maid in 1948, Ernie took them to Burrishoole. They were home-schooled by him there, while Helen remained in Dublin and travelled to London and America.

Imagine the traumatic effect the kidnapping must have had on the two children when they were taken away from their father and young brother, not to see them again for years. In some ways they had simply lost Ernie and Cormac. When Helen brought them back in 1953 for a short visit to their father, Cathal reported that he felt estranged from Ernie and had difficulty relating to him. Ernie, as well, may have felt estranged from Cathal and Etain, but they were the innocent victims of their forced separation. Ernie tried to correspond with each of his older children from their departure until his death in 1957, but it was challenging. The last letter he wrote was to Cathal.

What had happened to bring Helen and Ernie to the tragedy where Helen felt compelled to kidnap the two older children? Who could answer this query better than Ernie's mother-in-law, Blanche Hooker, who had been observing how the couple interacted together. When their marriage problems began to surface, she wrote to Ernie in December 1946:

> I had high hopes that you and Helen, with patience and increased understanding would in time make a success of your life together ... One of the points I made was the absolute necessity of keeping respect for each other. That was a year ago and there has been a turn for the worse ... I also wrote this in my letter to you a year ago, 'I am a woman and I know a woman must have some attention shown her by her husband or she starves.' Helen has very marvellously strong qualities and equally strong weak ones. I should say the same of you and neither of you is likely to change under the method you have been pursuing most of the time since you have been married. I have with some unhappiness come to the conclusion that you should continue no longer together.[34]

Another family member later opined that the marriage could not have worked. In a letter to Cormac after his father's death, Ernie's cousin Sylvia Laithwaite wrote, 'You will readily understand from all this that your father should never have married – particularly to someone who is used to a completely formal and set way of life, such as your mother. She made the dreadful mistake of trying to refashion him into something quite alien to his nature.'[35]

CHAPTER 10

LAST YEARS: *QUIET MAN,* COMRADE INTERVIEWS, 1950–1957

Ernie felt the kidnapping was just another in the series of episodes that plagued his life: the defeat of the IRA in the Civil War; his long imprisonment followed by a lack of support from countrymen he fought for; his struggle to manage without enough money while travelling in America and Mexico; his difficulties getting his memoir published, and the ruinous libel suit that followed; his marriage break-up with Helen; his continual health issues; and now his failure to keep his children safe in Ireland. In September 1950, when he was still reeling from this latest setback, Ernie received encouraging news from his film director friend in California, John Ford. Ford wrote that he would be shooting a film in Ireland the following year starring John Wayne and Maureen O'Hara. He wanted Ernie to be there as a consultant on Irish matters. Ernie was delighted and immediately accepted this new role.

The Quiet Man is about the life of Sean Thornton, played by John Wayne. Sean is an Irishman whose mother takes him from the west of Ireland to America as a child after his father tragically drowns. They are poor and struggle for survival. The boy becomes a professional heavyweight boxer in the United States and marries a red-haired young wife there only to lose her to blood poisoning. After he unwittingly kills a young boxing opponent in the ring, he returns to the fictional village of his nativity, Innisfree, where he eventually woos and marries a lovely red-haired Irish girl, played by Maureen O'Hara, who reminds him of his first wife. The movie was filmed in the small Mayo village of Cong. It is still a staple in Irish American cinema for its many colourful scenes featuring Wayne courting O'Hara, fighting her bully brother, participating in a horse race, and having his courting supervised by a local Irish matchmaker played by the Irish actor Barry Fitzgerald.[1]

John Ford could trace his family's origins back to Connemara, where his family's home had purportedly been torched by the Black and Tans during the War of Independence. He liked to claim he had been involved in the IRA fight against Britain, but it appears that any involvement of his was peripheral. Like many Irish Americans at the time, it is possible he may have supported the IRA financially. Coincidentally, late in 1921, he was a fellow passenger on the ship that brought Michael Collins back to Ireland from London, where Collins had been negotiating the treaty ending the War of Independence.[2]

One of the key reasons he had asked Ernie to join his movie crew was that Ford had enjoyed his company when the men met in California back in 1929. Ernie fit the image of the gallant Irish revolutionary that Ford so much admired. Some of his prior movies had featured an underdog hero who overcame superior odds, just as Ernie had in his military career. Ernie could authenticate not only the local Irish settings but also the native Irishness of the actors and extras, be it in their lines, accents, behaviours, or how they reacted in each scene. A newspaper account of the time had John Ford roaring through a megaphone for Ernie O'Malley to bring on the extras, and Ernie assisting Ford in the direction of the crowd scenes.[3] Finally, there is an account of Ford urging Ernie to get Wayne to drink late into the evening before the actor was featured in the fistfight scene the next morning. This was in order to ensure that Wayne was relaxed.

Ford and Ernie would often talk together well into the night about military and naval history. Over time each had become an impatient, demanding older man who occasionally frightened people off, yet despite this they became very fond of each other. Later, during Ford's second film visit to Ireland in 1956, Ernie described their relationship to his friend Jean McGrail:

> I was Ford's assistant ... I like Ford. He is difficult to work with and fun at times as he has a cyclonic temper ... He can stand inefficiency patiently enough before he explodes. In that he is like my former self ... My function, among others, seemed to be to get him up in the morning, stay by him until he was on the set, smooth him down and break the storm if it threatened to break.[4]

In 1953, a few years after the filming of *The Quiet Man*, Michael Feeney, a cousin of Ford's, was applying for an Irish government pension for his IRA service in the War of Independence. Ford naturally asked Ernie to help his cousin with a recommendation. Ernie's reply showed how he always put his integrity and service to the IRA above friendship. He wrote to Ford that neither Ford himself nor de Valera nor Ernie could support Feeney's application for a pension. Only officers or comrades of Feeney who personally knew his service or had directed or seen him in action could vouch for him. Ernie concluded, 'I ... can not give evidence about a man whom I consider to be a good man unless I was in control of him in action. Michael must know this, and if he does not, he should.'[5]

During this time Ernie also became friendly with John Wayne and Maureen O'Hara. O'Hara reported that Ford and Ernie became pals who would chatter away like old buddies together. There are photos showing Wayne and O'Hara together with Ernie and his son Cormac, who occasionally accompanied his father to the movie set. He was 9 years old then and had a wonderful time. Cormac even had a part in one scene; he was driving a horse cart carrying Wayne in pursuit of O'Hara after the famous horse race in the film. Unfortunately, this sequence never made it into the final movie.[6]

To this day Cormac has fond memories of Maureen O'Hara. They both had red hair, and for that reason she took many photos of him as a boy on the set. During a visit Cormac made to Hollywood when he was 20 years old, Maureen invited him to a shoot on a movie she was making with Henry Fonda. In the mid-1980s they met again in New York City, where she presented him with an album of photographs she had taken of him on the set of The Quiet Man.

Ford returned to Ireland in 1956 to make another movie, The Rising of the Moon. This time Ernie received a prominent screen credit as Technical Advisor, Earnan O'Malley. This led to an occurrence that demonstrated Ernie's capacity to be extremely difficult when he felt he had been slighted. Ford had rented a special car on a train headed for Limerick City, where parts of the film would be shot. By mistake, his assistant left Ernie off the list of those travelling in the car. Instead, Ernie had to buy himself a second-class ticket in a car where he sat back morosely by himself. When Ford found out what had happened, he sent his man back to find Ernie, apologise to him and bring him up to the movie group's private car.

Furious, Ernie refused to budge and would not even answer when the fellow tried to make conversation to mollify him so he would join the film crowd. As the train arrived in Limerick, he made one last attempt and said to Ernie, 'That's Limerick. Do you know it?' Ernie turned and said, 'Of course, I do. I took it once.'[7]

Despite Ernie's role in Ford's internationally recognised films made in Ireland, the most intense, sustained project that Ernie undertook from the late 1940s until the end of his life were his personal interviews with 450 survivors about their direct experiences in the War of Independence and the Civil War. He made these during his itinerant travels to interview former comrades all over Ireland. Many of his early interviews had been completed by 1952. After he suffered a heart attack in 1953, Ernie worked on the remaining ones every day he could to preserve them for posterity.[8]

The Irish historian Eve Morrison has made a valuable study of Ernie's effort to create an oral history of the warring period. In her comments on his Northern Division interviews, she wrote, 'All record both the experiences and *mentalité* of Ireland's revolutionary generation. At their best, O'Malley's interviews are uniquely gritty, atmospheric, occasionally profane, punctuated with graphic descriptions of political violence and, in terms of their Civil War (1922–23) content, unrivalled.'[9]

In October 1951, Ernie wrote a letter explaining his interview project to James Johnson Sweeney, who had now become his neighbour in Mayo near Burrishoole: 'the Tan and the Civil War must be done now for the men are dying fast even as I move around, and I don't expect to last. Hence my hurry … In a strange way I am a member of their families and our ties are as strong as good blood.'[10]

Ernie had begun these interviews years earlier, originally to obtain needed material so he could finish his memoir on the Civil War. However, after he had given up his memoir project, he continued to interview prior combatants all over Ireland to cover the entire period. In 1947 the Irish Bureau of Military History began an official programme that ultimately typed up 1,773 interviews with former combatants, concentrating on the War of Independence. Ernie's interviewing efforts consumed much of his life after he left Dublin to live at Burrishoole with the children in the autumn of 1948. The warring period had been the defining chapter in his life, and perhaps this was his way of continuing its meaning, not only for the men and himself but also for posterity.

In a letter to Paul Strand, Ernie provided useful insight regarding why he undertook this oral history, much as the bards had done in ancient Ireland:

> I am working on these notes I have taken for the past 5 years. When I was too disturbed I thought it better to collect information, because in Ireland the men will tell me the truth about themselves. I take the notes at speed as fast as they talk, but again that had to be rewritten into notebooks. It is a long piece of work. So far I must have written about 2¾ million words … It is material to use at some time.[11]

The key to Ernie's motivation may lie in his words: 'in Ireland the men will tell me the truth about themselves.' Would the survivor of three imprisonments and fourteen wounds have trusted anyone else, including the governmental bureau, to have his IRA men tell the world what had really happened? As noted in Ernie's interview with Joe Sweeney about Collins's involvement with General Wilson's assassination in June 1922, these interviews have often offered unique insight into contested aspects of the warring period.

There is another interpretation of Ernie's enormous efforts to collect so many pages of verbal histories. Roy Foster points out that it could have been an effort to justify to the world a struggle which eventually failed and might never have been worth the suffering caused by bringing on the violence. This might have been a factor in Ernie's efforts to record so many interviews. When one is on the losing side, there may be a special urgency in trying to assure the 'correct' story is preserved for posterity. Of course, the correct story always depends on who is the storyteller.[12]

At first, Ernie bought an old Ford car to take him to interview the men in the counties in the south and west of Ireland, but this broke down constantly. He often had to spend his nights in or under it. The interviews also took his time away from Cormac during his summer vacations, and he had to find suitable families to take the boy in for a month or two. He faced both communicative and psychological challenges in arranging to have 450 men – some living in rural areas where the telephone service was not yet common – agree to share their personal experiences with him.

By the spring of 1952 he had begun to write up some of these interviews for publication. Dan Nolan, editor of the *Kerryman* newspaper, was preparing to publish these stories in connection with reports on specific raids on RIC barracks and other events during the War of Independence. Dan and Ernie had a disagreement about editing that caused Ernie to end this relationship. He then turned to Raidió Éireann, where he gave some lectures on the raids early the next year.

During the next year Ernie's oral history project received a new life when Lt Colonel Matt Feehan, editor of the *Sunday Press* newspaper, became enthusiastic about Ernie's project. He offered a car and photographer; the photographer was to accompany Ernie, taking pictures of both the former combatants and their battle sites. This was the most expensive project the paper had ever funded, and it ran Ernie's 'IRA Raids' series from September 1955 until June 1956.

Cormac took on the responsibility of publishing Ernie's interviews of his comrades' experiences. So far the following county interviews have been published: Kerry (2012), Galway (2013), Mayo (2014), West Cork (2015), Clare (2016) – all by Mercier Press – and the Northern Divisions (2018) – by Merrion Press. The Irish Manuscripts Commission plans to publish the entire set of interviews.

Ernie's relationship with John Ford during *The Quiet Man* shooting also reveals the lingering effects that the kidnapping of his two older children had on him in the years that followed. It was clear that Ford had become fond of young Cormac. However, no matter how close Ernie's relationship was with Ford, he would not even give his friend the name or address of the boy's school at the time so he could send him presents. Instead, Ernie insisted that all correspondence to Cormac should go through him so that the boy's location always remained hidden. Ford honoured his friend's request and sent his letters to Cormac through his father, signing himself as 'Uncle Jack'. This unusual practice was not limited to Ford. Ernie kept his son's whereabouts a total secret from everyone except the family who may have been putting him up at the time. Ernie took these seemingly excessive precautions for years after the kidnapping for fear that Helen, or someone acting under her orders, would take his son from him.

In June of 1949 Helen had asked a leading law firm she used in Dublin, A. & L. Goodbody, to put the house and lands at Burrishoole on the market for sale. She had given a high price and no offers came forth. Then, shortly after the kidnapping, Helen hired a moving company in Dublin to go to Burrishoole to collect her personal property there, such as furniture and paintings. Ernie must have got wind of this. When the driver arrived, he found a group of Ernie's neighbours, armed with shotguns behind the outside wall, barring the way into the house. The driver saluted the group and drove back with an empty van.

Helen instructed her lawyers to proceed again with the sale of the property, but Ernie resisted this effort as well in whatever ways he could. In a letter to Paul Strand he wrote, 'Burrishoole Lodge is mine and it is not mine. It was given to me as a wedding present, but I put the purchase in Helen's name.'[13]

Helen's lawyers then brought a formal legal action in Dublin's High Court against Ernie. In contrast to the large, prominent Dublin law firm serving Helen, Ernie was represented by Michael Noyk, a modest individual solicitor with a small office in Dublin. His clientele included many prominent republicans; he notably defended republican prisoners during and after the War of Independence, and was Arthur Griffith's solicitor until his death. Solicitors like Noyk do the background legal work to prepare the cases for court, where the case is argued before the judge and jury by a barrister. They also handle the many legal issues that never go to court, such as contracts, trust and estate matters, varied corporate issues, and real estate closings.

Ernie was particularly vulnerable to this legal action because of the couple's financial and legal history. When he lost the libel suit against him in October 1937 and bailiffs came to their house in Dublin to seize its furnishings, Ernie had to borrow a large sum to settle the libel judgement. When he became aware that his writings could subject him to future libel actions, he decided to try to avoid such a future liability by having the real estate they bought in Ireland registered in Helen's name.

In addition, the couple had regularly made purchases of both land and paintings in their own names after their marriage. Part of this tendency towards owning assets individually could have been because Helen, through her allowance from her father and her inheritance of his estate, simply had much more money than Ernie. His lawyer argued that Ernie had dedicated some of his royalties from *On Another Man's Wound* to purchasing Burrishoole and adjoining land, but some of these purchase monies may have been advanced by Helen.

Ernie wrote in a letter to Strand, 'Helen owes money, rates [taxes], on Burrishoole, which she promised to pay, but did not pay.'[14] During their early 1940s at Burrishoole together, Ernie had somehow to pay these bills from his limited resources to keep the place going.

The action was brought by Helen's lawyers in Dublin's High Court of Justice in June 1950. The complaint alleged that Burrishoole, its possessions, its cattle and its adjoining land had all been purchased by Helen and were registered in her name. It requested the court to order Ernie to leave the premises and exercise no control over it, to forbid him from removing any property or cattle, and to enjoin him from interfering in any way with Helen's right to sell Burrishoole, its furnishings, its cattle and its adjoining lands.[15]

The defendant's brief denied that Helen owned Burrishoole, its possessions and adjoining lands. It alleged that Ernie had paid his part towards their purchase, so they were joint owners. Further, Helen and Ernie had intended that it serve as a dwelling for them and their three children. They had also agreed for special reasons that Burrishoole be registered in her name. It denied that Helen had the right to sell the property, its contents, its cattle or its adjoining lands.

Ernie's lawyer also raised another issue that would prove to be a determining factor in the final adjudication of the case. The defence brief stated:

Plaintiff [Helen] has in breach of her duty as the wife of the Defendant to reside in the matrimonial home [Burrishoole] absented herself from the said home of the Defendant and has wrongfully and without just cause or excuse deserted the Defendant and further has without the consent of the Defendant and contrary to his express wishes removed the said two elder children out of the jurisdiction of this Honourable Court.[16]

In March 1951, ten months later, a draft judgement was prepared by Justice George Gavan Duffy. He noted that the case had been brought in a court of equity. Equity courts consider cases where there is no specific legal remedy available to the plaintiff in an ordinary court of law. There are ancient rules under English law which provide that whoever comes into a court of equity requesting its special help must, themselves, be free of any wrongdoing. In his draft decision, Justice Duffy wrote:

Mrs. O'Malley, seeking the aid of a Court of Equity against her husband, has not seen fit to put before this Court any reason whatever for her very singular desertion of her husband; nor are there any matrimonial proceedings between the parties; no cause what ever for the estrangement has appeared in this action. Equally remarkable is her failure to bring before this Court any semblance of a reason to justify or even palliate her very grave breach of duty as wife and mother in secretly removing two of the children across the Atlantic Ocean. In my opinion this Court was entitled to such explanations as she may be able to give of conduct which, if wholly unexplained, was shocking and outrageous, especially in a country which has solemnly recognised the Family as the basis of the social order.[17]

The justice went on to write:

> So the plain object of this unhappy suit is to invoke the aid of
> this Court for a judicial order to complete the ruin wrought
> by her vagaries ... I do not think that Mrs. O'Malley realised
> the temerity of these proceedings against her husband when
> she was herself to emerge in her suit as the wrong-doer. It
> is an ancient maxim of Equity that a suitor coming into
> a Court of Equity for equitable relief must come ... 'with
> clean hands.'

The action for restraining orders against Ernie was dismissed in
the draft judgement. Justice Duffy was editing his final judgement
when he unexpectedly died in June. Although it was never formally
recorded, Helen's lawyers may have learned of its contents – or the
justice's questioning at the trial may have made his sentiments clear
to them. In any event, Helen did not pursue the case further. The
above quotes are from Justice Duffy's annotated draft judgement,
made available to Cormac years later.

In August 1951, Ernie gave a celebratory dinner at Burrishoole
in honour of his solicitor, Michael Noyk, and the barrister who
argued the case. Noyk was a loyal republican who had great
respect for Ernie. Neither he nor the barrister had charged Ernie
for their services; they had successfully defended his case pro
bono.

The food courses served with their accompanying wines[18]
would have met or exceeded the standards of the Savoy in
London or the Ritz in Paris:

Hors d'oeuvres	Malmsey 1920
Liver – Kidney, Rosgibblin	Marsala 1925
Mackerel, Grilled, Carrowkeel	

Rice Clare Island – Indian Corn	Bernkasteler-Doctor 1929
Artichoke Hearts, Burrishoole	Krug 1919
Olives, Tir Nar	
Mountain Lamb, Skerdagh – New Potatoes	Chianti Montalbano 1941
Cauliflower alla Pietmontese	Ch Ausone 1937
Salad Dressing, Carrigahowley	Ch Mouton Rothschild 1929
Artichokes Sauce, Island More	
Raspberries Cream	
Minced Chicken Giblets, Murrisk	Ch Filhot 1929
Camembert – Pecan Nuts	
Oven Fresh Short Bread	Marc de Bourgogne 1933
	Brandy 1875

Many of the courses were from, and named for, local sources. Ernie had found the artichokes growing wild on islands in Clew Bay; Rosgibblin refers to local land Ernie had purchased; Carrowkeel, to nearby lands Helen bought; Clare Island guards the entrance to Clew Bay; Skerdagh refers to a location near Newport where the Mayo flying column fought Auxiliary forces during the War of Independence; Giblets Murrisk refers to the abbey on the south side of Clew Bay founded by an O'Malley in 1457.

Burrishoole was in a deteriorated physical state, and it lacked electricity as well as a kitchen staff to prepare the food when the dinner was given. Ernie had limited funds and yet he managed to provide this magnificent feast for his victorious lawyers.

Ernie and Cormac remained living at Burrishoole until the summer of 1954, when they moved to a four-room apartment in Dublin, mainly because of Ernie's declining health. Ernie established an initial schedule for Cormac. The boy went away to boarding school in September, returning for the Christmas and Easter vacations, and the long summer vacation from late June through August.

Sometimes Ernie took Cormac along to his military interviews all over Ireland. He also established safe havens, with various protective families, for Cormac to stay. Cormac was with the Josie Gill family on Island More in Clew Bay for several weeks during the summer of 1950; in 1952 he spent a month with Dr Sarsfield Kerrigan and his wife in Lifford, Donegal; he was with his Uncle Paddy for June–July 1953; and in 1954 he visited Luke Duffy and his family on a farm near Strokestown, Roscommon.

Helen had terminated the staff at Burrishoole and pulled all of her financial support. Ernie's financial resources were dwindling. In the mid-1940s the wind charger that generated electricity was blown down in a storm. At some point in 1950–51, the pump that brought drinking water to the house from the well failed. From that point on, drinking water was obtained when someone, like Cormac, walked the mile or two to a potable water source with buckets in each hand. Runoff water from the roof was used to flush the toilets. Ernie did not have the funds to pay for the connection to the new rural electrification plan when the poles were erected on the road close to the house in 1954.

Burrishoole is now owned by a family who uses it regularly as a vacation home. The couple has transformed it to its former state as a charming, large country house suitable for a family and its house guests. When I visited Burrishoole with Cormac, he took me to a small room in the back of the house with a fireplace and a door opening to the lawn. The room appeared to have been kept much as it must have been in the 1950s. Cormac said he and his father had lived together in this room during cold weather, eating and sleeping there. Ernie burned peat in the fireplace and cooked meals in it that they would share for several days. They read by Aladdin oil lamps or candles in the evenings.

In the years following the kidnapping in 1950 until Ernie's death in 1957, Cormac's growing up as an Irish boy, his academic and sports programmes in school, and his development into a healthy, happy young man were foremost in his father's heart and mind. Cormac represented the continuance of the O'Malley tradition; he was the joy of his father's life. A 1953 letter to Cathal stated, 'Please be kind to Etain and thank you for writing to Cormac. He works hard at school and at home he does his housework and cooking kindly and graciously.' To Paul Strand, he wrote, 'when Cormac is home for the holidays, we cook together and we sail in the Bay.' In a 1955 letter to Eithne Golden, he noted the emerging differences between Cormac and his two older children being brought up in the United States: 'I have one child, Cormac, whom I must bring up as an Irishman, and if his intelligence and integrity are of use, he could help this country.'[19]

From 1954 to 1957, when his health was failing, Ernie had an open invitation from his loyal friends Bobs and Harry Walston to visit Newton Hall, their large country estate in Cambridgeshire, England. Most of his visits were for three to four months over the long Irish winters, but he came for recuperative visits at other times as well. During one such visit, Harry was running for parliament as a local Labour candidate and Ernie volunteered to do local campaigning for him. His host quickly observed that the only quality more harmful than being a Roman Catholic as a vote-getter in his predominantly Protestant farming district was to be a Roman Catholic who was also an Irishman from Dublin. Harry nevertheless let Ernie go on canvassing his neighbours. It appears that Harry's neighbouring farmers enjoyed sharing their conservative ideas with Ernie as much as he enjoyed sharing his distinct political ideas with them. More often than not, his interviews with them ended amicably.

Cormac joined his father at Newton Hall whenever school vacations permitted. The Walstons had six children, and Cormac became an integral part of their children's mess. Ernie and Cormac each had their own room assigned to them there. By 1954 father and son had become partners in spite of the fact that the boy was then only 12 years old. Ernie wrote a letter to his friend Frank Gallagher describing Cormac as 'blooming'. He ended it by the signatory, 'With many kind thoughts to you and Cecilia, Ernie and Cormac.'[20]

Despite the couple's troubled past, Helen returned to Ireland to visit Ernie and Cormac on several occasions. Their first meeting took place early in July 1952, in Dublin. She had written to Ernie asking that he meet her in London, but he replied that they would have to meet in Dublin. He wrote a 'To whom it may concern' notice giving her permission to enter and leave Ireland to discuss family matters. Otherwise, Helen could have been at risk of being arrested for the kidnapping in 1950. She and Ernie had long talks about the future, and she was allowed to take Cormac out on several occasions.

It does not appear that they were able to work out the matters which Helen had come to Dublin to resolve that summer. In May she had received a divorce under Colorado law, which gave her custody of the two older children. Ernie's draft letter to Helen after she left for America outlined the outstanding issues that they tried to resolve during their Dublin meetings:

a. That the children write to each other.
b. That Etain be sent to school in Ireland.

c.   That Burrishoole be sold in our joint names. [With one third going to Helen, one third to Ernie, and the other third to buy a Dublin house.]

d.   That my money in America be returned prior to sale of Burrishoole, as a sale meant removal of furniture.

e.   That a home be purchased in Dublin, be inspected and agreed on.

f.   That you and I live with the children … You are divorced and you wanted a remarriage. This cannot take place as long as I am a Catholic. On the other hand you can annul your divorce.[21]

Ernie ended this long draft letter by requesting of Helen, 'Would you kindly put on paper what you consider was the agreement tentatively arrived at between us two.' If Helen ever received this letter, she never followed up on this request, and none of the above issues were resolved between them.

Their next meeting occurred in September 1953 when Helen decided she would return to London to continue her theatrical career. She and Etain visited Ernie and Cormac at the Walstons' in Cambridge before she put Etain in an English boarding school.

Helen's final visits to see Ernie and Cormac before Ernie's death were in Mayo and Dublin during September 1955. She had brought her two older children to a weekend at Newport House in Mayo, specifically to be with their father. Ernie was not able to communicate easily with the two older children he had not seen for so long. Many years later, Cathal recalled the meeting with his father: 'The visit was awkward. I had just completed my first year at Harvard. We were like two ships passing in the night. There was hardly any connection. I felt he had renounced me.'[22]

Helen also invited Ernie and Cormac to a dinner at the Shelbourne Hotel in Dublin. She had brought an American man she was seeing named Richard Roelofs Jr with her to Ireland for this visit. At dinner Helen turned to Ernie and said she wished to remarry him. He declined, citing their irrevocable differences, the fact that married life with her would be too complicated for him, and finally his failing health. After this Helen told him she would marry Richard Roelofs, and Ernie wished the couple well. Helen married Richard at her mother's home in Connecticut in August 1956, shortly after her mother's death.

In 1973 Cathal O'Shannon of Raidió Teilifís Éireann interviewed Helen to discuss her career as an artist who had been involved with Ireland, and her marriage to Ernie. Helen was then a woman of almost 70. He pointedly asked her why, after all their difficulties together, she asked Ernie to remarry her during her visit to Ireland in September 1955. She had kidnapped the children and divorced Ernie in America, and she was travelling with another man whom she would later marry. Helen replied simply, 'There was no one like him. I would have done it all over again. To have had those years with him was a great privilege to me.'[23]

Ernie decided that he and Cormac should go to the Aran Islands off the coast of Galway each August. The islands had been a refuge and source of inspiration for Ernie during the many years he visited by himself. Back in 1919, early in the War of Independence, he had first gone to Inisheer, the smallest of the islands, to establish a company of Irish Volunteers. He developed an early appreciation of the distinct character of the hardy local fishermen and farmers who lived there year-round, and he made the effort to become familiar with their local tradition of telling stories in the evening seated around a turf fire. In 1941 he had visited Inishmore, the largest island, staying by himself at a boarding house owned by Elizabeth Rivers, an English artist who had moved there before the Second World War. The dwelling had been pictured in Robert Flaherty's famous documentary movie *Man of Aran.*

In August 1954, after Ernie and Cormac had packed up his paintings, books and furniture at Burrishoole in preparation for moving to their new flat in Dublin, they stayed in Kilmurvey House on Inishmore. They were exhausted after their ordeal, and the guest house offered rooms and three meals a day so that they would not have to worry about cooking. One of its disadvantages was that Ernie had brought Cormac there so he could learn Irish from speaking with the local children, but none were available in the vicinity where they were staying.

During the next two summers, Ernie took Cormac to the island of Inisheer. Although a smaller community, it had guest houses that took in visitors, and there were local families nearby with children who spoke Irish. Various people Ernie knew spent time there in the summer. He brought books to read during his visits, and he kept diaries where he assiduously wrote down his thoughts, made corrections, and kept count of the words he wrote each day. He made fresh, spontaneous observations in these diaries reminiscent of his memoir *On Another Man's Wound.* The diaries explain local folklore and the fishing techniques used in the teeming seas around the islands. Cormac later arranged for his father's Aran diaries to be published.

Aran was one of the least developed areas in Ireland, and the people lived simply. So did Ernie and Cormac. He described the situation in their guest house at Inisheer:

> Cormac and I have a double bed, a small table which holds a looking glass, a small table of support for a zinc basin, a chamber pot of metal. Three nails on the back of the door. A small hanging whiskey bottle with a feather duster in it for sprinkling holy water, and a ledge under the window. At

first glance one thinks this an impossible situation. Where will I hang my clothes, where will I place my books, my toilet articles ... But [jail] has already solved many things in one's mind.[24]

This was a hard life. Fishing had been the basic industry, and the men fished in long boats, called currachs. These were constructed by putting heavily tar-coated canvas over light wooden slats. They were rowed by two or three oarsmen with an occasional sail; they were at the mercy of strong currents and fierce Atlantic winds. Ernie noted that the local people sometimes exhibited curious habits, such as when they, native Irish speakers, spoke only English when talking to their animals. Ernie wondered if this came from early Cromwellian days when the English conquered the islands. The islanders refused to eat crabs, which were plentiful, using them only for bait. They considered the French to be 'dirty eaters' because they ate fish in stews, whereas the locals preferred to eat bacon and eggs.

In the 1940s, some marriages were still arranged, and the women were often not to be seen. Ernie reflected:

This absence of women is important enough. Only occasionally does one see a red skirt, that of an elderly woman ... A few young girls normally wander about the strand ... and an odd woman may bring down an ass for the turf to the pier, but the bulk of women are absent save at Mass on Sunday.[25]

Ernie was teaching his son to appreciate the old Irish ways. They were an odd couple. His father shared experiences with him, hoping he would serve Ireland one day in keeping the O'Malley name alive and well.

Beginning in the early 1950s, Ernie experienced increasingly serious problems with his health. His wounds and imprisonment may have weakened him, but his basic issue was a heart condition dating back to a heart tremor he had in his youth. His brother Kevin, a noted heart specialist, understood Ernie's health challenges and watched over him. In the spring of 1953, at Burrishoole, it was apparent that Ernie had had a massive heart attack and needed hospital care. He went to Dublin at Kevin's urging but had difficulty getting admitted into St Bricin's Military Hospital at Arbour Hill, Dublin, which cared for serving military and war veterans. He was eventually admitted in April, remaining there through July 1953. Ernie described this period in a letter to Paul Strand: 'Kevin this year when I expected to die took charge of me in hospital and has been very kind.'[26]

When he left the hospital, Kevin and Ernie's former IRA comrade Tony Woods took care of the bills that Ernie had expected would be paid by the department of defence because of his service in the two wars. When he discovered that the government had determined he was not eligible for free hospital care, he became furious and insisted on paying Kevin and Tony back.

By 1953 the Irish government had determined that its military hospitals were supposed to serve the active armed forces and retirees of the Free State army as of 1949 going forward. They no longer served military veterans from the pre-1949 period, including veterans who had been involved in the warring period from 1919 to 1921. Even pensioners with earlier disabilities, like Ernie, were not covered. Apparently, Ernie was not informed of this policy when he was admitted to St Bricin's. His brother Kevin was probably aware of it and intended from the beginning to pay for Ernie's treatment himself, or with the help of Tony Woods. Regardless, Ernie's condition improved in the months he had spent in hospital to the extent that he could continue raising Cormac, interviewing his comrades and supporting the arts in Ireland for another four years. Tony Woods and Ernie's old friend Johnny Raleigh ended up paying the St Bricin's bill of £153.[27]

When he left the hospital in July, he was taken in for a month by his old IRA comrade Christy Smith. Smith was a civil servant living with his wife in Dublin. They brought Ernie to their modest house, where they generously insisted that he have their marital bed for his convalescence while they slept in a smaller room. The Smiths took Ernie in when he had no place to go in Dublin.

Ernie was able to go on with his life after this episode, but he was never the same again. In late August 1954, he moved with Cormac to 52 Mespil House, Sussex Road, Dublin, a four-room apartment with a small kitchen that Tony Woods had found for them. Cormac recalls that his father's books, paintings and interview notebooks were stored in every room. Cormac was a weekday boarder at the nearby Willow Park school and came home to be with his father on weekends. Ernie took refuge with the Walstons at Newton Hall in the winter, bringing Cormac along on his holidays. When his friend Evie Hone died in 1955, Ernie led the effort to hold a retrospective exhibition in her honour. Though suffering from poor health, he was still able to take Cormac to the Aran Islands every summer during his last three years.

On 9 May 1955 Ernie wrote a letter to Helen presenting a poignant picture, both of his financial struggles at that time and the deterioration of their relationship. As precarious as his money situation was, and despite her failure to pay for Cormac's schooling in Ireland, he neither complained nor criticised her. In January 1954 he had belatedly received Helen's previously promised school fees for Cormac, which she had withheld for several years. He wrote to Helen:

I received money, which I think you forwarded to the bank in January 1954, but not until the end of the year did I realise what the money meant. Thank you for sending it as I did not know who it belonged to I did not make use of it and as I was in debt, hospitals, etc., I sold my Rossgiblin land [near Burrishoole] at a big loss to come clean. Sincerely yours, Ernie O'Malley.[28]

In a later letter on 5 September, Ernie wrote to her again, 'Please do not hold up Cormac's money for I must continue at times to borrow money for schooling.' He wrote another letter to Helen that September, 'As I told you I have a short time to live. I require peace of mind and I must avoid worry. Somehow Cormac and I will manage … This happens to be my country and it is here one son of mine must be brought up.'[29]

In the autumn of 1956 Ernie became seriously ill again and went to the Mater Private Hospital in Dublin and then to the Walstons for a long Christmas break. In January 1957, he returned to the hospital, where Kevin followed his treatment. In February his sister Kaye took him into her comfortable house in Howth, where she nursed him as his siblings began to visit. The last letter Ernie ever wrote was to his son Cathal in February. The last time Cormac saw him alive was during a weekend visit from his English boarding school in early March. On 25 March he died of a pulmonary embolism blood clot. This was the culmination of his failing heart condition and all of his other physical distresses.

In his will, made just nine days before he died and witnessed by his sister Kaye, Ernie left all of his possessions to his son Cormac. He named his brother Paddy as his executor and his brother Kevin as Cormac's guardian.

Kevin did not attempt to prevent Helen from taking Cormac to America with his brother and sister after the funeral. Cormac's older siblings were already enrolled in university and boarding school. They all spent that summer in Colorado, and Helen had a caretaker for Cormac for the next school year while he attended a local Colorado boarding school as a day student, spending his holidays in New York with his family. During that year, Helen visited him in Colorado on several occasions. She was busy in New York trying to buy a house in Greenwich to settle in with her partially invalided second husband. The next school year, Cormac was sent to Deerfield Academy, a boarding school in Massachusetts.

Shortly after Ernie's death, his sister Kaye wrote a letter to their cousin Sylvia Laithwaite describing Ernie's last days and his reconciliation with the Catholic Church, which had excommunicated him at one time:

> The priests here were very good; he was given Holy Communion ... every time he asked for it ... Cormac came on March 18th ... and it seemed to give Ernie great joy ... During the night I was awakened by a shout. He must have had a bad dream ... Suddenly I heard a little sound and when I got beside him he was dying ... He was dead, 9.20 a.m. quietly and with no distress and no fuss ... The Lord have mercy on him. He looked so peaceful and at rest. No wasted appearance, just calm.[30]

Ernie had hoped his children would continue in their original Roman Catholic faith, and Kaye asked a family friend to tell them before the funeral about their father's concern.

The rebel-intellectual had passed on. It was now time for his family, his IRA comrades, his friends, and Irish men and women to honour him.

Ernie had made it clear that he did not wish to have a big affair made over his funeral. He bore no animus to his former opponents in the War of Independence or the Civil War. He never sought fame or recognition; he would have wanted to be buried in peace.

Éamon de Valera, who had recently been returned to power as taoiseach, and his ministers, some of whom had served under Ernie's command, had other ideas. They honoured Ernie with a state funeral held in Howth and Glasnevin Cemetery even though he had never held political office. They wanted a serious celebration for the man who had become an Irish hero to his countrymen; the man still remembered for his cry, 'No Surrender Here' when he ran out alone to confront the multitude of Free State soldiers surrounding the Humphreys' house early that morning in November 1922.

The protocol for a state funeral involves 300 members of the defence forces providing a guard of honour while a gun carriage carrying the deceased is draped with appropriate colours; in this case it was the battered flag from the Four Courts complex, which Ernie had been ordered to surrender. Buglers played the 'Last Post'. There was a final gun salute. There is a photograph showing Ernie's former senior comrades de Valera, Seán Lemass and Frank Aiken marching in the funeral possession; the taoiseach and the two cabinet ministers are solemnly dressed in black suits, black topcoats and black fedoras. There is another photograph showing minister Seán Moylan giving the funeral oration for the Irish hero at the graveside while dignitaries, Ernie's children and Helen look on; Cathal stands with head bowed alongside his mother, sister, and brother.[31]

His IRA comrades in battle came to Ernie's funeral from all over the country. Dan Breen came all the way from Tipperary. At the service, someone noted that Dan was crying. No one had ever seen him weep. A brother who had taught Ernie at the Christian Brothers School remembered a phrase from a poem, 'tears of warlike men'.[32]

When men encounter a deeply respected military hero, they often hold him in awe in spite of their own worldly achievements. They are never sure they would have behaved the way he did on the battlefield. This awe never goes away; the military hero carries it with him the rest of his life. This explains why publishers, political figures, newspaper editors and famous film directors continued to call Ernie 'General', although he had shed that title long ago.

In 1964, years after Ernie's funeral, John Ford was addressing a large group of newspaper reporters and members of the public at the Shelbourne Hotel in Dublin. They were asking questions about a new film he was about to make in Ireland. Ford was beginning to falter and his mind wandered. He went off script and shouted a question to the crowd: '"Tell me," he asked the assembly, "who was at Ernie O'Malley's funeral ... Did he get military honours?"'[33]

ENDNOTES

CHAPTER ONE: BOYHOOD TO EASTER RISING, 1897–1916

1   E. O'Malley to Molly Childers, 26 November–1 December 1923, Ernie O'Malley Papers, New York University Library, Archives of Irish America 060 (hereafter 'EOMP-AIA060'), Box 4, Folders 120, 121; Cormac K.H. O'Malley and Anne Dolan, eds, *'No Surrender Here!': The Civil War Papers of Ernie O'Malley, 1922–1924* (Dublin: Lilliput Press, 2007), 243.

2   Ernie O'Malley, unpublished draft, *On Another Man's Wound*, 1–2, EOMP-AIA060, Box 1, Folder 24.

3   Ernie O'Malley, *On Another Man's Wound* (Cork: Mercier Press, 2013) (hereafter *Wound*), 17.

4   E. O'Malley, *Wound*, 20.

5   Ibid, 20.

6   Ibid, 29.

7   Ibid, 28.

8   Fearghal McGarry, *The Rising: Ireland, Easter 1916* (Oxford: Oxford University Press, 2016), 120.

9   Ibid, 188.

10 Ibid, 102, 120–21.

11 Richard D. Finneran, ed., *Collected Poems, W.B. Yeats* (New York: Scribner Paper Back Poetry, Simon & Schuster, 1996), 181–3.

12 R.F. Foster, *Vivid Faces: The Revolutionary Generation in Ireland, 1890–1923* (New York: W.W. Norton & Co., 2015), 5–25.

13 Liam Ó Briain to Frances-Mary Blake, March 1973, FMB Papers, University College Dublin Archives (hereafter 'Blake Papers'), 244/27-1.

CHAPTER TWO: IRELAND PREPARES FOR WAR, 1916–1918

1   E. O'Malley to Molly Childers, 26 November, in *'No Surrender Here!'*, 425.

2   Ernie O'Malley, *The Singing Flame* (Cork: Mercier Press, 2012) (hereafter *Flame*), 354–5, cited by Francis Costello, *The Irish Revolution and Its Aftermath, 1916–1923* (Dublin: Irish Academic Press, 2003), 12.

3   E. O'Malley, *Wound*, 149.

4   E. O'Malley to Childers, 26 November 1923, in *'No Surrender Here!'*, 426–7.

5   Tomas Malone interview by Cormac O'Malley, Tipperary, October 1970, EOMP-AIA060, Box 24, Folder 20.

6   E. O'Malley to Childers, 26 November 1923, in *'No Surrender Here!'*, 428–9.

7   Ibid, 431.

8   E. O'Malley, *Wound*, 135–6.

CHAPTER THREE: WAR OF INDEPENDENCE, 1919–1921

1   J.J. Lee, 'The Background, Anglo Irish Relations, 1898–1921', in *'No Surrender Here!'*, xxii.

2   Ibid; Royal Irish Constabulary, *History of Policing in Ireland*, www.RoyalIrishConstabulary.com.

3   Dan Breen, *My Fight for Irish Freedom* (Cork: Mercier Press, 2010), 32.

4   Breen, *My Fight*, back cover.

5   E. O'Malley, *Wound*, 147.

6   Peadar O'Donnell interview by Cormac O'Malley, Dublin, October 1970, EOMP-AIA060, Box 24, Folder 20.

7   E. O'Malley, *Wound*, 180.

8   Ernie O'Malley, *Raids and Rallies* (Cork: Mercier Press, 2011), 22–6.

9   E. O'Malley, *Wound*, 193–4.

10   Ibid, 203; E. O'Malley, *Raids*, 42–58.

11   Tomás Malone interview by Cormac O'Malley, Tipperary, October 1970, EOMP-AIA060, Box 24, Folder 20.

12   E. O'Malley, *Wound*, 239–46.

13   Ibid, 246.

14   Seán Lemass interview by Cormac O'Malley, Dublin, October 1970, EOMP-AIA060, Box 24, Folder 20; Blake Papers, P244/40.

15   E. O'Malley, *Wound*, 214–15.

16   Ibid, 236–7.

17   E. O'Malley, *Flame*, 31.

18   J.J. Lee, 'The Background, Anglo-Irish Relations', in *'No Surrender Here!'*, xxii.

19   Peter Hart, *The IRA and Its Enemies: Violence and Community in Cork, 1916–1923* (Oxford: Clarendon Press, 1999), 22–30.

20   E. O'Malley, *Wound*, 275; references to *Wound*, 288–357, are made on the immediately following pages without specific references.

21 Tom Barry, *Guerilla Days in Ireland* (Tralee: Anvil Books, 1971), 124. Some senior IRA officers opined later that both Tom Barry and Dan Breen had exaggerated their warfare feats in the books they wrote about the roles they played.

22 John Crowley, Donal Ó Drisceoil and Mike Murphy, eds, *Atlas of the Irish Revolution* (Cork: Cork University Press, 2017), 553.

23 Crowley, Ó Drisceoil and Murphy, *Atlas*, 564.

24 Ibid, 555–6.

25 Ibid, 564.

26 Ibid, 553–4.

27 E. O'Malley, *Raids*, 130.

28 Charles Townshend, *The Republic: The Fight for Irish Independence* (London: Penguin Books, 2014), 273–80.

29 E. O'Malley, *Wound*, 374–5.

30 Barry, *Guerilla Days*, 145–7.

31 Ernie O'Malley to Mother Scholastica, 12–14 January 1923, National Archives of Ireland, Bureau of Military History, CD 6/36/21, 7–8.

32 E. O'Malley to Molly Childers, 26 November, in *'No Surrender Here!'*, 432.

33 Ibid, 431.

34 E. O'Malley, *Wound*, 379.

35 Ibid, 421.

36 Ibid, 425–31.

37 O'Malley to Childers, 26 November 1923, in *'No Surrender Here!'*, 430.

38 Ibid, 432–3.

39 E. O'Malley, *Wound*, 435.

CHAPTER FOUR: TRUCE TO CIVIL WAR, 1921–1922

1 Barry, *Guerilla Days*, 160–1.

2 Ibid, 166–7.

3 Ibid, 175.

4 Crowley, Ó Drisceoill and Murphy, *Atlas*, 381.

5 Michael Collins, *The Path to Freedom* (Cork: Mercier Press, 1968), 86; Michael Hopkinson, *Green Against Green, The Irish Civil War* (Dublin: Gill and Macmillan, 1988), 9.

6 E. O'Malley, *Flame*, 39.

7 Ibid, 41–2.

8 E. O'Malley, *Wound*, 145.

9 Hopkinson, *Green Against Green*, 110–11.

10 E. O'Malley, *Flame*, 65.

11 Gavin M. Foster, *The Irish Civil War and Society: Politics, Class and Conflict* (London & New York: Palgrave Macmillan, 2015).

12 E. O'Malley, *Flame*, 72.

13 Calton Younger, *Ireland's Civil War* (New York: Taplinger Publishing, 1969), 232–3.

14 E. O'Malley, *Flame*, 82.

CHAPTER FIVE: IRELAND'S CIVIL WAR, JUNE 1922–MAY 1923

1 Ibid, 112, 114, 196.

2 Síobhra Aiken, Fearghal Mac Bhloscaidh, Liam Ó Duibhir and Diarmuid Ó Tuama, eds, *The Men Will Talk to Me: Ernie O'Malley's Interviews with the Northern Divisions* (Dublin: Merrion Press, 2018), 33.

3 Frank O'Connor, *The Big Fellow: Michael Collins and the Irish Revolution* (Dublin: Poolbeg, 1979), 203.

4 Younger, *Irish Civil War*, 306–7; E. O'Malley, *Flame*, 119.

5 E. O'Malley, *Flame*, 273; quotations from *Flame* made on following pages are without specific page references.

6 John O'Callaghan, *The Battle for Kilmallock* (Cork: Mercier Press, 2011), 55–7, 76.

7 Ibid, 57; Mac Eoin, *Survivors*, 232.

8 Charles Townshend, *The Republic: The Fight for Irish Independence, 1918–1923* (Dublin: Penguin, 2014), 419–20.

9 Madge Clifford Comer interview by Cormac O'Malley, Tralee, October 1970, EOMP-AIA060, Box 24, Folder 20.

10 E. O'Malley to P. Hooper, Editor, *Freeman's Journal*, 24 August 1922, in 'No Surrender Here!', 116–17.

11 E. O'Malley to C. Moloney, 18 September 1922 and Mike Price to E. O'Malley, 30 September 1922, Ernie O'Malley Papers, UCDA (hereafter EOMP-UCDA, P17a/63), in 'No Surrender Here!', 192–3, 204.

12 Frank Aiken to E. O'Malley, 16 September 1922, Seán Lehane to E. O'Malley, 19 September 1922, E. O'Malley to Liam Lynch, 22 and 24 September 1922, in 'No Surrender Here!', 187, 199, 211, 221.

13 E. O'Malley to Liam Lynch, 22 September 1922, 'No Surrender Here!', 212.

14 Lemass interview by C. O'Malley, October 1970.

15 E. O'Malley, *Flame*, 231; quotations from *Flame*, 231–39, made on the immediately following pages are without specific page references.

16 Richard Mulcahy to William T. Cosgrave, 29 December 1922, in 'No Surrender Here!', 341.

17 Ibid, lvi; Cormac K.H. O'Malley and Nicholas Allen, eds, *Broken Landscapes: Selected Letters of Ernie O'Malley, 1924–1957* (Dublin: Lilliput Press, 2011), 5.

18 E. O'Malley, *Flame*, 241; quotations from *Flame*, 241–56, made on the immediately following pages are without specific page references.

19 Marion O'Malley to Desmond Fitzgerald, 22 May 1923, 'No Surrender Here!', 376.

20 Kevin Malley interview by Frances-Mary Blake, Dublin, 6 July 1973, Blake Papers, P244/41-10, /43.

21 E. O'Malley to Childers, 'No Surrender Here!', 415.

22 K. Malley interview by Blake, 6 July 1973.

23 E. O'Malley, *Flame*, 312–13.

24 O'Donnell interview by C. O'Malley, October 1970.

25 O'Malley, *Flame*, 320–22.

26 Ibid, 333.

27 Meda Ryan, *The Day Michael Collins Was Shot* (Dublin: Poolbeg, 1989), 96, 105.

28 Liam Lynch to all divisions, 26 November 1922, 'No Surrender Here!', 337.

29 Florence O'Donoghue, *No Other Law* (Dublin: Anvil Book, 1986), 297.

30 Crowley, O'Driscoil and Murphy, *Atlas*, 719.

31 Tom Malone, *Alias Seán Forde: The Story of Commandant Tomás Malone, Vice O.C. East Limerick Flying Column, Irish Republican Army* (Dublin: Elo Press, 2000), 92, 111.

32 O'Donoghue, *No Other Law*, 301.

33 Ibid, 305.

34 Ibid, 305.

35 O'Malley, *Flame*, 179.

36 Ibid, 196.

37 Lynch to E. O'Malley, 27 August 1922, 'No Surrender Here!', 127.

38 Anne Dolan, *Commemorating the Irish Civil War: History and Memory, 1923–2000* (Cambridge: Cambridge University Press, 2003), 67.

39 Todd Andrews interview by Blake, Dublin, 26–7 October 1974, Blake Papers.

40 Máire Comerford interview by Blake, Dublin, 26–7 October 1974, Blake Papers.

41 E. O'Malley to Childers, citing poem to L. Lynch, 'No Surrender Here!', 476.

CHAPTER SIX: POST-JAIL: IRELAND AND EUROPE, 1924–1928

1 Gavin Foster, *Irish Civil War*, 158, 264, fn 96.
2 K. Malley interview by Blake, July 1973.
3 Interview Notes, Blake, 1974, Blake Papers, P244/40.
4 E. O'Malley to Kay Brady, 27 December 1925, in *Broken Landscapes*, 15.
5 Minutes of [IRA] Executive Committee Meeting, 10–11 August 1924, EOMP-UCDA, P17a/12.
6 O'Donnell interview by C. O'Malley, October 1970.
7 E. O'Malley European Notebook, 1925–27, 11–12, Cormac O'Malley Private Papers [hereafter cited as COMPP].
8 E. O'Malley European Diary, 19 February 1925, 5–6, EOMP-AIA060, Box 9, Folder 28A.
9 EOM Events Chronology, 1925, COMPP.
10 E. O'Malley, *Tramping the Pyrenees, 1925–26*, TMS, 4–5, EOMP-AIA060, Box 9, Folder 30.
11 Ibid, 88–9.
12 E. O'Malley to K. Brady, 27 December 1925, in *Broken Landscapes*, 14.
13 Ibid, 17.
14 Catriona Lawlor, ed., *Seán MacBride, That Day's Struggle: A Memoir, 1904–1951* (Dublin: Currach Press, 2005), 101.
15 E. O'Malley to Harriet Monroe, 10 January 1935, in *Landscapes*, 109; E. O'Malley, *Tramping the Pyrenees*, 87.
16 Lawlor, *Seán MacBride*, 102–3.
17 Ibid, 104–5.
18 O'Donnell interview by C. O'Malley, October 1970.
19 President of San Mareno (B.J. O'Malley) to Chairman of Senate of San Mareno (Kevin O'Malley), letter No. X22, 3 January 1927, and Chairman to President, letter No. A/150, 3 January 1927, EOMP-AIA060, *San Mareno Letters*, Box 2, Folder 10.
20 E. O'Malley to Monroe, 10 January 1935, in *Broken Landscapes*, 110.

CHAPTER SEVEN: CREATIVE JOURNEY: AMERICA AND MEXICO, 1928–1935

1 E. O'Malley, American Diary, New York, 12 October 1928, EOMP-AIA060, Box 9, Folder 34A; *Broken Landscapes*, 46.
2 *Irish World*, 27 October 1928, Blake Papers, UCDA, P244/12.
3 E. O'Malley, American Diary, Carmel, 21 April 1929, EOMP-AIA060, Box 9, Folder 38A; *Broken Landscapes*, 64–5.

4   Edward Weston to E. O'Malley, 28 February 1931, EOMP-AIA060, Box 4, Folder 102.

5   *Seattle Daily Times*, 8 March 1929; *Broken Landscapes*, 45.

6   E. O'Malley, New Mexican Diary, 14 September 1929, 15–16, EOMP-AIA060, Box 42, Folder 31.

7   E. O'Malley to Helen Golden, May 1930, in *Broken Landscapes*, 70.

8   E. O'Malley, New Mexican Diary, 30 November 1929, 5, EOMP-AIA060, Box 42, Folder 34.

9   Dorothea McDowell, *Ella Young and Her World: Celtic Mythology, the Irish Revival and the California Avant-Garde* (California: printed privately, 2017), 339.

10 Miriam Hapgood DeWitt, *Taos: A Memoir* (Albuquerque: University of New Mexico Press, 1992), 26–7, 31.

11 H. Golden to Patricia Golden Smith, 20 August 1932, COMPP.

12 Dorothy Brett to E. O'Malley, March 1930, EOMP-AIA060, Box 3, Folder 29.

13 E. O'Malley to Brett, 11 March 1930, EOPM-AIA060, Box 4, Folder 118; *Broken Landscapes*, 69.

14 E. O'Malley, New Mexican Diary, 19 September 1929, 43–5, 46, EOMP-AIA060, Box 42, Folder 31.

15 *The New Mexican*, Santa Fe, NM, in *Broken Landscapes*, 76.

16 E. O'Malley, Mexican Diary, 20 January 1931, 8–9, EOMP-AIA060, Box 42, Folder 36.

17 E. O'Malley to Harriet Monroe, 10 January 1935, in *Broken Landscapes*, 109.

18 E. O'Malley to H. Golden, 19 January 1931, in *Broken Landscapes*, 80–1.

19 Hart Crane to E. O'Malley, June 1931, in Langdon Hammer, ed., *Hart Crane: Complete Poems and Selected Letters* (New York: Library of America, 2006), 678.

20 Crane to Malcolm Cowley, 2 June 1931, in Hammer, ed., *Hart Crane*, 674.

21 E. O'Malley, Mexican Diary, 20 January 1930, 7, EOMP-AIA060, Box 42, Folder 36.

22 E. O'Malley to Countess Plunkett, 15 March 1931, in *Broken Landscapes*, 85.

23 Notes on E. O'Malley by Eithne Golden, 1983, 9, COMPP.

24 E. O'Malley, New Mexican Diary, 8 December 1929, 72–3, in EOMP-AIA060, Box 42, Folder 34.

25 E. O'Malley to Paul Strand, 13 July 1932, in *Broken Landscapes*, 87–9.

26 Ibid. Yaddo is now known as the Corporation of Yaddo.
27 Strand to E. O'Malley, 8 July 1932, EOMP-AIA060, Box 4, Folder 88.
28 E. O'Malley to H. Golden, 24 July 1932, in *Broken Landscapes*, 89.
29 E. O'Malley to Strand, 19 August 1932, in *Broken Landscapes*, 92.
30 E. O'Malley to H. Golden, 30 June 1934, in *Broken Landscapes*, 100–2.
31 Ibid.
32 E. O'Malley to H. Golden, 9 April 1935, in *Broken Landscapes*, 112.
33 Ibid, 114.
34 E. O'Malley to Strand, 28 December 1934, in *Broken Landscapes*, 107.
35 E. O'Malley autobiographical statement, TMS, 1950, EOMP-AIA060, Box 1, Folder 7, in *Broken Landscapes*, 218.
36 H. Hooker to Elon Hooker, 2 January 1931, COMPP.
37 H. Hooker to Blanche Hooker, 15 February 1934, COMPP.
38 H. Hooker to B. Hooker, 21 February 1934, COMPP.
39 E. O'Malley to Strand, 12 July 1934, in *Broken Landscapes*, 102–3.
40 E. O'Malley to Helen Hooker, 9 July 1933, 17 December 1933, in *Broken Landscapes*, 94, 96–7.
41 E. O'Malley to H. Hooker, 23 April 1935, 8 May 1935, 10 May 1935, in *Broken Landscapes*, 114–16, 116–18, 119.

CHAPTER EIGHT: DUBLIN: HUSBAND, AUTHOR, LIBEL DEFENDANT, 1935–1939

1 E. O'Malley statement, in *Broken Landscapes*, 217–19.
2 Strand to E. O'Malley, 6 August 1953, EOMP-AIA60, Box 4, Folder 88.
3 E. O'Malley statement, in *Broken Landscapes*, 218–19.
4 Ibid, 219.
5 Elon H. Hooker to E. O'Malley, 24 December 1935, EOMP-AIA060, Box 5, Folder 48; in English, *Ernie O'Malley*, 183–4.
6 E. O'Malley statement, in *Broken Landscapes*, 219.
7 Lois Dwight Cole to E. O'Malley, 6 October 1933, EOMP-AIA060, Box 3, Folder 39.
8 Philip Kolb, ed., *Selected Letters, Marcel Proust, A Life, 1910–17*, Vol. 3 (New York: Harper & Collins, 1992), 135; William C. Carter, *Marcel Proust* (New Haven: Yale University Press, 2000), 525.
9 E. O'Malley, *Army Without Banners: Adventures of an Irish Volunteer* (Boston: Houghton Mifflin, 1937), 288–95.
10 E. O'Malley, *Rebellen in Irland* (Berlin: Alfred Metzner, 1938).

11 E. O'Malley, *Wound*, 175.

12 Ibid, 229.

13 *New York Times*, in Padraic O'Farrell, *The Ernie O'Malley Story* (Cork: Mercier Press, 1983), 96.

14 *New York Herald Tribune*, in O'Farrell, *O'Malley Story*, 94–5.

15 Ó Faoláin, book review of *Wound*, *Ireland Today*, October 1936, in O'Farrell, *O'Malley Story*, 93–4.

16 E. O'Malley, *Flame*, 19.

17 Frank O'Connor, *My Father's Son* (London: Macmillan, 1978), 106.

18 E. O'Malley to Desmond Ryan, 22 December 1936, in *Broken Landscapes*, 136.

19 Various Irish newspaper articles referencing the libel case during the course of the trial, EOMP-AIA060, Box 9, Folders 21, 22.

20 E. O'Malley, *Wound*, 142.

21 E. O'Malley statement, in *Broken Landscapes*, 220.

22 Ibid.

23 Ibid.

24 H. Hooker to B. Hooker, 12 June 1936, COMPP.

25 E. O'Malley to Eithne Golden, 4 October 1936, in *Broken Landscapes*, 132.

26 E. O'Malley, 1937 Diary, 6 August 1937, EOMP-AIA060, Box 9, Folder 45.

27 E. O'Malley to H. Hooker, 28 February 1937, 20 March 1937, 6 April 1937, in *Broken Landscapes*, 139, 143–6.

28 E. O'Malley to H. Hooker, 7 June 1938, in *Broken Landscapes*, 155.

29 E. O'Malley to H. Hooker, 11 June 1938, in *Broken Landscapes*, 157.

30 E. O'Malley, 1939 Diary, May–July 1939, EOMP-AIA060, Box 10, Folder 1.

CHAPTER NINE: MAYO: IRISH ARTS SPONSOR, MARRIAGE DIFFICULTIES, KIDNAPPING, 1940–1950

1 E. O'Malley, 1939 Diary, EOMP-AIA060, Box 10, Folder 1.

2 E. O'Malley to H. Hooker, 5 August 1940, in *Broken Landscapes*, 192.

3 Cathal O'Malley to H. Hooker, 24 July 1940, in *Broken Landscapes*, 190–1.

4 E. O'Malley to Sylvia Laithwaite, February 1942, in *Broken Landscapes*, 202.

5 E. O'Malley statement, in *Broken Landscapes*, 222. This incident occurred after the 1798 French invasion in north Mayo to help the Irish fight the

English, but the effort failed.

6   E. O'Malley to N. Naughton, 9 November 1943, E. O'Malley to John Raleigh, 31 January 1944, in *Broken Landscapes,* 209–10.

7   E. O'Malley Farm Notebooks, EOMP-AIA060, Box 10, Folders 5 and 6.

8   E. O'Malley to Laithwaite, February 1942, in *Broken Landscapes,* 201.

9   Ibid, 201–2.

10 E. O'Malley statement, in *Broken Landscapes,* 223.

11 Helen persuaded de Valera to allow her to do a sculpture of him in 1973 long after Ernie died.

12 C. O'Malley, unpublished TMS, *HHH Chronology,* 2007, 19, COMPP.

13 E. O'Malley to Jean McGrail, 5 March 1956, in *Broken Landscapes,* 362.

14 E. O'Malley, book review of Thomas MacGreevy's *Appreciation and Interpretation of Jack B. Yeats,* in *The Bell,* 1946, in *Broken Landscapes,* 397.

15 E. O'Malley to Thomas MacGreevy, 1 May 1939, in *Broken Landscapes,* 165.

16 E. O'Malley to James Johnson Sweeney, 18 January 1946, in *Broken Landscapes,* 234.

17 Jack B. Yeats to E. O'Malley, 9 December 1945, EOMP-AIA060, Box 7, Folder 59.

18 English, *Ernie O'Malley: IRA – Intellectual* (Oxford: Clarendon Press, 1998), 57.

19 E. O'Malley, 'Louis le Brocquy', *Horizon,* XIV, 79, 1946, in *Broken Landscapes,* 397–401.

20 Ibid, 400.

21 Louis le Brocquy to C. O'Malley, 22 October 1989, EOMP-AIA060, Box 2, Folder 4.

22 MacGreevy to E. O'Malley, 9 February 1940, EOMP-AIA060, Box 4, Folder 30.

23 All critical articles are included in Appendix I, *Broken Landscapes,* 389–430.

24 Transcript of E. O'Malley's radio lecture, EOMP-AIA060, Box 1, Folder 22. Quotations in the next few paragraphs are from the same source.

25 H. Hooker to E. O'Malley, 22 October 1946, EOMP-AIA060, Box 5, Folder 64.

26 E. O'Malley to B. Hooker, 9 January 1947; E. O'Malley to Cathal O'Malley, 21 September 1947, in *Broken Landscapes,* 247, 256.

27 Cathal O'Malley to Harry Martin, 2 February 2017, Martin Private Papers.

28 E. O'Malley Diaries, July–August 1948, COMPP.

29 E. O'Malley to Strand, 7 November 1953, in *Broken Landscapes,* 310–11.

30 Auction E. O'Malley's books at Sotheby, London, 15 December 1949, English, *Ernie O'Malley*, 61; catalogue in EOMP-AIA060, Box 6, Folder 3.

31 E. O'Malley to John Kelleher, 30 January 1950, in *Broken Landscapes*, 274.

32 List of paintings loaned to Limerick City Library Gallery, 30 October 1948, EOMP-AIA060, Box 4, Folder 3.

33 Cathal O'Malley to Martin, 2 February 2017, Martin Private Papers.

34 B. Hooker to E. O'Malley, 11 December 1946, EOMP-AIA060, Box 5, Folder 47; English, *O'Malley*, 190.

35 Laithwaite to C. O'Malley, 14 February 1973, Blake Papers P244/52.

CHAPTER TEN: LAST YEARS: *QUIET MAN,* COMRADE INTERVIEWS, 1950–1957

1 Des MacHale, *Picture The Quiet Man: An Illustrated Celebration* (Belfast: Appletree Press, 2009), 9–18.

2 MacHale, *Picture*, 43; Joseph McBride, *Searching for John Ford: A Life* (New York: St Martin's Press, 1999), 139–40.

3 MacHale, *Picture*, 46.

4 E. O'Malley to McGrail, 27 May 1956, in *Broken Landscapes*, 364.

5 E. O'Malley to John Ford, 9 December 1953, in *Broken Landscapes*, 314.

6 MacHale, *Picture,* 46–7.

7 Mary Lavin to C. O'Malley, 18 May 1985, fn 2, EOMP-AIA060, Box 25, Folder 3.

8 Eve Morrison, 'Witnessing the Republic, The Ernie O'Malley Notebook Interviews and the Bureau of Military History Compared', in C. O'Malley, ed., *Modern Ireland and Revolution, Ernie O'Malley in Context* (Dublin: Irish Academic Press, 2016), 126–7.

9 Eve Morrison, 'The Ernie O'Malley Interviews, Methodology, Chronology, Interviewees', in Síobhra Aiken et al., *The Men Will Talk to Me: Ernie O'Malley's Interviews with the Northern Divisions* (Dublin: Merrion Press, 2018), 244.

10 E. O'Malley to Sweeney, October 1951, COMPP.

11 E. O'Malley to Strand, 9 December 1953, in *Broken Landscapes*, 313.

12 Foster, *Vivid Faces*, 309–11.

13 E. O'Malley to Strand, 7 November 1953, in *Broken Landscapes*, 310.

14 Ibid, 311.

15 Plaintiff's Originating, Statement of Claim, 15 June 1950, EOMP-AIA060, Box 6, Folder 25.

16 Defendant's Defense and Counterclaim, 29 June 1950, EOMP-AIA060, Box 6, Folder 25.

17 Draft, unsigned, undelivered, unrecorded judgement with corrections by Justice George Gavin Duffy, 30 March 1951, EOMP-AIA060, Box 6, Folder 24.

18 Burrishoole Celebratory Dinner Menu, August 1951, COMPP.

19 E. O'Malley to Cathal O'Malley, 2 May 1953, to Strand, 19 July 1953, and to E. Golden, 10 July 1955, in *Broken Landscapes*, 304, 305, 342.

20 E. O'Malley to Frank Gallagher, 17 August 1954, in *Broken Landscapes*, 322–33.

21 E. O'Malley, To Whom It May Concern Letter, 28 May 1952, and letter concerning the children to H. Hooker, 28 June 1952, in *Broken Landscapes*, 292–4.

22 Cathal O'Malley to Martin, 2 February 2017, Martin Private Papers.

23 H. Hooker interview by Cathal O'Shannon, Raidió Teilifís Éireann, 1973, included in documentary film, *Sceal Ernie O'Malley*, directed by Jerry O'Callaghan, Blackwood Pictures, 2008.

24 C. O'Malley and Roísin Kennedy, eds, *Nobody's Business: The Aran Diaries of Ernie O'Malley* (Dublin: Lilliput Press, 2017), 92.

25 Ibid, 75.

26 E. O'Malley to Strand, 7 November 1953, in *Broken Landscapes*, 311.

27 Tony Woods to E. O'Malley, 1954, EOMP-AIA060, Box 4, Folder 105.

28 E. O'Malley to H. Hooker, 9 May 1955, EOMP-AIA060, Box 5, Folder 64.

29 E. O'Malley to H. Hooker, 3, 5 September 1955, EMOP-AIA060, Box 5, Folder 64, in *Broken Landscapes*, 347–8.

30 Kaye Malley Hogan to Laithwaite, 2 April 1957, COMPP.

31 Photos in *Broken Landscapes* opposite 259.

32 O'Farrell, *O'Malley Story*, 107; the words are a line in a poem, 'Bernardo del Carpio', by British poet Felecia Dorothea Hemans, first published in the *New Monthly Magazine* in 1825.

33 J. McBride, *Searching for John Ford*, 662.

BIBLIOGRAPHY

Aiken, Frank, Frank Aiken Papers, University College Dublin Archives.

Aiken, Síobhra, Fearghal Mac Bhloscaidh, Liam Ó Duibhir and Diarmuid Ó Tuama, eds, *The Men Will Talk to Me: Ernie O'Malley's Interviews with the Northern Divisions* (Dublin: Merrion Press, 2018).

Barry, Tom, *Guerilla Days in Ireland* (Tralee: Anvil Books, 1971).

Blake, Frances-Mary, Frances-Mary Blake Papers, University College Dublin Archives.

Breen, Dan, *My Fight for Irish Freedom* (Cork: Mercier Press, 2010).

Carter, William C., *Marcel Proust, A Life* (New Haven: Yale University Press, 2000).

Collins, Michael, *The Path to Freedom* (Cork: Mercier Press, 1968).

Costello, Francis, *The Irish Revolution and its Aftermath, 1916–1923* (Dublin: Irish Academic Press, 2003).

Crane, Hart, *Hart Crane: Complete Poems and Selected Letters*, ed. Langdon Hammer (New York: Library of America, 2006).

Crowley, John, Donal Ó Drisceoil and Mike Murphy, eds, *Atlas of the Irish Revolution* (Cork: University College Cork Press, 2017).

DeWitt, Miriam Hapgood, *Taos: A Memory* (Albuquerque: University of New Mexico Press, 1992).

Dolan, Anne, *Commemorating the Irish Civil War: History and Memory, 1923–2000* (Cambridge: Cambridge University Press, 2003).

English, Richard, *Ernie O'Malley: IRA Intellectual* (Oxford: Clarendon Press, 1998).

——, *Armed Struggle: A History of the IRA* (London: Macmillan, 2003).

Foster, Gavin M., *The Irish Civil War and Society: Politics, Class and Conflict* (London & New York: Palgrave Macmillan, 2015).

Foster, R.F., *Vivid Faces: The Revolutionary Generation in Ireland, 1890–1923* (New York: W.W. Norton & Co., 2015).

Hart, Peter, *The IRA and Its Enemies: Violence and Community in Cork, 1916–1923* (Oxford: Oxford University Press, 1999).

Hopkinson, Michael, *Green Against Green: The Irish Civil War* (Dublin: Gill and Macmillan, 1988).

Kolb, Philip, ed., *Selected Letters, Marcel Proust, 1910–17*, Vol. 3 (New York: HarperCollins, 1992).

Lawlor, Catriona, ed., *Seán MacBride, That Day's Struggle: A Memoir, 1904–1951* (Dublin: Currach Press, 2005).

Lee, J.J., 'The Background, Anglo-Irish Relations, 1898–1921', in eds Cormac O'Malley and Anne Dolan, *'No Surrender Here!': The Civil War Papers of Ernie O'Malley, 1922–1924* (Dublin: Lilliput Press, 2007), pp. xi–xxxii.

Mac Eoin, Uinseann, *Survivors: The story of Ireland's struggle as told through some of her outstanding living people recalling events former days of Davitt through James Connolly, Brugha, Collins, Liam Mellows, and Rory O'Connor to the present time* (Dublin: Argenta Publications, 1980).

MacHale, Des, *Picture The Quiet Man: An Illustrated Celebration* (Belfast: Appletree Press, 2009).

———, *The Complete Guide to The Quiet Man* (Belfast: Appletree Press, 2001).

McBride, Joseph, *Searching for John Ford: A Life* (New York: St Martin's Press, 1999).

McDowell, Dorothea, *Ella Young and Her World: Celtic Mythology, the Irish Revival and the Californian Avant-Garde* (California: printed privately, 2017).

McGarry, Fearghal, *The Rising-Ireland: Easter 1916* (Oxford: Oxford University Press, 2016).

Malone, Tom, *Alias Seán Forde: The Story of Commandant Tomás Malone, Vice O. C. East Limerick Flying Column, Irish Republican Army* (Dublin: Danesfort Publications, 2000).

Martin, Harry F., Harry F. Martin Private Papers, Stonington, CT.

Military Archives of Ireland, Bureau of Military History, Childers Papers, Dublin.

Morrison, Eve, 'The Ernie O'Malley Interviews: Methodology, Chronology and Interviewees', in Síobhra Aiken, Fearghal Bhloscaidh, Liam Ó Duibhir and Diarmuid Ó Tuama, eds, *The Men Will Talk to Me, Ernie O'Malley's Interviews with the Northern Divisions* (Dublin: Merrion Press, 2018), 244–8.

———, 'Witnessing the Republic: The Ernie O'Malley Notebook Interviews and the Bureau of Military History Compared', in Cormac K.H. O'Malley, ed., *Modern Ireland and Revolution: Ernie O'Malley in Context* (Dublin: Irish Academic Press, 2016), 124–40.

O'Callaghan, John, *The Battle for Kilmallock* (Cork: Mercier Press, 2011).

O'Connor, Frank, *The Big Fellow: Michael Collins and the Irish Revolution* (Dublin: Poolbeg Press, 1979).

———, *My Father's Son* (London: Macmillan, 1968).

O'Donoghue, Florence, *No Other Law* (Dublin: Anvil Books, 1986).

O'Farrell, Padraic, *The Ernie O'Malley Story* (Cork: Mercier Press, 1983).

O'Malley, Cormac K.H., ed., *Modern Ireland and Revolution: Ernie O'Malley in Context* (Dublin: Irish Academic Press, 2016).

O'Malley, Cormac K.H. and Nicholas Allen, eds, *Broken Landscapes: Selected Letters of Ernie O'Malley, 1924–1957* (Dublin: Lilliput Press, 2011).

O'Malley, Cormac K.H. and Anne Dolan, eds, *'No Surrender Here!': The Civil War Papers of Ernie O'Malley, 1922–1924* (Dublin: Lilliput Press, 2007).

O'Malley, Cormac K.H. and Róisín Kennedy, eds, *Nobody's Business: Aran Diaries of Ernie O'Malley* (Dublin: Lilliput Press, 2017).

O'Malley, Cormac K.H., Cormac K. H. O'Malley Private Papers, Stonington, CT.

O'Malley, Ernie, *Army Without Banners: Adventures of an Irish Volunteer* (Boston: Houghton Mifflin, 1937).

———, *On Another Man's Wound* (Cork: Mercier Press, 2013).

———, *Raids and Rallies* (Cork: Mercier Press, 2011).

———, *Rebellen in Irland* (Berlin: Alfred Metzner, 1938).

———, *The Singing Flame* (Cork: Mercier Press, 2012).

———, Ernie O'Malley Papers, Archives of Irish America, New York University Library.

———, Ernie O'Malley Papers, University College Dublin Archives.

O'Shannon, Cathal, 'Cathal O'Shannon Interviews, 1973, Helen Hooker', in 'Sceal Ernie O'Malley, On Another Man's Wound', *The Path to Irish Freedom* [DVD] (2008).

Royal Irish Constabulary, History of policing in Ireland, www.RoyalIrishConstabulary.com

Ryan, Desmond, *Remembering Scion* (London: MacMillan, 1937).

Ryan, Meda, *The Day Michael Collins Was Shot* (Dublin: Poolbeg Press, 1989).

'Sceal Ernie O'Malley, On Another Man's Wound', Disc 3 in *The Path to Irish Freedom* [DVD], directed by Jerry O'Callaghan (2008).

Townshend, Charles, *The Republic: The Fight for Irish Independence* (London: Penguin Books, 2014).

Yeats, W.B., *Collected Poems: W.B. Yeats*, ed. Richard D. Finneran (New York: Scribner Paper Back Poetry, Simon & Schuster, 1996).

Younger, Calton, *Ireland's Civil War* (New York: Taplinger Publishing, 1969).

INDEX